SPEAK MORE!

SPEAK MORE!

Marketing Strategies to Get More Speaking Business

NATIONAL SPEAKERS ASSOCIATION

RIVER GROVE
BOOKS

The National Speakers Association (NSA) is a not-for-profit professional association comprised of more than 3,000 professional speakers. Founded by Cavett Robert, CSP, CPAE, in 1973, NSA is the leading organization for professional speakers, providing resources and education designed to advance the skills, integrity, and value of its members and the speaking profession. In addition to membership, National Speakers Association offers the highly acclaimed certification for Certified Speaking Professionals (CSP), online education programs, *Speaker* magazine publication, *Voices of Experience* audio publication, conferences, research, and networking opportunities. Members are able to connect locally through 39 state and regional chapters, and NSA is also a member of the Global Speakers Federation.

National Speakers Association
1500 South Priest Drive, Tempe, AZ 85281
480.968.2552 Fax: 480.968.0911
www.nsaspeaker.org

This publication is designed to provide accurate and authoritative information in regard to the subject matter covered. It is sold with the understanding that the publisher and author are not engaged in rendering legal, accounting, or other professional services. If legal advice or other expert assistance is required, the services of a competent professional should be sought.

Published by River Grove Books
Austin, Texas
www.gbgpress.com
Copyright ©2012 National Speakers Association
All rights reserved.

Distributed by River Grove Books

For ordering information or special discounts for bulk purchases, please contact
Greenleaf Book Group LLC at PO Box 91869, Austin, TX 78709, 512.891.6100.

Design and composition by Greenleaf Book Group LLC
Cover design by Greenleaf Book Group LLC
Publisher's Cataloging-In-Publication Data
(Prepared by The Donohue Group, Inc.)
Speak more! : marketing strategies to get more speaking business / National
Speakers Association.—1st ed.
    p. : ill., charts ; cm.
  ISBN: 978-1-938416-02-6

  1. Public speaking—Marketing. 2. Public speaking—Vocational guidance. 3. Strategic planning. 4. Success in business. I. National Speakers Association (U.S.)
PN4098 .S64 2012
808.5/1/023   2012907658

Part of the Tree Neutral® program, which offsets the number of trees consumed in the production and printing of this book by taking proactive steps, such as planting trees in direct proportion to the number of trees used: www.treeneutral.com

Printed in the United States of America on acid-free paper

12 13 14 15 16   10 9 8 7 6 5 4 3 2 1

First Edition

CONTENTS

Networking and Public Relations

Social Media and Technology

Business Operations

Potpourri of Proven Practices

ACKNOWLEDGMENTS

This book is the result of the combined efforts of individuals who were willing to share their expertise with the National Speakers Association (NSA). In addition to the authors who contributed their rich content knowledge, NSA also acknowledges the following individuals for their roles in the completion of this book:

Content Advisors/Reviewers

Wally Adamcik, CMC, CSP
Vickie Axford Austin
Allison Blankenship
Shane Browning, CGP
Dick Bruso
Deborah Crowder
Jennifer FitzPatrick, MSW, LCSW-C
Shari Frisinger
Bob Goodyear
Michael Gouveia
Stuart Gray
Ian Griffin
Roberta Guise
Jonathan Halls, MEd
Jean Houston Shore, MBA, CSP, CPA
Lorna Kibbey, MBA
Gregory Lay
Snowden McFall, MAT
Barbara McNichol
Dave McSpadden
Debra Moorhead
David Newman
Helen Osborne, MEd, OTR/L
L. Paul Ouellette, CSP
Beth M. Ramsay

Patricia Raymond, MD, FACP, FACG
Gary Rifkin
Deborah Rivers, PhD, CMC, CPT, MCT, PCC, BCC
Sheryl Roush
David Ryback
Natalie J. Sayer
Steve Schumann
Steve Taubman
Gail Tycer, MS
Mike Wakshull
Monica Wofford, MA, CSP
Mara Woloshin

Project Leader

Barbara Parus

Project Support

Kim Cook

Editors

Barbara Parus
Stephanie R. Conner
Jake Poinier

Design, Marketing, and Publishing

Greenleaf Book Group, LLC

FOREWORD

This is all new to me.

The truth is it's all new to all of us.

I've been in the speaking business for thirty years and I've been fortunate to have experienced a degree of success. That means I know what used to work. In the spirit of fabulous bragging, let me assure you that I can compete and win . . . in markets that no longer exist.

Those who truly are brand-new to what we call the "speaking business" have a decided advantage over those who have been around for a long time. Beginners have no preconceived notions of how things are supposed to work. They aren't stuck in a business model that has worked for decades but now may have little relevance to the realities of today's marketplace.

Some in this business say that the recession that began in 2008 changed things forever. Some say that the pie is smaller. Maybe so. But if that is true, it's equally true that a lot of new pies have been baked and are waiting for us to start taking slices.

A survey of NSA members revealed that speakers define themselves in many ways. We are authors, consultants, trainers, keynote speakers, coaches, and more. We reach our markets and audiences through speeches and face-to-face networking and via Facebook, LinkedIn, and Twitter. We post videos everywhere. There are printed books, e-books, downloadable chapters, webinars, teleseminars, and Skype. For many speakers, our activities create a self-sustaining synergy. My writing supports and creates opportunities for speaking, which helps drive my consulting. It's all interconnected. The most popular three words in the speaking business seem to be "multiple income streams."

For some, these changes are liberating. For others, it all just seems overwhelming. Take heart. In this book, you'll find strategies, tactics, and, yes, even wisdom that will help you make smart marketing choices. Don't think that you have to do everything. You just have to do what feels right and works for you.

As you look at the chapter titles in this book, you see that the contributors cover a very wide range of material, and a lot of the ideas here will be brand-new to some of you. With thirty years of experience in this business, though, I see two success factors that have remained constant for a long time, and are just as true today as they ever were.

For me, the most important factor in growing your business is the same as when I began. It's the quality of your work. All of the ideas in this book can help you tremendously if, and only if, you begin with quality work.

You will succeed to the extent that you can create value for your customers. All of the branding, positioning, and tweeting in the world can't help you if the market doesn't perceive value in what you do. That's where we have to begin, and it's why, to this day, the biggest part of my marketing efforts is spent making sure that my platform performances, writing, and consulting work are as good as they can possibly be. That's the foundation upon which all our businesses must be built.

As I read the book, I felt the message of "quality" running like a thread throughout each chapter. You don't need to get "something" up on a blog. You need to get something really valuable and useful up on a blog. If you're going to fascinate your market, then you have to be, well, fascinating. You can't fake it. The marketplace never tolerates pretenders for long. Creating real value is the most powerful marketing tool ever known. In my humble opinion, the best marketing for any of us is to always get better. Never stop improving.

Along with the importance of quality of work, I see one other factor that, fortunately, holds true today just as it did decades ago. It is simply this: There are a thousand ways to be successful in this business. There are probably as many ways to succeed in speaking as there are speakers. For someone like me, who refuses to be put in a box and rebels whenever someone tells me that "this is the only way to do it," it's the perfect career. I'll do it the way I want to do it, thank you very much. How many careers give people that incredible opportunity?

The beauty of this book is that I can focus on and take action on the ideas that apply to how I want to do business. If I want to build a more prominent online presence, the ideas are here. To get help in creating a brand that drives business, I can turn to multiple chapters. Ideas for harnessing the power of the media, growing my line of written products (in whatever form they may take), networking, public relations, and tons of ideas about the effective use of social media are all in this book.

If this book doesn't help your career, then you didn't read it.

My final thought about this book and, more specifically, the professionals who contributed to it, is simply "How cool is this?" *Speak More!* embodies the very essence of what NSA is all about: incredibly accomplished and successful people telling you how they've succeeded, spilling the beans on their "secrets," giving away the very ideas and strategies that they use to create a competitive edge. It makes you want to say "Really? Why would they do this? What's in it for them?"

Well, it's what's already in them that makes them do it. We work in a profession of classy, caring, giving people.

As you begin to explore the opportunities presented in this book, I leave you with one of my favorite quotes, which is generally attributed to Michelangelo (although there's some debate about that):

> *The greatest danger for most of us is not that our aim is too high and*
> *we miss it, but that it is too low and we reach it.*
> *Aim high.*

—Joe Calloway, CSP, CPAE
Author, *Becoming a Category of One: How Extraordinary*
Companies Transcend Commodity and Defy Comparison

BRANDING AND NICHES

FIRST THINGS FIRST.
YOU NEED A STRATEGY.

Bruce Turkel

Because I run an advertising agency and I speak on branding at National Speakers Association conferences, walking the halls of an NSA meeting can be a dangerous place.

"Hey, Bruce, can I pick your brain about what kind of ads I should run?"

"Bruce, would you take a look at my iPad? I've got my new website loaded up and I'd love to know what you think."

"Bruce, buddy, how do I use Twitter and social media to get more speaking gigs?"

Needless to say, I want to be helpful (why else would I write this chapter?) and I want to be friendly. But I also want to be realistic and honest. And the realistic and honest answer usually sounds something like this:

"You don't need social media. You don't need a website. You don't need ads. You need a strategy."

Now don't take my dramatic rant too far and become a marketing miser. You do need all of those tools. They're exactly the devices you're going to use to market yourself and your business and get the word out about who you are and what you do. But before you start creating noise, you've got to know what you're creating noise about and why anyone should care. Because if you don't know what you're yelling and screaming about, you're just wasting your breath.

This isn't an issue that affects only the speaking business, by the way. It's branding at its most basic. Look at the leaders in any field—you can describe who they are and what they do in one or two words. Volvo? Safety. Walmart? Low prices.

Ferrari? Performance. Sure, they're big companies with millions and millions of dollars in advertising money, but the real secret is that they know who they are, what they sell, and—more importantly—what people buy.

SO WHAT DO YOU STAND FOR?

What do you stand for? Can you describe it in just a few words? If you can't, how can you expect your clients and your prospective clients to do it? What difference will it make if you're tweeting your little heart out and Facebooking right and left if you're sending out random shotgun blasts instead of laser-accurate focused marketing messages?

Believe it or not, I already know what you're thinking. "Sure, Bruce, defining an issue and standing for something makes a lot of sense and I can see how it works for all those companies . . . (big sigh) . . . but I'm different. After all, my business is much more diverse, much more creative, and much more customized to my clients' specific needs . . . (pause) . . . I do too many different things. There's just no way I could shoehorn everything I offer into a couple of words."

Really? Your business is too complicated to brand? Well, before we accept that and give up, let's look at one of the giants on the list above. How about Volvo? Think about the various businesses that company is in. Transportation, manufacturing, research and development, metallurgy, engineering, upholstery, design, import/export, and logistics, to name just a few. Plus, retail stores (for both new and used products), sales and service, and accessories. They operate under the governmental regulations of not just one country but hundreds of countries, states, and municipalities. They work in multiple languages, with multiple consumers, and in multiple industries. And let's not forget that they don't just make consumer automobiles. Volvo also manufactures busses and trucks and provides engines and engineering for lots of other companies. Yet despite this incredible amount of complexity, they can still describe themselves with their commitment to one word.

Safety.

This brand positioning is so valuable to Volvo that when they introduced an SUV, arguably the new American suburban family car, their XC70 outsold all foreign SUVs (European and Asian) combined!

What's more, Volvo's brand description isn't even about what they actually provide. Nowhere in their branding do they talk about transportation or about getting from point A to point B. They talk about safety.

New York is the Big Apple. Chicago is solidly Midwestern. Los Angeles is movies. Las Vegas is sin. Miami is hip. What do you stand for?

The Fox News Channel is on the right. MSNBC is on the left. CNN is firmly in the middle. Where are you?

The funny thing is that we use these designations every single day without thinking twice. Yet, when it comes to our own brand identity, the cobbler's kids have no shoes.

WHAT YOUR BRAND POSITION IS. AND WHAT IT'S NOT.

So how do you figure out your brand position? Well, first let's talk about what it's not. Your brand position is not what you talk about when you're in front of an audience (that's your vocation or your avocation). Your brand is not what you believe in (those are your values). Your brand is not even what you do onstage— juggling, comedy, storytelling, whatever (those are your tools).

Your brand position is not your business card, your tagline, or your talent. It's not your Facebook page, your Twitter handle, or your LinkedIn account. And it's certainly not your logo.

Your brand position is the place you occupy in the heads and hearts of your customers and your potential customers. And if you don't know what that is, you can be sure they don't, either.

That's the bad news.

The good news is that it's simple to figure out. With some time and a lot of soul-searching, you can distill all of the great things you provide your customers down to a single, powerful, and compelling essence. Please note that I said *simple,* not easy. Figuring out your brand positioning takes a lot of hard work and soul-searching. But if you follow one simple diagram and apply yourself to do the work, you'll create a brand positioning that will help inform everything else you do and assure that your future marketing efforts will be efficient and effective.

SCALING THE PYRAMID TO SUCCESS

Ready to get started?

Figure 1-1

Take a look at Figure 1-1: a classic brand pyramid. Hundreds or maybe even thousands of great brands have been created using this simple triangle, and it will work just as well for you.

The way it works is simple—you just start filling in the boxes, going from the general (bottom) to the specific (top). When you reach the apex, you'll have a very good idea what your brand position is and how to promote it to the world.

WHAT YOU HAVE

The bottom box is titled *Features and Attributes* and it's where you inventory everything your business has to offer. And I really mean everything. Here's where you'll list your products and services, your talents, skills, and experience, and everything you use to run your business. Got a computer or two? Write it down. American Airlines frequent flier status? Down it goes. Suits and heels, brochures, and online products? Start scribbling. Specific industry experience, a unique life story, a killer resume? They all belong in the box.

Needless to say, you don't have to actually write on the pyramid; you can create your files in Word or Excel or whatever program you like. The way you record the information is unimportant. What matters is that you do it clearly and well.

The more comprehensive you are with your list, the easier filling out the next level will be. Because the more complete your portfolio of attributes, the more you'll have to draw from as you ladder up the pyramid. It's no accident that the first section, *Features and Attributes,* is on the bottom of the diagram. It will create the foundation that you'll build the rest of your brand messaging on. The more comprehensive it is, the stronger your structure will be.

You also don't have to do this alone. If you have an assistant or there are other professionals in your business, they should participate as well. Your husband or wife or significant other can be a good source of information. Friends are good, too, as well as clients with whom you have a good personal relationship. You may even want to schedule an ideation session and have a bunch of people work together to list all of your company's features and attributes on big flip charts in your conference room or living room. The bottom line is that you want to assemble as much pertinent data as possible. And don't worry about doing this all in one sitting. Often, ideas will keep popping into your head long after you've turned off the computer and gone home. I don't care when you generate the list; I only care that you build it carefully and well.

WHAT YOU DO BETTER THAN ANYONE ELSE

Once this is done it's time to move up to section two—POD, or *Points of Difference.* Here's where you'll list the things that are uniquely yours. Perhaps you play harmonica when you speak (oh wait, that's what I do). That would go in this section. Maybe you have a proprietary coaching technique. That goes here, too. Unusual physical or racial characteristics? If you use them to your advantage, write them down. Chances are that anything you consider your intellectual property (IP) or have trademarked or copyrighted belongs on this list, too.

Please don't take the word *unique* at its most literal definition. Because there's nothing new under the sun, there's a pretty good chance that whatever your special qualities and characteristics are, you're not the only person in the entire universe who would list them. Still, they should be things for which you have a unique slant, a unique delivery, or even a unique combination of items. If they're not special, they belong in the first tier, not the second.

For example, Volvo isn't the only car company that spends time and money on safety. It's even arguable whether or not a Volvo is safer than similar models from its competition. But Volvo has spent so much effort on building its brand around safety that it's become one of its most unique attributes. Therefore, other companies probably wouldn't write "Safety" in this slot. But Volvo would.

When you're done, this list should be a lot smaller than the *Features and Attributes* list. It should contain only the items that are uniquely yours—specific deliverables that you own and that your clients and audiences would readily identify with you and you alone. You don't need to worry if you don't have a lot of items on this list—many fortunes have been built on just one powerful POD. But if you don't have anything compelling on the list or anything that is truly unique and special, then your problem isn't branding; it's much more fundamental. If you've got nothing that's uniquely your own, you'd better get to work on your product before even thinking about marketing. After all, Paul Revere probably would not have gone down in history if he'd rode through the colonial night warning the populace that "the British may or may not be coming."

WHAT YOU DO

Okay, now it's time to ratchet up to the next level—*Functional Benefits*. To fill out this section, you've got to put on a different hat and start thinking like your customer. You want to list the functional benefits your consumer will get from doing business with you. So if you consult on safety preparedness, your clients will know how to outfit and organize their business for a disaster. If you speak on succession strategies for family businesses, then after a keynote, your audience will understand how to plan for the successful transition between generations. And if you write about social media, then your readers will understand how to incorporate Twitter, Facebook, LinkedIn, etc., into their businesses.

This section is the easiest because it's the most obvious. And it's where most businesses stop when they think about their brands, if they think about them at all. But it's the next level of the pyramid where the magic starts to happen. Because this level—*Emotional Benefits*—is where you really begin to connect with your audiences. And you can only get there if you are clear about your functional benefits.

HOW THEY FEEL

Remember that Volvo's brand doesn't really talk about its functional benefit, which is transportation. Instead, Volvo has built a powerful brand based on the emotional benefits of safety. So Volvo drivers can feel that they're better parents, better spouses, or better citizens because they're driving a safer car. Because this is a benefit of the heart and not the head, it stands to reason that it's less intellectual but much more powerful. Words that fit in this category include "confidence," "reassurance," "fulfillment," "relief," and "love."

TOP O' THE WORLD, MA!

Once you've filled in the emotional benefits, look back at the pyramid and look for the connection between what you offer (POD) and what your customer will feel when you've done your job (emotional benefits). These patterns become the fuel for the creative inspiration that you'll need to fill in the final triangle at the very top of the pyramid. This section is where great brand definitions live. Here's where you'll find "Just Do It," "There Is No Substitute," "The Relentless Pursuit of Perfection," "I Love New York," and "We'll Leave the Light on for You."

These lines, none more than seven words long, are exemplary examples of how great brands connect viscerally and emotionally with their consumers. You'll notice that none of them talk about what the products actually do. Instead they evoke the feelings that users will enjoy when they engage with the brand itself. And this is where you want your brand to live.

CONGRATULATIONS. YOU DID IT!

This is also the hardest part of constructing your brand positioning. Besides the craftsmanship and eloquence required, figuring out a truly unique consumer-focused and emotional brand message takes a lot of work and trial and error. But once you climb to the top of the pyramid and proclaim who you are and what you stand for, the rest of your marketing is easy. With your brand positioning firmly established, you'll know what your ads should look like, how your website should function, and what you should tweet. Knowing what your powerful brand positioning is will also help you pick subjects to speak on and topics to write about. And, most importantly, when you begin to promote and distribute your brand messaging, it will tell your customers and potential customers what to expect from you and what leads to refer to you. Because once you, and your audiences, know what you stand for, the rest of the business is easy.

Bruce Turkel makes brands more valuable. Bruce is the executive creative director of brand consultancy TURKEL, where he's worked with great brands such as Miami,

Discovery Channel, and HBO; spoken at MIT, Harvard, University of Miami, and Babson and hundreds of conferences; been interviewed on NPR, CBS, Fox, and CNN; and been featured in *The New York Times, Fast Company*, and *Communication Arts* magazines. He's published three books on branding, including his latest, *Building Brand Value*. Bruce writes a weekly blog on branding at www.TurkelTalks.com and can be reached at bturkel@turkel.info.

GET PASSIONATE ABOUT YOUR PERSONAL BRAND

Pamela Gilchrist, MA, APR, CPT

Branding isn't just for Coke® and cattle. For professional speakers, it's more important than ever to develop a strong personal brand. Not only does it separate you from a million other speakers, but personal branding also allows you to successfully ride the social media rocket ship. By understanding the key elements that underpin your personal brand, you can learn how to leverage it to grow your speaking business. Here's how to get passionate about your personal brand.

As a professional speaker, you know there are proven best practices (better known as methods to the madness) in developing and delivering a great speech. From signature stories to your platform presence, all is carefully planned. For improved business results, your marketing and branding deserve that same attention to detail.

Getting to a clear brand position is a bit more like a cross-country journey in a covered wagon than nonstop jet service to LAX. You'll need some grit and determination. There will likely be some bumps, potholes, storms, unplanned expenses, and days when you wonder why you took this path. The journey will clarify and crystallize your brand. The destination is well worth the effort. And, once there—you've carved a roadbed that will be your marketing on-ramp.

WHY BUILD A PERSONAL BRAND?

Take a page from the celebrity and athlete marketing playbook. You're a thought leader; it's time to position yourself as an industry rock star or information czar.

A clear, compelling personal brand enhances your value to your speaking clients. It gives you a professional edge and sends a message to the marketplace that you are professional and buttoned-up and that you know who you are, what you are about, and what value you bring to the table.

Let's face it—like any business, professional speaking is competitive. NSA founder Cavett Robert, CSP, CPAE, strongly believed in the "more pie theory," meaning there is enough business for all of us to find our place at the banquet. Personally, I love more pie and totally agree with Cavett. He also understood, however, that eloquence involves the power of persuasion, including how you position yourself—onstage and off. This eloquence is complemented by another key competency: enterprise. Part of running a successful business is understanding how you go to market. By developing a powerful personal brand, you are more easily able to grow your prominence among prospects. As your target market becomes more aware of you and your brand promise, it becomes much easier to build your business.

By building a strong personal brand, you are better able to share your expertise. It's one thing to have a great body of knowledge and to be a subject-matter expert—successfully packaging that expertise in a way that sells is both art and science.

5 KEYS TO PERSONAL BRANDING

Think about the top speakers in NSA for a moment. What words come to mind to describe them? Those words that are closely associated with a particular speaker represent a large part of his or her personal brand. Speakers who have a fuzzy personal brand haven't done the mental heavy lifting required to make their brand clear, compelling, relevant, and salable. Now, let's get started.

1. Identify Your Target Market (Who)

Whether you are an emerging speaker or a seasoned professional, a personal brand doesn't start with a clever tagline. Great speakers who have developed a sustainable business model understand that it's not all about them. It's about clarifying who needs to hear your message and what value or benefit you bring to them. This is where you start to define your brand.

Instead of focusing on yourself, define your target market first by figuring out who you want to reach. This might sound like an odd place to begin the journey, but it is the proven starting line for brands around the globe. Is the target a market that you currently serve or a new market? Is geography an important factor? Find your geographic sweet spot. Is it local, regional, national, or global? Finally, when analyzing your target market, give thought to whether it's horizontal or vertical. Ask yourself: "Am I an oil rigger or a strip-miner?"

Some speakers have extremely deep subject matter expertise in a narrow area. Let's take a speaker who is an oil and gas engineer; he probably has more knowledge about fracking and OSHA in his pinky than most mere mortals will learn in a lifetime. This speaker is drilling an oil well. It's vertical. It's deep. It's strong. On the flip side, if you speak on leadership, marketing, or motivational topics, you appeal to a broader audience across many industry sectors. Imagine strip-mining. You travel back and forth across these industries, but don't dig too deeply into any of them.

As you evaluate your target market, investigate if there's money in "them thar hills." (Can you make a living by targeting this audience?) There's no one "right path." But the path you choose will dictate how you focus your brand and your marketing resources.

2. What's Your Why? (Why)

Clarify your value proposition for your target audience. You became a speaker because you had something to say—something that was bubbling up inside of you. What is it, and why should this audience care? Why do they need to hear your message? Why do they need it right *now*? How is it relevant to the current trends and times? And why are you the right person to deliver that message? Once you have answered these questions, translate them into key branding statements that you can use consistently in all of your marketing communications.

Speaker DeLores Pressley is an international powerhouse. From long before her Oprah moment to her latest UP Woman Circles, she lives her passion daily to create a world of confident women. She has continued to clarify her "why" over her speaking career. DeLores's personal power expertise goes above and beyond "teaching success" into the realm of confidence coaching. Her unique approach and inspirational mind-set help her engage, energize, and excite diverse audiences from all walks of life. DeLores has truly mastered the art of inspiring these qualities in others. Her keynote motivational speeches have garnered international acclaim, and she's been featured on ABC, CBS, NBC, and more. Why? Because she first understood her why.

3. Do You Have an Objective? (What)

Next, establish a clear objective (motivation) for developing your personal brand. What is it that you are trying to accomplish? Is it to teach/train? Is it to impart wisdom that audiences need to hear? Is it to inspire, enlighten, or entertain? Is it to make money? If you're like most speakers, the answer is some combination of the above. By defining your primary objective, you are one step closer to developing a personal brand that stands out from the crowd.

4. Does It Make Business Sense? (How)

Both emerging and seasoned professional speakers may have a personal passion, or topical area, they feel strongly about. As I learned early in my NSA Ohio Pro-Track sessions, a passion is not necessarily salable—and therefore, may not be a strong basis for a viable business. You may need to do a little more market research to find out if prospects are interested in your topic and willing to pay for it.

Research the price point that your target market will bear. Is it in line with the value that you have to offer? If not, you have a couple of options. Circle back to step one and make sure this target audience is the right fit. Redefine your audience if necessary. Or if you're on track with the right target audience, you may still need to change up your message or value proposition. Another option is to rewrap your message in a different package that will have broader market appeal. Think of repainting an airplane, or those advertising vehicle wraps that are gaining traction. Inside, it's the same stuff . . . but it looks different and attracts attention in a new way. Whatever works.

Patrick Henry's bio, for example, reads: "Patrick Henry is a professional musician and songwriter who turned his passion into a profession . . . Patrick traded in his pickup truck for a minivan and his pickup lines for a love song . . . Patrick still enjoys playing music, but instead of performing in honky-tonks and bars, Patrick travels the country speaking to associations and corporations, as he entertains, inspires, and teaches his audiences how to 'Keep Your Team in Tune . . . and Have Customers, Clients, and Co-workers Singing Your Praises.'"

Patrick has artfully wrapped his music into a message, and built a brand that can be marketed and sold.

Your brand strategy is all about booking yourself solid. Want more bookings?

Wrap your message in a package that the market wants to buy. (Yummy chocolate candy coating outside—I want it. Vitamin inside—I need it.) You get the idea.

5. Commit Resources for Success (How Much)

If you want to build a brand to last, it will take resources and some sweat equity as you work through targeting and developing your objectives and key messages. It will also take time. Great brands aren't birthed overnight. Tiny seeds are tucked in some dirt and carefully nurtured into a strong, fruitful plant. (This is time that otherwise might be spent on speaking engagements, consulting, book writing, family, and friends. You're making a short-term sacrifice for long-term gain.) Finally, it will take some financial resources. Whether you work with a firm to develop your personal brand or choose a variety of ad-hoc resources, you will need marketing, copywriting, graphic design, and online and print production, as well as social media and PR, to launch successfully. Carefully vet these resources. Look for those who have deep expertise and go beyond the headline.

DISCOVER YOUR STRENGTHS

On your branding journey, you will discover your strengths. These strengths can then be translated into the foundation that supports your personal branding statement. The best place to start is to look at what your clients have to say.

Review client testimonials and speaker evaluation sheets to glean keywords and phrases. Also, consider how these elements might be used as part of your marketing platform. Next, review your expertise and experience. Your expertise includes the specific training and knowledge base that you have, while your experience looks at how you have applied that knowledge through your speaking and professional career.

Now, articulate what makes you a credible expert. Consider breadth and depth of experience, industry training and certifications, and a strong client list. External confirmation of your expertise, such as industry awards, media attention, or anything else that provides third-party validation, demonstrates that you are who you say you are. Credibility is earned. Your credibility also gives you the earned right to the platform.

Although credibility is the external confirmation of your brand, authenticity is the reflection of your essence, or the internal truth, that you bring to every conversation and presentation. Clients and prospects will see right through a paper-thin veil of vain self-promotion. Your authentic self is where your passion comes into play. Are you willing to remove the mask and put yourself out there—to be consistent in who you are in all aspects of your life? Credibility and authenticity go hand in hand to help develop a strong personal brand.

The final area of strength is to look at what personal character traits you bring to your brand. Make a list. Again, it's a good reason to look back at evaluations—plus, ask clients, friends, and family to share what it is they love about you. These traits translate into your brand personality and determine the tone color of your messaging. They could include: a sense of humor, playful spirit, creativity, dedication, perseverance, trustworthiness, or wisdom. These are the traits that make you unique. They separate you from the pack and speak to your brand promise. They define who your clients get when they book you to speak.

YOUR BRAND PROMISE STATEMENT

The work that you have done to create the elements of your personal brand can now be translated into your brand promise. Your brand promise is what customers can expect from you, your company, and any of your products or services. Often, your brand promise becomes your tagline. NSA speaker Mark Sanborn, CSP, CPAE, past president and Cavett award winner, has branded "Developing Leaders in Business and in Life®." This promise is supported by his brand positioning statement, "An international bestselling author and noted authority on leadership, team building, customer service, and change."

Your brand promise should make a compelling case for the value that you can deliver to your clients. Make it short, sweet, and powerful. It clarifies what you offer and why it matters. Don't expect to come up with a great brand promise statement over a quick cup of joe. Like a great advertising slogan, it takes time to develop. I've just spent a full year refreshing a brand for a client. It needed to be distinct and easily recognizable and to gel. (Yes, this is why branding costs big companies millions of dollars.)

Organizations and speakers who rush to market with an ill-thought-out brand promise often find themselves needing a "do-over" in no time. Instead, take time to let your brand mature before going for a big launch campaign. Build a sustainable model for the long term.

Are you ready to get passionate about your personal branding and begin the journey? Here are **9 Personal Branding Action Steps** to get started. Once this foundational work is complete, your next milestone is to build your go-to-market road map so you can book yourself solid.

9 Personal Branding Action Steps

Get Clear and Get Going

1. Answer your Who, Why, What, How, When, Where, and How Much questions.
2. Review testimonials and speaker evaluation sheets.
3. Articulate your expertise and authenticity.
4. Be true to yourself.
5. Answer the question: "What gives you the 'earned right' to the platform?"
6. Write your brand promise statement and get feedback from a variety of sources.
7. Write your bio and boilerplate.
8. Write your Twitter and LinkedIn handles.
9. Begin to create content based on your expertise that delivers on your brand promise.

Passionate about personal branding, speaker/author Pamela Gilchrist, MA, APR, CPT, has earned the trust and respect of clients across the country from Fortune 500 companies to entrepreneurs. As Chief Strategist at the Gilchrist Group®, Pam optimizes outcomes and adds impact for organizations during times of growth and change. She is well-known for her business strategy, change leadership, go-to-market roadmaps, and high-impact communications. Her insights and expertise will help you break through barriers and move forward. Pam's proprietary thought leadership training program, *Expert with Influence*™, turns thought leaders into rock stars and information czars. For more than 25 years, Pam's proven results have repeatedly earned top national industry honors for excellence and strategy. You can connect with Pam at www.gilchristgroup.com, e-mail info@gilchristgroup.com, or follow @pamgilchrist.

YOUR IN-DEMAND BRAND

Dick Bruso

An in-demand brand must have power, needs to encompass all you have to offer, and gives back to the world. As professional speakers, it's absolutely critical that we position ourselves uniquely in the marketplace by creating a brand that makes us truly stand out. We need to be heard above the noise. "Same old, same old" brands don't attract very much attention. Unfortunately, this holds true for a number of those in the speaking community.

The importance of branding can't be overemphasized. As a speaker, your brand—by necessity—is up close and personal. We also live in an age where your brand/reputation, good or bad, can be quickly communicated all over the world via the Internet.

Thus, it's essential to create a brand that's both relevant and extraordinary. Marketing guru Seth Godin tells us, "It's no longer good enough to be good enough. Only the exceptional, the amazing, and the remarkable have a chance to build awareness, word of mouth, and profits."

How do you begin the process of creating an exceptional, amazing, and remarkable brand—a brand that's always in demand? To go from bland to grand, you need to have three brands in one—a power brand, an umbrella brand, and a giving brand.

AN IN-DEMAND BRAND IS A POWER BRAND

A power brand has to be a brand where there's absolutely no substitute! To create an in-demand brand that's powerful involves focusing on your essence, your passion, and your uniqueness. Let's explore these factors in greater depth.

Your Essence (Who You Are)

Focusing on who you are allows you to ultimately build a brand that will stand the test of time. Keep in mind that such a brand will always be of great value because it's based on your authentic self. Hold true to your core principles and you won't go wrong.

In NSA's highly regarded book, *Paid to Speak*, in the chapter, "Simply the Best," I featured three different types of speakers, all of whom are living their lives and careers from a place of absolute authenticity. Their talents, gifts, and abilities may be quite different, but they are totally focused on being true to themselves. They each have created trusted brands of genuine significance in a very crowded marketplace.

Your Passion (Why You Do What You Do)

Mother Teresa said it best: "To work without love is slavery." So, are you speaking on topics you love to talk about and addressing the audiences with whom you most want to interact? Or are you just following the crowd?

Follow your passion and then build your brand accordingly. It's essential that you tune out the naysayers and tune in the cheerleaders. Steve Jobs put it all in perspective: "Don't let the noise of others' opinions drown out your own inner voice. Your time is limited, so don't waste it living someone else's life. Have the courage to follow your heart and intuition. They somehow already know what you truly want to become. Everything else is secondary."

So, let's assume for a moment you were given a once-in-a-lifetime opportunity to give one speech for forty-five minutes to one million people at a very large venue and never be allowed to speak in front of an audience again. What would you talk about? And why? Is that message in alignment, either directly or indirectly, with what you speak about today?

If not, perhaps you should consider revisiting your existing presentations. You may be surprised to discover that in most instances your ultimate message and the topic(s) of your current programs can work very effectively together.

Your Uniqueness (What Sets You Apart in the Marketplace)

The process of creating a unique and distinctive in-demand brand takes time and commitment. It needs to be a top priority if you're going to succeed in a very crowded marketplace as a professional speaker. Howard Putnam, CSP, CPAE, and former CEO of Southwest Airlines, says, "Until you figure out who you are, understand what business or businesses you are in, and establish your uniqueness, success will be difficult to attain."

It's critical that you set yourself apart, as the meetings industry has many excellent choices when it comes to hiring speakers. How you uniquely brand yourself will be the key differentiator in maintaining an ongoing competitive advantage.

Your audiences need to engage with both your brand and your presentations. What is unique about your point of view in your area of expertise? What is your innovative or creative approach to your topic? And is your brand so compelling and distinctive that you are the only source for what you have to offer?

Take a hard look at these questions and drill down deep to get the answers. Focusing on developing a unique and differentiated brand will prove to be a major step on your road to a more successful and fulfilling career.

AN IN-DEMAND BRAND IS AN UMBRELLA BRAND

To create your in-demand brand requires that it be all-encompassing—an umbrella brand consisting of three essential elements. It must be congruent, consistent, and comprehensive. Let's take a closer look at each of these elements.

Be Congruent

Is your brand congruent with who you are and what you do (your expertise), and in particular, the target audiences you want to reach? Many speakers operate in diffused light and don't have a laser-beam focus when it comes to establishing their brand in the marketplace. How often have we heard a fellow speaker say, "Everyone can benefit from my area of expertise"?

Many of us have topics that can help a vast array of audiences. However, in building your brand you need to reflect upon the following two very essential questions: "Who can benefit *most* from what I have to offer?" and "Who do I want to really hang around with for the rest of my life?"

Once you have answered these questions, you just might want to dig a little deeper:

- Who *needs* what I have to offer?
- Who *wants* what I have to offer?

- Who can afford what I have to offer?
- Who is willing to pay me for what I have to offer?

By focusing on a few primary markets or niches, you can become much more knowledgeable about those markets and what their needs and wants are. As a result, you'll be able to more effectively relate to your audiences.

Be Consistent

Think of Coca-Cola® or McDonald's®. Whether you're in your own hometown or in China, the look and feel of these brands remain consistent.

In 2007, Interbrand, one of the world's premier branding consultancies, published a survey report of brand managers from around the world that asked these experts to share the most critical aspects of building and maintaining a successful brand. By far, consistency was referenced more than any other response.

In this same report, understanding the customer/target market was the second greatest response cited by these branding experts.

There are numerous ways to get your message out other than from speaking to a live audience. In addition to coaching and consulting, the opportunities are endless for creating viable touch points with your market(s), including, but not limited to:

- Websites, blogs, and e-zines
- Media (social, new, and traditional)
- Teleseminars and webinars
- Books and mini-books
- E-books
- Articles, columns, newsletters, and white papers
- Market surveys
- CDs and podcasts
- YouTube® videos and DVDs
- Apps
- QR codes
- Other promotional and commercial products

Many of these tools can and should work hand in glove with each other. Whatever tools you do choose to use, be sure you're always consistent in the various ways your brand is presented to your target market(s).

Be Comprehensive

Does your brand encompass everything you do? Does it work at every level? The speaking community comprises keynoters, trainers, workshop/seminar leaders, facilitators, actors, and entertainers. Most professional speakers bring other services and skill sets to the marketplace. Many are very successful authors, consultants, and/or coaches.

By combining these attributes with speaking, they are more apt to ride the ups and downs of the economy. In addition, they are able to expand on their expertise by writing about it and/or working one-on-one with others. On a personal note, I determined, after several attempts at branding myself, that I wanted to be recognized as a branding/creative marketing expert who positions his clients to be "heard above the noise®" in the marketplace. My brand is now congruent with who I am (the oldest of nine children, former broadcaster, media producer, professional speaker, and branding consultant) and conveys what I do in a clear yet distinctive manner.

When you build a brand that's comprehensive as well as congruent and consistent, you'll be well on your way to achieving the success you desire. There's one more key aspect, which can't be overlooked in brand building—creating a brand that truly gives back.

AN IN-DEMAND BRAND IS A GIVING BRAND

We all need to use our talents, gifts, and abilities to serve others. Earlier we addressed the importance of focusing on the specific target markets benefiting most from what you have to offer. It's imperative that you craft a positioning statement, essentially a 30-second commercial, focused on your distinctive brand and target markets, to convey how you can be of particular benefit.

Creating a compelling 30-second commercial includes these three key components:

- What you do/your expertise

- Whom it benefits/target market(s)
- Hook/attention grabber

Of course, the first two components in your 30-second commercial are foundational. However, the third component, creating your hook, is where you add sizzle to the steak and ultimately get someone's attention. In the classic book *How to Get Your Point Across in 30 Seconds or Less,* author Milo Frank devoted an entire chapter to crafting a hook and how it can relate to and garner the interest of your listener.

Another outstanding book, *Give Your Elevator Speech a Lift,* by media specialist Lorraine Howell, shows you how to craft your own 30-second commercial focused on what makes your business truly unique and the positive results you can provide to the listener. In addition, Howell emphasizes, "People will respond favorably if what you say is interesting and they feel you are authentic."

You'll find that both these essential books will help you better define what you have to offer—and express it in a manner that's sure to grab the attention of those you wish to serve.

Making a Lasting Difference

What is the legacy you want to leave for others? As William James so beautifully states, "The great use of life is to spend it for something that will outlast it."

Does your brand impart principles and values that will provide a lasting and meaningful impact? It's a question well worth addressing.

GIVING VOICE TO YOUR BRAND

There's no doubt, by living an authentic and passionate life, you'll inspire many others to do the same and ultimately enrich their lives. So, give voice to your brand by living your life to the fullest and rendering a service to others that will resonate loud and clear.

Building your in-demand brand, a brand that has power, is all-encompassing, and is giving by nature, requires total commitment on your part. But it's well worth the effort. Your brand is your most important asset. When you create an in-demand brand, your value to the marketplace will increase accordingly, and you'll find your speaking career will be better than ever.

Dick Bruso, international speaker and founder of Heard Above The Noise®, is a highly regarded branding and marketing expert. For nearly two decades he has worked one-on-one with hundreds of professional speakers, authors, entrepreneurs, and executives to create and implement powerful branding, marketing, and relationship-building strategies. He is also a contributing author to *Paid to Speak*, published by NSA. Visit www.heardabove.com or e-mail dickbruso@heardabove.com.

AUTHOR-SPEAKER-COACH-SNOOZE: SET YOUR PROFILE APART TO ATTRACT CLIENTS NOW

Nancy Juetten

Speakers who want to be sought after, well compensated, and frequently booked do themselves (and the people who hire them) a great service by making clear what sets them apart with a few well-chosen words. "Author-Speaker-Coach" is not the way to wake up decision makers. These are generic words that read like a grocery list of roles as opposed to specific words that are infused with results and emotional resonance.

Discriminating decision makers value experts and specialists. Set yourself apart by claiming a niche you can call your own and having a message people can remember. What makes you special, memorable, and remarkable among the decision makers most likely to be interested in what you have to bring to the marketplace?

Make your points of differentiation clear. For example, "Author-Speaker-Coach" isn't nearly as compelling as "Humorous Keynote Speaker, Beatles Expert, and Comedy Writer Bill Stainton." One is generic. The other is memorable, remarkable, and preferred.

Most important, be clear about what you want your profile to accomplish for you. If you want your profile to invite speaking invitations, say so. If you want your profile to attract clients, write it with that objective in mind. Words on paper or showcased online that guide the reader to take a desired action are worth their weight in gold.

FROM-WALLPAPER-TO-WOW BIO TRANSFORMATIONS

These "before" and "after" makeovers demonstrate how these ideas can pay off with more compelling messaging.

Case 1/Before:

Laura Fenamore, CPCC, is the CEO of Body Image Mastery, LLC, and founder of www.OnePinky.com, a global online community that extends support and friendship to women who wish to change the way they feel about themselves and their bodies. Her forthcoming book, *Weightless: A Body Image Revolution*, a memoir/self-help book, is currently in submission for publication, and her 12-week Body Image Mastery Course supports her private coaching practice. She lives a healthy, joyful life of faith and gratitude in Northern California.

Comments:

- This bio lacks a compelling headline.
- The first line of text reads like "alphabet soup" with credentials
  that may not be meaningful to the average reader.
- There is no call to action.

Case 1/After:

Body Image Mastery Coach and Speaker Laura Fenamore Guides Women to Love What They See in the Mirror, One Pinky at a Time

Body Image Mastery Coach Laura Fenamore is on a mission to guide women around the world to love what they see in the mirror, one pinky at a time, so they can unlock the secrets to a healthy weight and start loving their lives as soon as possible.

Her popular Body Image Mastery program is celebrated by hundreds of women who have lost weight, reclaimed self-esteem, and started bold, happy lives, with Laura and her proven programs as their guide.

Having overcome her own battle with addiction, obesity, and eating disorders, Laura released over 100 pounds 24 years ago to begin a journey to guide other women to live more joyous, balanced lives. The author of the forthcoming book *Weightless: 7 Tools to Love Your Body (and Lose Weight for Good),* Laura is a frequent contributor to local and national media, including *First for Women* magazine and the *Dr. Pat Show.*

Laura believes that self-love and self-care are where the transformation begins. Learn more about her programs, invite her to speak or contribute to your program or conference, or place pre-orders for her book today at OnePinky.com.

Case 2/Before:

As an award-winning CEO and the author of *37 What Were They Thinking Moments in Marketing*, Olalah has been known to break a fire code or two with her standing-room-only events. A member of the National Speakers Association (NSA), Olalah speaks to audiences across the United States about strategic marketing, the alignment of marketing and sales, competitive differentiation, and market leader positioning.

A featured expert on Forbes.com, Fox News, and *Small Business Trends*, Olalah is a champion for small business success, and she has developed a game-changing system called Breakthrough Advantage™ to help business owners identify, leverage, and profit from their unfair competitive advantage. Currently, Olalah writes a column for *Carolina Business Connection* and is a featured expert in the 2011 and 2012 Woman's Advantage calendar. She also sits as the chair of the Community Relations committee for the National Association of Women Business Owners (NAWBO) of Greater Raleigh.

In 2009 and 2010, Olalah was honored as an International Stevie® Award Women in Business finalist. Business Leader Media tapped Olalah as a Top 50 Catalyst Entrepreneur in 2010 and 2011 for seeing her company to record profitability.

Comments:

- The bio lacks a compelling headline.
- This reads like a summary of everything accomplished to date as opposed to inviting a specific call to action.

Case 2/After:

Breakthrough Advantage Catalyst Olalah Njenga Inspires Audiences to Identify, Leverage, and Profit from Their Unfair Competitive Advantage

"Olalah Delivers Solid Gold Value You Can Take to the Bank"

That's what clients say about the value Olalah brings through her speaking and consulting. An award-winning CEO and the author of *37 What Were They Thinking Moments in Marketing*, Olalah's events are standing room only. Olalah teaches her game-changing system, called Breakthrough Advantage™, to help business owners identify, leverage, and profit from their competitive advantages.

Whether she is speaking about strategic marketing, the alignment of marketing and sales, competitive differentiation, or market leader positioning, this National Speaker Association member shares rich content in a straight-talking way that speaks the truth and gets people moving forward fast to achieve big bottom-line impact.

A featured expert on Forbes.com, Fox News, and Small Business Trends, Olalah is the strategic marketing columnist for *Carolina Business Connection*. In 2009 and 2010, Olalah was honored as an International Stevie® Award Women in Business finalist. Business Leader Media tapped Olalah as a Top 50 Catalyst Entrepreneur in 2010 and 2011 for leading her company to record profitability.

Invite Olalah to make a memorable contribution to conferences, events, and conventions that welcome her tell-it-like-it-is and how-it-can-be-a-whole-lot-better approach to strategic marketing. Visit www.olalah.com to learn more and engage.

TIMELESS TIPS FOR GETTING NOTICED

Take a stand about who you serve, and be clear about it. It will serve you and your business well and make it easy for a decision maker to know you are a perfect fit for the opportunity at hand.

Here are three time-tested tips to stand out and get noticed:

1. Offer a compelling, descriptive headline for your most popular speaking topic that sizzles with benefits your audience can't wait to enjoy. **Example:** Transform Your Boring Bio from Wallpaper to Wow to Attract Clients Now with Nancy "Broadcast Your Brilliance" Juetten

2. Make the ultimate result that your ideal client will enjoy crystal clear. **Example:** Deliver Powerful Presentations and Enjoy a Competitive Advantage with Hall of Fame Speaker Patricia Fripp, CSP, CPAE

3. Offer a call to action to invite phone calls and e-mail inquiries to discuss your availability. **Example:** To hire Liz Goodgold to speak at your next event or purchase her book—*Red Fire Branding: Creating a Hot Personal Brand So That Customers Choose You*—connect by phone or e-mail today.

By making the invitation clear with well-chosen and specific words, decision makers can get to an "easy yes" decision. Best of all, you can invite more opportunities to share your message and grow your business.

RIGHT CONTENT, RIGHT SITUATION

Telesummits, webinars, live events, and media interviews are leveraged ways to share your information with decision makers who have the influence to bring your message to more of the right people. A one-size profile does not suit all situations in today's technology-charged, interactive, and global marketplace.

Speakers who want to be ready to say "yes" when opportunity calls need to anticipate content needs long before speaking invitations flow in. To that end, prepare bios of varying lengths—50, 100, and 300 words—and post them to your website or blog where a meeting planner can easily find them.

Write a speaker introduction as well. If you have a name that is difficult to say, spell it out phonetically so there is no mistake about the correct pronunciation. Then, you can share that message with the meeting planner at any time, and you'll know you will be introduced properly.

BE READY WHEN OPPORTUNITY CALLS

It is often said that how you do anything is how you do everything. For example, if you are ready to submit your materials in advance of a stated deadline, you will show up as a joy to work with and set the stage to do a great job and make a valuable contribution. Then when you deliver your messages with impact as promised and expected, the event producer, reporter, or other person of influence is more likely to extend repeat invitations and refer others to you. My advice: Get ready in advance so when an opportunity comes up, you're ready to show up at your best.

Here is a checklist to make sure you can quickly respond to opportunities when they come your way:

- Two-sentence introduction
- 50-, 100-, and 300-word bios
- Speaker introduction, including phonetic spelling for names that are unusual
- Five questions that open the door to an engaging and content-rich interview
- The three to five main points your audience will enjoy as a direct result of your talk

- Digital photograph of you looking your best
- Book cover or product image
- Web address
- Link to offer a free gift in exchange for an opt-in e-mail address
- Emergency phone number
- Call to action
- Affiliate program link if appropriate for the situation

By taking time to prepare the right content for the right situations, you save valuable time, avoid the "11th-hour bio scramble," and stand above the competitive crowd to welcome new engagements, clients, and referrals with ease and grace.

SHARE YOUR STORY

Once your story is well prepared, take steps to share your story in a variety of ways to invite more of the right opportunities. Share your story in the "About Me" section of your website or blog, in a custom e-mail signature, in the "bio box" for every article you submit to an online article directory, via social media profiles, in the "boilerplate" paragraph of every press release, and in the teleseminar information you share with your joint venture partners.

Here are additional ideas to share your story in ways that can bring you to the attention of decision-makers who can engage your expertise and services.

- Refer to your short bio in every pitch you send to the media, using services such as www.helpareporter.com, www.pitchrate.com, and www.reporterconnection.com.

- Post to your own blog three times a week with compelling content that engages your readers in a relationship that will bloom and grow over time.

- Post meaningful comments to the blogs that your ideal clients read so you can start engaging those readers and inviting them to take interest in what you have to say.

- Contribute articles to the most prestigious business journal or trade publication that serves your ideal audience. Make sure your "bio box" packs a punch and invites readers to become fans and followers of your work.

- Launch and sustain a quality e-zine that offers news and resources to support the success of your readers and gives them ample and ongoing opportunities to sample your expertise and stories about your results.

- Respond to media queries that are well targeted for your expertise so your expertise can travel to more of the right media outlets and readers who can one day make the wise choice to become your clients.

- Target the top ten media outlets within which you want your expertise to be seen, heard, and celebrated. Then, plan your approach so that you can make compelling pitches the media can't resist and earn the leveraged media attention you seek, step by deliberate step.

- Issue news releases to the media on a systematic and timely basis to keep your perspectives in the news.

- Seek out quality joint venture partnerships with like-minded professionals so that your expertise can travel beyond the reach of your own list of fans and followers.

- Enter prestigious award competitions that are well supported by the media that matter for your message, as a way to set yourself apart from your competitors in a winning way.

The key is to focus on the big rocks that have the greatest potential to create awareness, excitement, and momentum in your business among your ideal clients and to use your time and resources wisely. Disregard the little pebbles: distractions have limited upside.

When you make it an ongoing priority to get seen, heard, and celebrated for your expert status with specific, compelling words that speak your points of differentiation, you invite more of the right kinds of opportunities. In doing so, you can create a rolling wheel of revenue-generating opportunity for your business that creates powerful momentum as you grow your influence, impact, and income.

Publicity expert, *Bye-Bye Boring Bio PLUS!* author, and speaker Nancy Juetten leads the Broadcast Your Brilliance Webinar Series so service professionals, speakers, and authors can get known to get paid. She speaks to thousands of business owners through webinars, teleseminars, and media interviews each year. Her expertise is showcased in articles on CNN Radio, *Success* magazine, *Fox Business*, NPR,

Marketing Sherpa, and the *American City Business Journals*, among other prestigious media outlets. To learn more and access a recorded webinar with tips to broadcast your brilliance and monetize your expertise, visit www.authenticvisibility.com/monetize.

NICHE SPEAKING: CASH IN WITH FEWER (BUT MORE DEVOTED) LISTENERS

Gordon Burgett

When I was new to public speaking, in the 1980s, every speaker seemed to have a different slant on what worked best, got the most and highest-paying bookings, and guaranteed fame and fortune—a few even hinted that, done right (their way), lots of fame and fabled fortune could be achieved within a year or two!

Yet most of their suggestions reminded me of an acquaintance living in Santa Barbara, California. He was a brain surgeon, and his favorite hobby was repairing Venetian blinds! He asked me whether he should get business cards printed as a brain surgeon and add the blinds repair in small type at the bottom, or advertise his expertise with Venetian blinds, and include brain surgery as a sort of footnote.

We both got a long laugh out of his quandary and agreed that either card was proof that somebody needed brain repair.

What confused me when I was new to speaking was that the biggest speaking names seemed to be able to talk about anything to anyone, with a long list of titles—and they could further parse each of those topics into a main speech, a keynote, a dinner presentation, a seminar or breakout session, a bout of emceeing, even a program for spouses! A lot of general stuff for huge crowds that also included Venetian blind repairpeople and brain surgeons.

You can imagine my concern because I only knew one thing better than my listeners, and at first, that worked well only as a workshop. I felt like a pitcher whose repertoire was a swooping sidearm screwball. A one-pitch Gordy. Worse yet, a talk that I was certain nobody would want to hear twice. I figured I'd better keep two day jobs even if I somehow backed profitably into the oral arts.

I HAD ONE SPEECH!

It took me many years to actually leave the day jobs because my booked speeches were getting in the way. I'd been wrong. My one speech, one topic deep, with modest improvements and a few simple slants, brought me more than 2,000 paid presentations. I had no idea that my goofy screwball, my swooper, was so special.

Except that my topic was about niches, and I really did have a singular perch (I wrote the book about it). And lots of "nichers" wanted to know how to make their niches permanent and profitable.

I told my audiences that if you know a very important piece of information—that a particular group or kind of person would travel long distances to hear you tell them how to do something better, faster, or more profitably if you were an expert and they needed your expertise—what you had to do was find out what those people had in common (like an association or specific training from applied experience) and let them know how you could help them.

That was easier to do if you wrote a legitimate book that was full of help and examples and advice; then you told all of the particular associations and conventions what your book was about and that you now spoke about it.

What I talked about was niche speaking, niche publishing, and niche writing. The crucial word was *niche*, and the rest was what you did to and with it once you found a niche that others were eager to pay a lot to learn more about.

If I pronounced the word "niche" like *leech*, half the listeners said it was pronounced like *witch*. Or *leash*.

But we all agreed that a niche by any pronunciation was a unique place, employment, or status such that the people in it resemble each other but are distinctly different from others. For example, brain surgery and Venetian blind repair are niches. So is plumbing—as is public speaking. Red-headed Porsche owners are a splashy niche, as are English Channel swimmers. Practitioners in each field do or know particular things that bind them together while distinguishing them from others not in their niche.

BUILD YOUR OWN NICHE

Selecting and building your own niche starts by identifying what core need those in a niche share. Travel writers need to know how to presell their articles before they take trips. K-12 school administrators need to hear how-to success stories in the areas where they hurt the most. Professional speakers need a blazing multimedia extravaganza built around a dozen of the best speeches dissected to find the techniques, topics, and delivery skills that always work.

Niche speakers don't stand out in their fields just by talking about any old topic. Sure, some people would listen to them, especially if they jumped around a lot, threw gifts into the crowd, and were very funny—or very odd.

But if they wanted to be invited back, again and again, they'd have to hone their themes to the specific topics or competences they uniquely share with their niche collaborators. Their listeners would expect to hear special knowledge or information or inspiration that is drawn from the speaker's depth of preparation, experience, or skill. The listeners would have to get much more back from the speech than they had invested in time, attention, and travel to hear it.

So anyone who wants to make a killing in a niche has to figure out what will make those listeners froth with fervor, take loads of notes, stand up and cheer at the conclusion, thank the programmer profusely, and rush to e-mail their niche friends that that very speaker *must* be heard as soon as possible!

Your task is to find a topic or field you love and want to embrace passionately, get on-site experience in it (or get bathed in others' experience and tips), and then make yourself an expert. Share that expertise, build an empire around it (more later), and make your name synonymous with your topic (and the reverse).

Sounds like a tall order even for a tall speaker, but it really isn't. A niche speaker knows his or her field, commands special knowledge in and of it, and is singularly polished in his or her facet of expertise.

EVEN A HUMBLE EXAMPLE HELPS

Let's take a seemingly innocuous topic: how to get patients to pay their bills in the dental field. No dentist or staff would have jobs for long if their patients (or their insurers) didn't pay for services rendered. So an expert who understands the travails and quirks of dental collections (by doing it or collecting the experiences of others) and who could explain how a surefire system could be implemented would be much sought-after, particularly if she was articulate and to-the-point and could share her solution with clarity, a process, and at least a whiff of humor. She would be in steady demand for the major dental conventions, the specialists' conventions, the state and regional gatherings, the county meetings, and for consultation at individual practices.

In other words, to dentists and the staff, that speaker would be a hero who must be heard, read, and consulted with. Her niche is dentistry.

Need that person be a dentist? Hardly. An accountant? Unlikely. Must she have years of dental in-practice experience? That wouldn't hurt—at least some hands-on know-how. But all she absolutely must have is a solid ability to speak well and a message that is based on truth, packaged to help the listeners make reliable (better, swift) dental practice collections.

(A tip: How do you find these gilded talking topics? Ask the veterans [or office managers] in any niche field if they could buy one book [or hear one speech] about the most important or most vexing niche topic right now, what would that topic be? That's what you deliver!)

TWO BURDENS: THE SPEAKING AND THE MESSAGE

Niche speakers in any field or occupation must make themselves and their services known, create the selling tools to get bookings, and do the same grunt marketing that all speakers must do, with one important exception: They need to focus only on their niche, within which they are a much-sought-after specialist, but outside of which they have no marketing distinction.

So, niche speakers have two burdens: They must speak well, and their message must be accurate, credible, and effective in their niche.

Learning to speak well is enhanced by attending speaking conventions and listening to and seeing the best performers from any field, whether they are talking about how to be more courageous, get better color coordinated, overcome insanity, or be more organized. Mind you, those generalists are seldom niche trained. But you are!

It is easier for niche speakers to find the bookers to whom they must pitch their program. And it's also easier to hear the competition, if any, by going to where they speak—and listening.

The best way to display their particular field knowledge is by having a published book or an article (or many) in, say, dental periodicals or journals that demonstrates their special expertise in print. That book or copies of the articles would be part of their sales kit, with the usual selling items, including videos, podcasts, testimonials, and perhaps workbooks or handout materials provided at workshops or breakout sessions.

That's why niche speaking is the kind of special gift that the gifted don't want to share too widely with their arm-waving colleagues. Just let the others speak magnificently to hundreds a few times a year, while, as a niche speaker, you can be booked several times a month, perhaps less flamboyantly but speaking more—and probably earning more too.

HIDDEN GOLD: NICHE SPEAKERS EMPIRE-BUILD!

Even better—much better—niche speakers are building their own empire from products about their core and related topics. The spin-off income keeps their coffers filling while the speakers sleep or perfect their special knowledge that is so vital to their well-being and to the members of their new niche tribe.

What is empire-building? And why does it bloom particularly and brazenly in niches?

Going back to the dental collections niche speaker, a typical empire starts with a book or a seminar (or workshop or breakout session). They are the best ways to show one's expertise in an in-depth way. Readers will know rather quickly if the author knows what they want more of. The same with an extended talk, often enhanced with some printed support material.

The two means are also rather intimately related as booking tools. Presuming the book is marketed widely to dentists and/or dental office managers, the author's qualifications are in evidence for all of the niche speaking bookers to see, particularly if comp copies and full tip sheets are sent with the speaker's marketing materials. With a good book, the speaker is almost preapproved, and readers of the book may even request the author for upcoming gatherings.

Conversely, at the time of the niche presentation, attendees can buy the book at a sales table, find out about it from a handout or flyer, or receive it as a gift from the event's sponsor.

Often, speaking sponsors will make the list of attendees available, with street and e-mail addresses. And if the books are purchased directly from the author-speaker's publishing branch, the addresses are also on hand.

Thus begins the e-list and direct mailing core of the empire. As the number of products continues to increase, or the book is updated and revised, flyers are sent to the earlier buyers. It may well be sent to other mailing lists or e-lists, too. Good things happen there: Recipients share the flyer with other dentists or their local association, and it moves up the rungs to the top associations. Bookers start contacting the author-speaker for future dates, and, assuming that the person speaks well, every appearance usually leads to one or several other contacts—where more books can be sold.

The range of products often increases, too, as the speaker-author identifies other needs and frustrations that he or she can also address. This usually begins with products close to the core book and speech.

From the first book may come a follow-up book, or if the book is, say, divided into twelve chapters, ten or so more books might be written, each based on one of the chapters. If there is a workbook that accompanies the speech or workshop, that, too, might be expanded into another full book. Or if there are standard operating procedures (SOPs) used in the collection process, those might be gathered into a specialized book/binder, perhaps with an accompanying CD so the SOPs can be immediately modified for the buyer's practice. Books are rather easily converted into how-to articles that might appear in the niche or association publications, which in turn strengthen the perception of the speaker's expertise. Finally, each of the printed products can probably be produced and sold in both printed (bound) and e-book formats.

There's a huge hidden asset in niche books, too. The followers read the same niche newsletters (often from their associations), and those publications review books! A good review there shines all the way to heaven!

Products from the speaking venues might include taped or digital copies of the presentation, with the workbook, all in a DVD; more specialized oral programs of key sections of the program; or a full video (or podcast) of the program. And if the program was, say, a speech, it could be offered to that group later as a breakout session or a workshop. Conversely, a breakout session or a workshop can be transformed into a speech. The program can also be broken into twenty- or thirty-minute study sessions and sold on video, CD, or DVD.

Related means of displaying continual expertise through the empire might include a website, with details about each product and the author-speaker, plus free sample book chapters and testimonials. There might also be a newsletter, blog, Q-and-A bulletin board, and social networking links. Every display of the needed information increases the likelihood of more purchases, more speaking engagements, and more supporters.

Finally, the above assumes that the core theme remains dental collections. There are hundreds more niche topics that beg to be explored and accrued expertise shared. You pick the niche, the need, the topic, and which information dissemination tool listeners want. Our dental expert might continue to branch out in dentistry, finding related topics just as popular for her now-familiar following. Or she might take a how-to collections formula and program to other professional fields, and create as much income again through her new empires. For example, she might modify her program, speech, and products for veterinarians, podiatrists, and chiropractors—each another empire!

It is, frankly, exhausting to consider all of the doors that niche speaking, and its related spin-offs, could open! Doors are easier to find because of the specific one-topic limitation in an intentionally tight niche, with bookings probably easier to get from less competition once the person's expertise is established and properly pitched.

What's really exhausting is thinking about finding sponsors for that foot-long list of general topics I mentioned earlier. As a nicher, you may have far less fame in the speaking world (how many dental collection experts have you heard at an NSA convention?), but done with diligence and love, you will very likely be speaking more often and earning more money (with an empire growing simultaneously)! The best thing is that your listeners also will keep asking you back so they can learn and earn more as you and they grow.

Now, go find that special target audience that can't wait to continually hear you and the magic you bring. Prosperous niching!

Gordon Burgett joined NSA in 1982 and has since given more than 2,000 paid presentations and published more than 1,700 articles and 42 books, including *Niche Publishing: Publish Profitably Every Time* and *Speaking for Money* (with Mike Frank). He currently reviews nonfiction adult book manuscripts, speaks, and directs a publishing company in Novato, California. Contact him at glburgett@aol.com, or visit him online at www.gordonburgett.com or http://blog.gordonburgett.com.

BRAINBRANDING: ACTIVATE THE BRAIN, STIMULATE YOUR BRAND

Robyn Winters, MA, and Ken Banks

Did you know that you might be limiting your business potential if you define your market niche too specifically, and if you focus your energies too precisely? That's because you might not consider that a broader market base will maximize both your potential and your income. How? It all starts with the brain.

As frequent attendees of National Speakers Association meetings and conventions for nearly two decades, we've noticed that one topic consistently emerges at every event: the suggestion to "find your niche and then capitalize on your brand within that niche." This advice still holds true today: You can always learn new lessons about understanding your market, and then differentiate yourself and your brand to audiences and clients.

Signature stories and effective delivery certainly make a presentation more interesting and effective by reaching out to the *hearts* of the audience. Yet, it's equally important to understand what's going on inside your audience's *heads* if you want your brand to appeal to more people. In the next few pages, we'll show you how—and why!

DISCOVERING THE SYNERGY BETWEEN BRAIN AND BRAND

How did BrainBranding develop? How did Ken (a brand strategy expert) uncover a synergistic connection with Robyn (a communications and buying style expert)? As NSA members, we discovered that, while our presentations were different, the principles were similar and the outcomes had the same results: greater brand recognition and staying power. The results of our discussions evolved into our book, *BrainBranding: Activate the Brain—Stimulate Your Brand.*

The book focuses on how the four thinking styles of the brain translate into the four instinctive buying styles of clients and customers, styles that can be effectively identified by following the four-step BrainBranding process. The number 4 continually emerged as a common thread—one that can significantly improve your brand's position in the marketplace and expand its appeal to your current markets.

THINKING STYLES, BUYING STYLES

You are most likely aware of left- and right-brain thinking. The concept of thinking styles breaks down the brain's left and right natural thought processes into four quadrants that mirror the way your brain makes decisions about what to buy and who to buy it from. We call these thought processes *buying styles*.

Each person in your audience is affected by buying styles. For example, the buying style of someone whose brain is dominated by logic and analysis is more likely to need facts and figures to help make a purchasing decision to get real value from your message. On the other hand, someone whose brain is more influenced by personal connection wants to form a relationship and prefers to "experience" service when making a selection, and so on.

What's important to note here is that very few individuals are influenced by a single buying style: All four come into play at some point, but they are utilized based on the strength of individual preference and an individual's basic physiology. This is particularly true when selecting a product or service. The brain's way of thinking affects how much interest and retention someone derives from a speech, seminar, or a sales presentation. The model we developed to illustrate this concept is shown at the top of the facing page.

FOUR BUYING STYLES . . . FOUR BRAND OPPORTUNITIES

This model illustrates the four buying styles that come into play during the decision-making process—whether a product, a service, or a plan. In other words, it's what your brain uses when it mentally "invests" in a person or a brand. Let's look at each of these buying styles in greater detail.

First is the TRENDSETTER buying style, which is influenced by vision and imagination. In this style, the person's decisions are impacted by creativity, innovation, and cutting-edge elements. It wants to visualize potential ways to use your brand and weigh the options not only for now, but in the future.

Second is the INVESTIGATOR buying style, which requires facts, statistics, and other relevant data to justify a decision. In this style, buyers will do research to have all the necessary information before considering your brand, products, or services and will then conduct comparative analyses before making a final decision.

Third is the RELATER buying style, typical of a buyer who wants to create an emotional connection to you and your brand. This style wants to form a relationship, one that specifies the benefits of his or her brand choice, and demonstrates the benefits of personalized service.

Fourth is the COORDINATOR buying style, which needs to see structure, organization, and detail in your brand and marketing strategy. People in this buying style want to know that using your brand's products and services (or taking action on your presentation's premise) will be practical, straightforward, and easy to understand. Add in convenience, and this buying style is ready to do business.

What's most important to remember is that every person you are trying to reach is *not* exclusively motivated by just one of these buying styles. There may be a dominant style, but all come into play to some extent and affect the decision-making process. And it's for this reason that you need to broaden your niche if you want to maximize your reach and profitability.

NEED AN EXAMPLE? LOOK AT AN NSA LEADER!

Mark Sanborn, CSP, CPAE, and a past president of NSA, intuitively knows the importance of appealing to the brain's four buying styles. This is how Mark's branding strategy reflects those styles:

Investigator: *Whether improving sales or strengthening leaders within an organization, Mark works with clients to set clear objectives and achieve bottom-line results—quickly and effectively.*

Coordinator: *Mark's presentations are carefully organized and planned.* Listening to his speeches or participating in his training programs, you know that there is a defined structure that leads you from point A to point B, as exemplified in his Six Principles of Leadership.

Relater: *Mark's stories pack enough emotional content to make you feel as if you are experiencing them yourself.* His sense of humor helps audiences and associates alike form an immediate relationship with him and his subject matter.

Trendsetter: *Mark has a vision, not only for his business but also for his audiences.* When he was president of NSA, part of his success—and appeal—was to look down the road and articulate that vision to NSA members. He places ROI in the bigger picture and emphasizes how it will lead to long-term improvement.

Those who have heard Mark speak, experienced his leadership at NSA, and interacted with him, recognize his ability to appeal to all four buying styles, all leading to a successful and sustained brand. What Mark and other savvy speakers discern is that, while it may appear that you can compartmentalize your audience members or clients by identifying which buying style their brains are most likely to use, it's not that simple.

That's where BrainBranding enters the picture.

You could be standing in front of an audience that is enthusiastically responsive, but not one of them is thinking or reacting to your message in exactly the same way as anyone else. More importantly, not one person is influenced *only* by your messages or *only* by information that is targeted to one particular buying style.

While your stories may emotionally win a relater's attention, that same person may also want to know how what you're saying fits into the long-term strategy of his or her business. Your presentation may be well organized and structured, but a coordinator may also want facts that verify your story or confirm that it is relevant to his or her situation.

Variations like this can go on endlessly, as each individual is motivated differently by his or her buying styles. Your task is to make sure that your message reaches each style throughout your presentation so that, in the end, each person believes that she or he has derived value from what you have to say and, more important, will take action.

DEVELOPING YOUR BRAND . . . IT'S YOUR DNA

As important as it is to understand individual buying styles for your speeches and presentations, it's equally important when developing a brand for your business. Whether you're a consultant or trainer, a motivator or coach, your business model and brand need to reflect the brain's four buying styles during the development process—as well as when it's presented to your potential clients and customers. This is why it's so important to "activate the brain" and "stimulate your brand," in order to both engage each person's buying styles and to keep your brand front and center in their hearts and their heads.

The development of an effective brand goes far beyond a memorable name for your business or presentation: It's not just a logo or slogan that's easy to recognize and understand. Your brand strategy must include a comprehensive marketing plan that will reach more potential clients than your competitor. Period. Now let's look at how you can develop your brand effectively by understanding and employing the BrainBranding process.

FOUR STEPS TO BRANDING TO THE FOUR BUYING STYLES

BrainBranding is the solution for developing a brand that has the ability to appeal to a greater number of people, and to have greater staying power. It's equally notable that each of the four buying styles comes into play for each of the four steps.

Step 1: Create Your Vision (Trendsetter)

In this first step, you articulate a clear and understandable *vision* for what you and your brand want to be famous for. How is your brand different from your competitors'? How will this knowledge help you to build a successful brand? Like the trendsetter, you must develop your vision to include future uses, cutting-edge applications, and innovations not available from other sources. This requires imbuing your brand with the creativity and originality to stand out. Finally, you must be able to communicate the vision to your organization as well as to your clients and customers.

It has been said that where there is no vision, the people perish. In the case of a professional speaker, where there is no vision, there may be no audiences, clients, or products, and the brand or career that goes with it may not be sustainable. In clarifying your vision, you'll discover those elements that most appeal to the trendsetter buying style, and you'll uncover the strategy that drives people to select your brand.

Step 2: Conduct Research (Investigator)

In the second step, you determine the viability of your brand through *research and systematic inquiry.* It's here that you establish whether there is a need for your message, your service, and your expertise. Like the investigator, you will want to analyze the competition, determine your differentiation, and see if there is a true need for what you offer. Gathering facts will steer the rest of your branding efforts toward your goal and provide you with the information you'll need to appeal to the investigator buying style.

Step 3: Communicate Emotional Value (Relater)

It's time to walk the talk by determining the *emotional value* of your brand and your message, which is essential if you want to appeal to the relater buying style. For example, in developing a brand for a new automobile, it's not sufficient to design a car with the latest technology. It's more important to recognize that the buyer wants to feel delighted about the car and the entire buying experience. In other words, if there is no relationship, there is no brand!

Step 4: Construct a Plan (Coordinator)

When you've successfully completed the first three steps, then you're ready for the fourth and final step: a well-organized, step-by-step action plan that will take your brand from conception to reality. The coordinator buying style recognizes and demands a detailed, uncomplicated way to use your product or service (or to implement the key points in your presentation), so that he or she can justify the buying decision.

Your presentations will be more effective if they are structured and sequential and provide a practical, reasonable, and understandable path that leads to the action you want audience members to take. In addition, your business will be more profitable if your services can be readily understood and activated in a simple, straightforward way.

HOW BRAINBRANDING CAN WORK FOR YOU

By now, you may be thinking that, to follow the BrainBranding principles, you have to be all things to all people. But really, the key to success is the degree to which you broaden your appeal to each of the buying styles, while developing meaningful points of difference.

Let's use your keynote presentation or seminar as an example of how to "activate the brain" to engage the four buying styles. First, you have to be clear about what you want your audience to walk away with after hearing your presentation (your vision). How will your content and message impact their lives or careers for the better once they leave the room? For example, it's not sufficient to provide information that enables people to receive four-star service. It's more important that you offer the kind of service that will increase revenues and strengthen loyalty within six months.

PUTTING IT ALL TOGETHER

First, the trendsetters want an original, unique brand that will enhance their current business situation and confidently position them for the future.

Second, the investigators need you to provide the facts, information, and numbers that verify your premise and help them understand how your premise, product, or service will positively impact their bottom line.

Third, the relaters want to know that you understand and identify with their unique circumstances, while connecting to their problems. In order for your brand to be memorable, your stories and examples should connect emotionally, demonstrate empathy, and be interesting and exciting as well.

Finally, the coordinators want to separate your message from the others that are competing for attention. They will be most drawn to one that is both practical and well organized. They are looking for the details that will enable them to formulate a plan and take action, and they can't be bothered with hassles and challenges. Make it easy for them to succeed.

THE BOTTOM LINE . . . DIFFERENTIATE YOURSELF

"Activate the brain, stimulate your brand" means that you combine the principles of an effective brand strategy with the four distinct ways that people make buying decisions. Why? To ensure that your brand stands head and shoulders above the competition, and creates an impression that is unforgettable.

Robyn Winters, MA, and Ken Banks have been professional speakers and members of NSA for more than 15 years. Each has served on the board of the NSA/Central Florida chapter, and each has presented internationally.

Robyn Winters, president of Stand Up, Stand Out!® International, brings more than 20 years of communication and buying style expertise. Ken Banks has been an expert in marketing and branding for more than 30 years, working with companies such as Eckerd Drugs, Circuit City®, and PetSmart. Their BrainBranding® concept provides a revolutionary way for brands to resonate with audiences, clients, and customers. It assists companies and individuals to make better use of their marketing budgets by appealing to a broader market of buying styles. Robyn and Ken are coauthors of the book *BrainBranding: Activate the Brain, Stimulate Your Brand.* Contact Robyn at info@robynwinters.com or visit www.standupstandout.com. Contact Ken at ken@kenbanks.com or visit www.kenbanks.com.

WRITING AND PUBLISHING

PYRAMID POWER: WRITE YOUR WAY TO MORE BUSINESS AND INCOME

Tyrone A. Holmes, EdD, CPT

If you're like most speakers, you are probably looking for new ways to increase sales, boost profits, and enhance your brand. Writing is not only a powerful way to demonstrate your expertise, promote your business, and generate significant income—it can enhance your credibility, increase your knowledge base, and position you as a leading authority in your field. While writing is a challenging endeavor, the process can be simplified with the Publishing Pyramid, which is a tool you can use to develop a wide variety of publications.

THE PUBLISHING PYRAMID

The Publishing Pyramid (see p.56) is a seven-level sequential model based on a simple principle: Content written at lower levels of the model can be used to develop content at higher levels of the model. These levels progress from easiest-to-write to hardest-to-write in ascending order. For example, website publications (e.g., tips, stories, and case studies) form the foundation of the pyramid, because they tend to be short and relatively easy to write. They are also published on a fairly infrequent basis, so there is little time pressure involved. More important, content posted to your website can then be used to develop newsletters and blogs, which in turn can be used to create booklets, articles and book chapters.

The pyramid methodology provides you with three benefits. First, it makes it easier to produce high-level content such as book chapters, manuals, and e-books.

Rather than develop a 200-page book from scratch, you can create a series of lower-level publications, such as articles or white papers, that form the chapters for your book. Second, the pyramid provides you with a variety of resources you can use to market your business. For instance, newsletters and blogs offer an excellent means to demonstrate your expertise and promote your speaking brand. Third, the pyramid provides you with potential revenue streams—especially at higher levels, such as booklets, articles, manuals, and books.

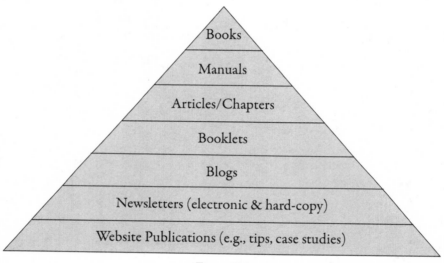

Figure 7-1

Using the Publishing Pyramid is a relatively simple process. It starts with answering two questions:

What does my Publishing Pyramid look like right now? Take a quick review of your writing and publishing history. What have you written in the past few years? Have you developed website publications, such as case studies, tip sheets, stories, or frequently asked questions? Do you publish a newsletter? Do you have a blog? Have you published any articles or book chapters? If you have, this content can be used to jump-start your progress on higher-level publications. If you haven't, no worries—just start your writing journey at the bottom of the pyramid.

Based on the current status of my Publishing Pyramid, what is the best place for me to start? If you have a newsletter, you can use it to create blog posts. If you have published a series of articles, you can use them to develop a manual, book, or e-book. Of course, you can also use the pyramid in reverse. If you have published a book or manual, that can help you create a newsletter, write a series of booklets, or start a blog.

The key is to consider how you can use every publication you create as the foundation for additional publications. For example, if you want to write a book that describes marketing strategies for small businesses in the health care industry, you need to make sure your lower-level publications are specifically geared to this topic. It won't help to have a blog or newsletter that discusses customer service in healthcare or marketing strategies in the automotive industry.

YOUR FIRST THREE STEPS UP THE PYRAMID

1. **Using Tips to Create Tips Booklets**. Your website is a powerful marketing tool for your business, providing information about your company, your background, and your brand. More significantly, it can house helpful resources that encourage visitors to return on a regular basis and purchase your goods and services. Website publications allow you to demonstrate your expertise, and provide your visitors with information, tools and suggestions that can enhance their performance.

Tips are among the easiest and most effective website publications. They consist of a series of recommendations designed to improve performance in a specific area. For example, a diversity expert can create a series of tips that help organizations reduce bias and create more inclusive environments. A leadership expert can create a tips series that helps managers and supervisors resolve conflict more effectively. A wellness authority might develop a sequence of tips that help readers lose weight and live healthier lifestyles.

Start with an action statement and use three or four sentences to describe that statement. For example, our wellness speaker might use the following tip to improve the eating habits of her clients:

HEALTHY TIP: Eat Breakfast Every Day

Eat a healthy breakfast within two hours of waking each morning. This will help boost your metabolism while reducing hunger. Studies have consistently shown that eating breakfast on a daily basis is the one behavior that most healthy-weight people have in common.

One of the most powerful aspects of tips is their ability to form the foundation for higher-level publications. Tips booklets, which occupy the fourth level of the pyramid, offer detailed tools, techniques, and ideas readers can use to improve their performance. They are concise, relatively small (3.5" x 8.5" to fit in a standard envelope), and typically describe specific steps one can take to accomplish a particular task. Booklets allow you to market your business, promote your brand, and generate income through individual and bulk sales—as well as licensing for distribution through client organizations. (See *How to Promote Your Business with Booklets* by Paulette Ensign for some terrific, practical ideas on the subject.)

You can easily use your website tips to develop tips booklets. Simply create a new tip in a particular series on a regular basis; once you've developed about 50 tips, you have the foundation for a booklet. For example, our wellness speaker might create a booklet titled "50 Ways to Lose Weight and Keep It Off Forever." Likewise, a customer service speaker might create a booklet called "75 Tips for Improving Service in Diverse Settings."

Tips on Tips

Develop tips for your website around a common theme (e.g., improving service in diverse settings, losing weight and keeping it off permanently, dealing with difficult employees).

- Update your website with a new tip on a consistent basis (e.g., weekly, semimonthly or monthly). The more often you add a new tip, the less time it will take you to create the content for a booklet. In addition, frequent updates can increase traffic to your website.

- Once you've accumulated enough website tips, put them together in a booklet format. Use a very specific title with a number, such as "101 Ways to Deal with Difficult Employees."

- Make sure you include information on your background, speaking business, products, and services. Place your product information on the back of the title page, and your biographical data on the last page of the booklet.

2. Turning Your Newsletters into Paid Articles

Articles and book chapters occupy the fifth level of the Publishing Pyramid. Creating articles can be an excellent way to demonstrate your expertise and to distribute valuable information to your readers. It can also be a great way to generate income. Many magazines and journals pay for high-quality, timely articles that offer unique perspectives on a specific issue or topic. The key is to develop valuable content that addresses the needs of your particular audience.

One way to do this is to use your newsletter as the foundation for your articles. Because most articles are between 500 and 1,500 words, you don't need a great deal of newsletter content to create a powerful article. Two or three issues will generally suffice. In addition, your newsletters do not have to be written in a serial format to serve as an effective foundation. For example, a business speaker might have an e-newsletter that is geared toward engineering consultants. He could develop a variety of articles on topics such as marketing trends for consultants, selling engineering services in a weak economy, and creating multiple revenue streams for an engineering business.

The first step in this process is to identify periodicals for your articles. *Writer's Market*, edited by Robert Lee Brewer and published annually by Writer's Digest Books, is a useful tool. It provides extensive information on consumer magazines and trade journals that accept queries from authors, including contact people, pay rates, and article requirements. You'll also find helpful information on topics such as feature article writing, developing a successful query letter, and using social media.

Once you have identified several magazines and journals that might be good fits, take the following steps to increase the likelihood of getting your articles approved for submission:

- Familiarize yourself with a few issues of each publication to get a sense of writing style and content.
- Request a copy of the submission guidelines (or find them on the publication's website) and make sure you follow them.
- Write an article that provides tangible benefits for the reader. Your goal is to provide valuable content for your target audience. This will enhance your credibility and increase reader interest in your services.

- Once published, order reprints of the article and distribute them to clients and potential clients. This is a very powerful marketing practice that clearly demonstrates your knowledge base and expertise—far better than your brochures can. You should also obtain digital copies of your articles and post them on your website.

- As you send out queries to various periodicals, include digital copies of your past articles as an example of your writing ability.

- If you have a blog, put links to your articles in your posts.

3. Blogging Your Way to a Book

A published book makes a powerful statement about your credibility and expertise. It positions you as a thought leader, increases your brand recognition, and boosts your speaking fees—which is why so many speakers want to write a book. It can be a formidable task, but the Publishing Pyramid can facilitate the process.

One way to develop book content is through your blog. An effective blog offers an inexpensive means to promote your speaking business, demonstrate your expertise, and bring people with similar interests together. Blogging can also facilitate content development, because it requires frequent updates, relatively short posts, and the ease of developing content in a serial fashion. This final point is critical if you want to develop book content from your individual blog posts. To be successful, you have to create posts that connect to one another in a systematic fashion.

For instance, an expert on motivation can develop a content stream that offers specific tips on motivating employees in the workplace. If she posts a new tip on her blog each week, she will have more than 100 tips in just two years—easily enough content for the foundation of a book on employee motivation. Likewise, a diversity expert could develop a book that offers advice on improving communication in diverse settings. He could develop two posts each week that provide readers with communication tips, tools, and suggestions. A year later, he would have tremendous amount of content for the development of his book.

Take the following steps to enhance the quality of your blog and boost the effectiveness of your content development process:

- Start with an end in mind by developing a detailed outline of the book you want to write. Your outline should include a working title, description, target market, outstanding features, and benefits for readers. Most significantly, it should include a description of each chapter.

- Use your chapter descriptions to identify topics for your blog posts. This allows you to develop book content through your blog over an extended period of time.

- Update your blog at least twice a week. This will increase your followers and allow you to develop book content more quickly. Feel free to include blog posts that are not connected to your book. This will enhance the overall quality of your blog.

- Keep your blog posts to 300–400 words. Your readers want to receive useful information in a concise manner and are more likely to read brief posts, while writing a minimum of 300 words will maximize the benefits of search engine optimization. It is also easier to create a series of short posts than one long post.

FIVE MORE WAYS TO REPURPOSE YOUR CONTENT

As they say in the infomercials, "But wait! There's more!" In addition to the aforementioned examples, here are five relatively simple ways to repurpose your content with the Publishing Pyramid:

1. **Make comments and use them for your own website publications.** Offering comments on blog posts, e-zine articles, and other online publications can give you a head start on becoming an author. You can use these comments to develop website publications, as described earlier in this chapter.

2. **Turn your LinkedIn question responses into blog posts**. One of the benefits of LinkedIn is that it allows you to respond to member questions, which is a great way to demonstrate your expertise and share your knowledge. You can repurpose your answers to these questions by turning them into blog posts.

3. **Turn your blog posts into white papers**. A white paper is an expert article designed to solve a particular problem or address a specific issue. Since

many blog posts offer tips, recommendations, and advice on a specific topic, you can use a series of posts as the foundation for a white paper in your particular area of expertise.

4. **Use a series of white papers to create a manual.** A series of white papers around a particular topic can serve as the foundation for a manual, which is a document that teaches readers how to carry out a particular task or achieve a specific goal. Manuals can be an excellent product for speakers because they are shorter and less expensive to produce than books, and they sell at a higher price point.

5. **Create lower-level publications from your book.** I mentioned earlier that you can use the Publishing Pyramid in reverse. Specifically, you can use high-level publications such as books, e-books, and manuals to create newsletters, blog posts, and articles. For example, you can create a series of articles from a book. You can also create a series of booklets, which you could then use to market your book and generate a separate stream of income. You can even create blog posts that could be used to promote your book. The possibilities are virtually unlimited!

Writing can be an extremely powerful tool for demonstrating your expertise, promoting your brand, generating multiple revenue streams, and establishing your credentials as a thought leader. The process can also enhance your ability as a speaker, because successful writing requires you to organize your thoughts and articulate your points in a coherent fashion. Put simply, writing improves your ability to think.

So, what does your Publishing Pyramid look like right now? What's the best place for you to start? Choose a simple publication, pull up a chair, power up your computer, and embark on your writing journey!

Tyrone A. Holmes, EdD, CPT, is a business and writing coach who helps his speaking, coaching, and consulting clients maximize income potential and write their way to more business. He has used the Publishing Pyramid to create two successful blogs; to develop a series of newsletters; to publish articles, booklets, and book chapters; and to publish two books: *Training and Coaching the Competitive Cyclist* and *Developing Training Plans for Cyclists and Triathletes*. Visit his websites at www.DoctorHolmes.net and www.HolmesFitness.com.

USE YOUR WRITING EXPERTISE TO ATTRACT MORE SPEAKING BUSINESS

Maura Schreier-Fleming

Anyone can write. Unfortunately, many of us don't enjoy it, thanks to lingering high school memories of painstaking work soaked in red ink. But here's the fact: You are no longer a teenager, and that ancient fear of writing has no place in your business today. Indeed, I'm here to tell you that writing is a fantastic way to sell your speaking talents—and I'm living proof.

Why write? Whether you verbalize it or not, you're in the business of making money. You do that through speaking, and you have to sell your speaking if you want to get booked. Yet the idea of selling, much like writing, induces fear for many speakers. It doesn't matter that they excel at the speaking part of their business, delivering presentations in an engaging, compelling way that draws the audience in and empowers them to act. But being a great presenter is not enough to make a sale.

The people who hire speakers are often risk averse, understandably, when it comes to hiring a speaker whom they haven't heard speak. That basic fact limits your options, unless you're speaking every day to groups where the audience includes decision makers who hire speakers. If that doesn't sound like you, you need some help to get booked. And that's where your writing can help.

What's your perception of someone who is published? Knowledgeable and professional, perhaps. When most people read a clever or thought-provoking article, they perceive the writer to be an expert. If it's a current or interesting subject, they might seek out other things the author has written, or even track them down at a conference or meeting.

You're that expert. You know you can speak. You just may not realize you can write. You can, and I can show you how.

STEP 1: YOUR STORY STARTS HERE.

Let's begin with the concept that as long as you can count, you can write. Why? Because writing is a four-step process. If you can count to four, you're already on your way to an article that you can submit for publishing.

Of course, before you can start jamming away at the keyboard, you need to have something to say. As an expert, that means tapping into your body of knowledge, such as what problems your clients face, how you helped them, and how others can prevent, avoid, or manage these problems. If you work primarily with business professionals, think about what they want to achieve, such as increasing revenues or decreasing costs. Again, if you've helped your clients do either or both, you could write about how you achieved those results—and how others can apply the same strategies.

Write what people like to read. Readers crave "how to" articles, so that's always a good framework. Using the examples above, your topic could be "7 Steps to Avoid (Big Problem)" or "5 Strategies to (Increase Revenues/Decrease Costs)." Some of my best-received stories have been "7 Habits of Less Successful Salespeople," "The Biggest Myth in Sales," and "Are You Making It Harder to Buy?" In "The Biggest Myth in Sales," I debunked the belief that being a gifted talker is what makes a salesperson successful. Actually, it's *listening* . . . and I gave readers practical tips on improving their skills.

As you generate possible topics, you'll think about the specifics of what you want to share with a reader that highlights your expertise. At the same time, you're also probably brainstorming possible titles, though it's not essential that you have your final title yet. Personally, I like to start with at least a working title, because it helps me organize my thoughts. It doesn't have to be perfect or final, just a guide for my creative thinking to get the ideas out.

A clever title catches readers' interest, perhaps with a question that challenges them or echoes a thought they've had in their own head; for example, "Do You Have What It Takes to Sell?" Titles that discuss pain (or avoiding it) also make for a good tease, such as "3 Easy Ways to Avoid Losing the Sale." Keep in mind that online publications or blogs also require attention to keywords in your article title to ensure that they're found and ranked well by search engines.

STEP 2: PICK 3 POINTS.

Appropriately enough, Step 2 deals with two dreaded words: writer's block. Staring at a computer screen in an empty gaze, wondering when the ideas will flow. Nothing happens and frustration increases. Rinse and repeat.

You can avoid writer's block by tapping into the way your brain wants to work. Here's how. Say you're writing about three, five, or seven points on increasing revenues. Start by putting that many bullets on the page or on your computer screen. If you haven't decided on how many points you're going to make, just put three bullets on the page.

Why? I call it the "Hangman Principle." You remember the old word game, where you wrote dashed lines on a page, with each line signifying a place for a letter in a word that the other person had to guess? Each correct guess filled the line with the correct letters, while each miss started to complete the hangman sketch. As the lines got filled in it, the person could guess the unknown word. That's how you got a winner.

Your brain likes completion. The blank lines invited your brain to think of the possible letters that could fill the line. Those three article bullets do the same thing: Your brain knows it must create three new ideas. It's a simple way to stimulate creativity and reduce writer's block.

I can promise you that you will always come up with ideas, tapping into both your conscious and unconscious mind. Relax as you think, and let your mind go from one idea to the next. If one thought leads you to another thought, that's perfect! This process, known as associating, is how the brain works. You will eventually come up with the ideas that work for your article.

Capture your ideas. The three bullets then will become the three main paragraphs that you're going to write. (Note: You don't have to do this all in one sitting. Your brain will be processing even when you're not sitting at the computer.) As an idea pops into your head, wherever you are, write it down. Sometimes other bullet points will come to mind. Add them. Before you go further, select the three most important bullets.

As other ideas relate to the bullets, jot them down. I like my bullets to have a phrase with a verb. In my "7 Habits" article, one of the bullets is "Talks too much." Another is "Expecting things to happen now." With phrases like these, I get an idea of what I will be writing. In the creative process, it's most important to get the ideas out of your head—you can worry about the order and grammatical construction later.

STEP 3: IT'S TIME TO START WRITING.

Based on the three most compelling bullets, you can begin crafting your message. These bullets will become your subheads, and can be used visually to guide your creativity. Make them bold so they catch your attention as you write and can serve as placeholders for your creative ideas. Subheads also help readers to understand what to expect and what's most important.

Sound conversational. It's usually appropriate to write the way you speak, while respecting good grammar. You're writing in an informal style for a business reader, not in a legal style suited for a court of law. (Does legalese make you want to read more? Unless you're a lawyer working on an important case, probably not.)

The goal is to sound conversational as you write, which is why you'll often hear an emphasis on using the active rather than passive voice: "He called the customer," not "The customer was called." Active voice is easier to read, because that's how people tend to speak.

Make it easier to write. It's common to focus on getting one sentence perfect before writing the next. Don't do it! You're wasting your creative energy if you focus on the perfect comma placement instead of the next good idea. Particularly during the first draft, it's more important to get the ideas out of your brain than it is for them to be perfect. You can, and will, edit later.

How long does it need to be? Most publications have a preferred word count range. An article with a few lines of introduction, three main points, and a conclusion will be about 500 to 700 words. Some journals want much longer articles, perhaps 2,500 words or more. How do you get there? Add a few more bullet points and start writing. Likewise, if you're running long, tighten your sentences and eliminate redundant or less important thoughts to reduce the number of words.

Read what you write. I'll generally reread my article several times before I find it's ready to send off for editorial review. I'm looking for major issues with clarity, sentence structure, and grammar—I want to make sure my ideas flow from one paragraph to the next, and try to reduce the number of words to the fewest, clearest words.

If there's time, it's helpful to reread the article the next day or at least after a brief break. I want my mind clear to get a fresh take on things. Sometimes an idea that appeared perfectly clear one day is confusing the next. That's when it's time to rewrite and improve the sentence to convey precisely what you mean.

Your bio is important. Even though your article is written, you still have one more writing step: the bio. After all, your objective is that the reader of your article will want to hear you speak. A solid bio showcases your expertise and confirms that you'd be a good match based on what you can produce for a client. Your readers also need to be able to contact you, so make sure to include your website, e-mail, and phone number. Obviously, an editor reserves the right to trim things down—but always provide a juicy pitch for them to work with.

STEP 4: PITCH AND GET PUBLISHED.

Want to get hired by more people like your clients? Ask them what trade journals they read, and make those your key targets. Before you contact the editor, check the publication's website to see if there's an editorial calendar and whether your particular topic fits an upcoming issue. If there are writer's guidelines available, great: Those will let you know the preferred method of making contact, whether regular mail, e-mail, or phone. When calling an editor, introduce yourself with a prepared introduction, including something that establishes you as someone who is familiar with their industry and readers.

Pitch your article. A solid pitch revolves around why a story is interesting for the publication's readers. Have that reason front and center, whether it's a verbal or written conversation, and pay close attention to the response to your proposal. Even if it's not a perfect fit, you might be able to modify your topic or word count to fit an editor's needs—and then stay within those limits. Be aware that e-mail queries don't always get a response, and never send attachments unless they're requested in the writer's guidelines.

You can write, if you're an expert who speaks. Now that you know how to write your first article, it's time to discover how good you are at writing—and experience that delightful feeling when speaking business starts to come to you.

4 Ways to Get Business by Writing

1. Write about a topic that will impact your customers' businesses.
2. Pick three main points.
3. Write without editing your thoughts.
4. Contact the editors of journals that your customers read.

Maura Schreier-Fleming founded Best@Selling in 1997. She works with sales professionals to shorten their sales cycles and increase sales. She is the author of *Real-World Selling for Out-of-This-World Results* and *Monday Morning Sales Tips* and writes several business columns, including "Customer Connections" for the Dallas, Austin, and Houston *Business Journals*. Maura's website is www.BestAtSelling.com and e-mail is Maura@BestAtSelling.com.

BREAK OUT WITH YOUR BEST BOOK

Mindy Gibbins-Klein

Speakers are often told, "You must have a book." Well, I disagree. I think the new imperative is: "You must have a *great* book." After all, the biggest reason for a speaker to write and publish a book is credibility. And only a great book stands out and builds real credibility in this increasingly competitive market.

So many speakers have written at least one book that it's not such a novelty anymore. Speakers bureaus and conference organizers used to ask, "Do you have a book? If so, what is the title?" Now, the question is often, "What is the title of your book?" Many booking forms even have room for you to list *all* of your books and other products! So, having a book has become table stakes—the minimum requirement to even play at the table.

WHY WRITE A BOOK?

There are many good reasons to write and publish your own book. I have chosen the ones that I have heard most often over the past ten years of coaching aspiring authors. As you read these, consider which ones are relevant for you. Reflecting on this for even a few minutes should get you excited about writing a book. You'll be ready to make a publishing commitment in no time!

Credibility. Are you impressed when you hear someone has written a book? Even though it's common among us speakers, remember that most people never write and publish a book, so they're likely to be impressed with those who have. I have lost count of the number of clients who said they had inquiries and booked business because someone was impressed by their book.

Being an author has an inherent authority; you can even see the resemblance in the two words. People assume you know what you are talking about and consider you an expert on the topic. But if someone reads it, the quality must stand up to scrutiny. So, again, it is not any old book that builds credibility, but a good one.

Income Stream. These days, you need to have several different ways of generating income. The economy has made it more challenging to rely only on live speaking, although there are some speakers who still make a great living doing that. For the majority of speakers, it is a good idea to diversify, using products like books to drive revenue.

Your core speaking business will benefit from the book. Internet marketing guru Bill Glazer estimates that a speaker with a best-selling book will be booked much more often and for twice the fee, compared with a speaker without a book. I know hundreds of speakers who prove that theory. For example, UK negotiation speaker Chris Merrington has kept his professional fees high and has won more speaking, training, and consulting business after the publication of his book, *Why Do Smart People Make Such Stupid Mistakes?* He estimates that the book has brought in $100,000 of new revenue for his speaking business in the first year alone.

You can make money with your book in lots of ways:

- Selling it directly to individuals online and at events
- Selling it in bulk to organizations
- Using it to enhance your speaker fee, or to negotiate with meeting planners
- Bundling it with other products and services you offer
- Having colleagues and affiliates sell it from their websites and at their programs
- Offering it as a bonus for people who do programs with you
- Turning sections or chapters of the book into separate e-books and other products that you can sell

With the ease of publishing, including digital and other formats, you can even have multiple versions of your book out there such as e-books, audio books, and multimedia versions, each earning its own income stream.

Wider Reach. Speakers who speak a lot may touch many people each year, but they still get to meet only those folks who can get to the events. Many other potential clients and fans will miss out on your great content if they are not able to travel, can't afford the conference fee, etc. Webinars and other online events help expand the numbers, but there are still so many others you could touch if you had the right book.

Sense of Achievement/Fulfillment. Finally, having a great sense of personal satisfaction, achievement, or fulfillment is a valid enough reason to do it. So many times, clients almost apologize for having this on their list of reasons, as if the commercial factors are the only ones that count. I rate writing and publishing your own book right up there with starting your own business, running a marathon, climbing a mountain, and any other big personal goal.

YOUR BEST BOOK

You are more than capable of writing your "best book." It probably has to do with the topic that you find yourself speaking, blogging, and thinking about most often. It is almost certainly about the things that inspire you to work as hard as you do, with the passion that inspires others.

A key reason to write your best book is to introduce new ideas or perspectives to your market. This is also called thought leadership.

New Perspectives/Thought Leadership. *Thought leadership* is a popular buzzword, but there is still real value in it. I believe it is essential for entrepreneurs and speakers scrambling around in a shrinking marketplace crowded with other experts to work toward being known as thought leaders. If you are going to go to the effort of writing a book, consider writing one that makes a big splash. People talk about it, share it, tweet it. Basically, it goes viral. Then, it remains in circulation for a long time. It has longevity because it presents an important idea (usually a new idea) in an exciting and accessible way. It sets the author up as a thought leader in his or her space. People associate that book with that author and vice versa.

Think Stephen Covey's *The Seven Habits of Highly Effective People*, Seth Godin's *Unleashing the Ideavirus* and *Tribes*, Malcolm Gladwell's *The Tipping Point* and *Blink*, and Sam Horn's *POP!* These are books that are exceptional, original, and talked about.

It's not about volume of production. I see people bragging on social media about having written 28 e-books, and yet, most of the time, none of them stand out or are remarkable in any way. Furthermore, it can even hurt your reputation to have too many books or e-books out there.

The more you produce, the more you diffuse, distract, and dilute. How can your readers or customers be expected to find the gems? I would suggest you not make them do the work. Your potential readers and clients need you to guide them and show them your absolute best stuff first.

If you have been lucky or smart enough to have written and published an iconic, thought-leading book, that book should be the main book featured on your websites, profiles, e-mail signatures, etc. If people are interested, they know how to Google you or trawl through websites and social media to find the rest.

One great book trumps a hundred mediocre ones. The bar has been raised. It's time to jump higher.

HOW TO ENSURE YOU WRITE YOUR BEST BOOK

Let's assume you are now convinced that you should have a great book to boost your speaking career. How do you go about creating a really great book? Below are ten key factors that will elevate your book, and you, to that next level.

1. **Be strategic.** My father, bless his soul, used to say that he could write only when he was inspired. He wrote some very good screenplays during his lifetime, but he also had long periods (months and even years) when he wrote nothing. Nothing at all. He was not inspired. I know others who have had a flash of inspiration at 2:00 a.m., wrote for a week straight, and ended up with a 100,000-word book that needed very heavy editing, which the author did not want to do, couldn't do, and couldn't afford to pay someone else to do. If you are a professional, then be professional about your book.

   Invest the time and money to do it right and do it well. The process I recommend requires only eight hours a week for twelve weeks, to get a great book planned and written and the final version ready to publish. If you can't invest that kind of time, you may want to wait until you can concentrate on it. In my opinion, there is no point dabbling and having it drag on for months or years. Decide if it is a *must* and carve out the time to do it. You can go back to your busy life in a few months, but with a book to your name.

2. **Write the book you want to write, not the book you think you should write.** As I mentioned, speakers are told they must have a book. Some panic, scratching around for something to write. Others pick random ideas they think will be popular in the market. There is a book you would love to write, one that excites you and would inspire others. That is the one you should write.

3. **Plan it**. It has been said that "if you fail to plan, you plan to fail." This is exceptionally accurate when it comes to something as important as a book that is meant to position you as a thought leader in your space. Really think about things before starting, then plan your time and plan your other products like blogs, articles, videos, and keynotes around the book. Some pointers to get you started:

   - A full-length book normally has between 150 and 250 pages.
   - It is now considered OK to write the way you speak.
   - Don't use too many footnotes and references if you want a mainstream book.
   - Keep chapters to a sensible length—2,500 to 3,000 words each. Shorter is also fine, if you want a book with many short chapters.
   - Ten to twelve chapters is a good number to aim for in a business book.
   - You do not need to do as much research as you may think. People want *your* ideas and point of view.

4. **Create the right plan for the right book.** Don't just plan the content; plan every aspect of your book: the outcomes you want, your exact target market, how you plan to use the book in your overall marketing efforts, whether illustrations are necessary, the ideal length of the book. Don't leave anything to chance. At The Book Midwife®, our clients spend several weeks on their plans before they are even allowed to write. Sound like a chore? Proper planning can reduce the project by up to 100 hours. Maybe now it sounds less like a chore.

5. **Get help if you need it.** Let go of any idea that you must do all of this by yourself. There are plenty of resources available now to help authors plan, write, edit, publish, and market books fast and effectively.

6. **Coaching.** I have seen what good coaching can do for people with big goals. Most people who want to run their best marathon or their best business have a coach or consultant to help them make it happen. I believe that having a good coach helping you with your book right from the start will ensure you actually do it (accountability and motivation), do it faster (tips and techniques for greater efficiency), and end up with a better result (having input as it takes shape, not just at the end).

7. **Editing.** Every serious entrepreneur and speaker must edit his or her book or have it edited before it goes to print. I cringe when I see typos and other errors that could have been avoided. They make the author look bad and often distract from good content. I recommend all speakers have their books edited by professionals, people who have been trained and who work with full-length books all the time. I am talking about copy editing—spelling, grammar, punctuation, sentence structure.

There are several schools of thought when it comes to content editing, or developmental editing. My personal belief is that the author, as subject matter expert, is the best judge of what needs to be in the book, how much, and where. New authors tend to doubt themselves and think that someone else would do a better job with the writing. You probably want to do one (or more) of three things with your book: educate, inspire, entertain. You can do this by writing from the heart about the subject you know best, and telling your own authentic stories.

8. **Publish professionally.** It is now so easy to publish a book that it has commoditized the process and the product. If you are not desperate to see your book out immediately, perhaps you want to see if you can get a traditional book deal. If you want it out quickly but want to outsource the entire job to a reputable independent or cooperative publisher, there are some good

ones around. Look at other books they have done, and find out what value the publishing partners added for the authors. A cheaply designed book can have a detrimental effect on the author's credibility!

9. **Don't be stingy with your books.** A client of mine was heading to a very important meeting with key influencers in her market. There were about twenty people on the list, and she asked me how many books she should take and what she should charge for them. I said, "Take twenty books, and give them all away!"

My good friend Dan Poynter, CSP, suggests that authors give the first 500 copies of their book away. Five hundred copies?! Absolutely. Some of the top entrepreneurial speakers I know give away thousands each year. People value a book very highly, and in many cases feel obliged to read it or at least skim through it.

I know the book is supposed to be an income stream, but as I mentioned above, that income does not all need to come directly from book sales. It is much easier to make the big bucks in other ways and use the book as a marketing tool. Say you net a $5 profit from each book you sell. For every 100 books sold, you will have made $500. Compare that with giving away some books to key influencers, prospective clients, and meeting planners. Every speaking engagement, training, or coaching contract that results from those giveaway books will make you the same $500 or, hopefully, much more.

And you can sell books at the back of the room, front of the room, or on your website, too, increasing the overall return on that investment.

10. **Love your audience.** I know you love your audience. It's easy when you are on the stage, getting live feedback, and enjoying the energy. How can you replicate that feeling with a book? I suggest that you pour the same amount of love into your book as you would if you were there live, so that it reaches the reader intact and they can feel it, even if they never get to meet you in person. Great books, just like great speeches, are the ones that resonate with the audience. And the best way to do that is to share your best content and wisdom with love.

Mindy Gibbins-Klein is an international speaker, author, and entrepreneur. Through her coaching company, The Book Midwife®, and publishing company, Ecademy Press, she and her team have helped more than 500 expert speakers and business owners write and publish great books fast. Seth Godin called Mindy's latest book, *24 Carat Bold,* "practical and inspiring." Mindy is the current president of the Professional Speaking Association's (PSA) London chapter. Mindy lives in London, England, with her husband and two teenage children. Visit www.mindygk.com or e-mail mindy@bookmidwife.com.

BETTER THAN A BUSINESS CARD: HOW A BOOK CAN BECOME YOUR TOP MARKETING TOOL

Les Kletke

When was the last time someone asked you to autograph your business card—or better, paid you for one? Yet, hand them a book and that is exactly what they'll want to do.

Many speakers think of writing a book as a chore that should return them some money from sales; others have dreams of crafting a best seller that leads to rock-star status and seven-figure advances from publishers. Reality lies somewhere between for most of us. A book can be thought of as a business card on steroids, and when you reframe it that way, you'll soon see how it's the best marketing tool in your arsenal.

The good news is that, although writing a book requires a good deal of hard work, you have done much of it in researching the topic that you speak about as a professional speaker. You've also attained a certain degree of visibility as an expert who people want to hear. A book allows you to turn that information into another marketable product and helps promote your career as a speaker.

OUT OF THE GARAGE AND INTO THE WORLD

Too many people publish a book and then complain that they have cases of them in their garage or basement. The day I figured out those books in my garage were not doing me any good—in fact, they were causing trouble in my marriage, because they were blocking access to the front of the garage—was the day I found the value in the books I had written.

My wife had been threatening to throw them out if I didn't sell them soon. On the other hand, no one was beating a path to my door, mostly because they didn't know I had written a half-dozen books. I started to give them away, not haphazardly, but with a purpose. Within a month, my speaking calendar showed the results.

I had a few hundred books left from a commissioned assignment I had done in Nepal, studying the agriculture of the country and writing a book on the advancements the country's farmers had made with small cooperatives. Much of the book was about the underdeveloped coffee industry in Nepal, which can't quite reach the critical mass for Starbucks to give the country its own brand.

So, when a new boutique coffee shop was about to open in our town, I approached the owner and asked if he would like 100 books for the grand opening. I offered to sign them and include an inscription about the opening. He was overjoyed, and within a month after the event, I had a call for a speaking engagement from a person who'd attended. That was an audience I would not have reached with my usual marketing program.

We can spend a lot of time dissecting the return on investment for giving those books to the coffee shop, but I know that the value of the speaking engagement and the books I sold there were very well received. I had the bonus of more space in my garage.

Books are a great way to promote yourself. I leave one at my dentist's office, doctor's office, accountant's, or any place that has a waiting room. You never know who the next person in the waiting room will be, and your book only has to beat out a four-year-old copy of *Time* to be the most interesting item on the table.

Drop off a copy at the local paper or radio and TV stations, and let them know that you are available for an interview. Don't expect one immediately, but on a slow news day you might just get a call. Never say you're too busy (even if you are). Make time for an interview, and you'll move up the expert list and will be called more regularly.

If you're a consultant, make sure that you send prospective clients copies of your book. Expensive? A fancy brochure will spend thirty seconds on a client's desk before getting round-filed, but a book might just get a place on the shelf where she will see it every day. What would you pay for that kind of exposure? The cost of that book is now very reasonable.

When you open a book and it is signed to someone, you feel like you are in the presence of someone special. You can give your potential client that feeling by giving them an autographed book, and they most likely will show it off in their office—to someone who is another perspective client.

I worked with one consultant who had no intention of ever selling a book. Instead, he expected to give every one of his books away, putting a price on the back cover only to have perceived value. You work hard to open the door; when it's open, step in—don't miss out on a $7 ticket, which is about what a book costs you.

As a published author, you go from someone who knows something to an expert. When I published my first book, I tripled my fee. I sold a few books, but the increased speaking revenues more than paid for the time it took to write out the stories that I'd told from the stage for years. Now people had a part of me to take home with them.

RETHINKING WHEN TO MAKE YOUR PITCH

Let me be clear: Don't sell from the podium! It's trashy, and it makes you and the event organizer look bad. The better play is to include the price of a copy of your book for everyone in the audience in your contract. Then you're available to mingle with the audience or personalize copies after you leave the stage. If you get just one more engagement, you're better off than selling a couple of cases of books.

The time to sell your books is after completing the negotiations for a speaking engagement. I offer the client a reduced rate, half the cover price if the client buys one for everyone in the audience. It might come from a different budget, and you may be asked to invoice the speaking and the books separately, but that's a small inconvenience for selling copies to the entire audience.

It's also about the value of your time, to you and your client, when you leave the stage. What works for them? Are you better off selling a few books . . . or connecting on a personal level with the audience?

Even better, help your client get local or national sponsorship for the books. It makes them look good to include a $20 or $25 book in the registration package (even if it only cost them $10). It's a much more memorable takeaway than a coffee mug, baseball hat, or cheap T-shirt, and it has more retention power for the advertiser, who can also include a business card as a bookmark. I offer to autograph each book and make a notation about the event—always using the same black pen when signing the books and personalizing them at the event. Have a few extras on hand for the client to give to folks who missed the meeting or in case attendance is higher than expected.

ONE KEY COPY TO GIVE OUT

Your book is a great "thank you" for the organizer, particularly one who was too busy to attend the event. A copy with a thank-you inscription is the best investment you will ever make. She is your reference and your advertising champion—so treat her like gold!

My role as a speaker is always to make a seamless event. No event organizer wants a prima donna who makes demands about what needs to be included in the dressing room; she needs someone who reduces her stress. I find my own way to the event, get there a day early, stay a bit longer than my presentation if that's what it takes, and give her a signed copy of my book to say thanks for choosing me to be a part of her event.

Hardcover copies are ideal—they cost under $20 a copy and are perfect for thank-you gifts and special presentations. They have the same content as my other books, but the dressed-up version features a full-color dust jacket, a ribbon book mark, and color pictures.

PUBLISH A BOOK IN 90 DAYS: A FOUR-STEP METHOD

Now that you are aware of the value and varied purposes of a book, it's a matter of getting one into print or e-book form. Either is fine; it is a matter of getting good material into a book that will leave readers with a message and a feeling of value when they are done reading. The retail price on the book is not the issue here, as long as your book has something of value for the reader. Time is our most valuable commodity—a book that sells for $8 and does not deliver a message is a far worse deal than a $30 book that generates one amazing idea or deliverable for the reader.

If you follow what I call the ISRI (Introduction, Story, Reason, and Impact), method you will be able to write a book in 30 days, and have it published in 90 days. This is not a linear process, and requires doing several things during the same time period.

The first is writing. The average book written by a speaker today contains about 50,000 words. So let's break that down into manageable tasks.

The first step is to make a list of the 25 concepts that you want to include in your book, whether it's a business book, autobiography, or any other genre. Make a list of the 25 most important concepts that come to mind; don't get hung up on having the right items on the list, just sit down and do it. This is a living document and can change—but you will find that about 22 or 23 of the items that you come up with are the right ones. No matter how long you spend thinking and changing them, you will come back to those that you listed on your first serious attempt. These are going to become the chapters in the book.

The other way to think of it is that your 50,000-word book is 25 chapters of 2,000 words each. That's still a formidable task, so let's break it down even further.

The ISRI system is so named because these are the components of each chapter. Start with an **introduction**: Set the stage for the reader (though you might sometimes write the story first and then set the stage later) in the first 500 words.

The **story** is the anecdote or story that came to mind when you made that original list to illustrate that point or concept. I assign about 500 words to this segment, though it may vary a little. (Without rules or guidelines, you might end up like my client who wrote an 8,000 word introduction to her book before she got started!) Just as you respect other peoples' time when you're on stage, so do the same thing for your book.

The next 500 words provide the **reason** you choose to put that story among your 25 items. Explain why that story is important. What was the lesson? What was learned?

The final 500 words of the chapter is the **impact**: More specifically, what was the long-term impact of this incident? The reason is why the story is important, while the impact is relates how it affected your life or those around you.

On day 2, you approach the next item on the list with the ISRI strategy. Doing this, you will have the content of a book completed in thirty days, with a couple of days for rewrites or just plain goofing off. Just like exercise, it is important to write every day—and once you get into the habit, you will feel a part of your day is missing if you don't sit down to do it.

The next thirty days on the program are intended for editing, and you need to hire a professional editor—not just a friend who is good at grammar. Editors are professionals whose job it is to make your writing look good. You can begin shopping for one once you have a couple of chapters of your book done. The first one you find may not be the one for you, so don't be afraid to shop around. Many will offer to do a chapter of your book on a trial basis, to give you an estimate of the cost and what the final product will look like.

The final thirty days are for printing. While most printers won't take the full thirty days, that includes time for checking the proofs and a final check. Don't leave cover design and back cover copy for the last minute—start that during your first few weeks, and the printing process will go much more smoothly. When you are deciding on a title or a cover design, think of who your market is, not your favorite doodle. This is a business card and represents you when you are not there, so do it professionally.

The ISRI method works. You'll get the book done in a relatively short time, but don't be afraid to enlist someone ask you the questions, to hear yourself tell the stories, for example. Transcribing a tape doesn't generate an instant chapter, but the interview can surely help you develop it. You might get a better idea of what the reader will be thinking, what they would like to hear more about, and when you are including too much detail.

There's no good reason to be afraid of getting assistance. I know people who bill themselves at $1,000 but refuse to pay a coach half that to help them write their books, or who use a "friend" to design the cover instead of a top-notch graphic designer. This is a business, and your book is your business card. Throughout the process, think of how proud you'll be the first time you're paid to hand out an autographed copy.

Les Kletke has authored seven books and helped scores of people write their own. He spent 15 years as the host of a daily news magazine radio show, where he honed his skills as an interviewer. As a freelance writer, he has contributed to more than 50 publications from local to national. Les has travelled to more than 30 countries and has had his passport stolen on 6 continents. He speaks about international business and how understanding other cultures can turn barricades to bridges. Along with working as a ghostwriter and book coach, Les conducts boot camps during which he guarantees clients will leave with three completed chapters after the two-day event. His website is www.TheGlobalGhostwriter.com, and he can be reached at lkletke@ mymts.net or (204) 324-6278.

HOW AUTHOR AND
BOOK PLATFORMS LEAD TO
ROCK-STAR BRANDING

Judith Briles

Picture this: You have an idea for a book that is rejected by every major publisher, a book that contains extensive research and interviews. You can feel it in every bone of your body. You know it's a breakout . . . a leap in your speaking career and a potential bestseller. Do you scrap it, or do you keep pushing, because in your heart of hearts, you know it's big?

That's where I was in late 1986—just coming through an embezzlement that personally cost me in excess of $1 million, a health crisis, and a challenge to my company. I had an idea. I had completed the work for my dissertation; had completed more than 300 one-on-one interviews with women; and had begun writing the commercial book . . . a book that hadn't been written on the topic I was immersed in . . . painfully immersed in.

I was passionate about the topic. I had a vision for the path it would take me on. I was committed in time, energy, and money to make it happen. It was the twenty-eight rejections that created a bit of a roadblock along the way. Everything from, "It doesn't fit our list," to "No media will ever cover this type of topic," to feminist Gloria Steinem telling me, "Don't write about this . . . don't publish this," over dinner one evening at a conference we were both speaking at in Milwaukee.

"But Gloria, *Ms.* magazine went under because of the backstabbing and undermining of your female staff," I responded.

That topic was women and sabotage. Or specifically, why women undermine other women and how to change it. A taboo topic . . . one that no one was speaking on and certainly no one was writing about. My niche to be.

Not knowing a lick about self-publishing (outside of its meaning "vanity press" and taboo for "legit" authors), I sold the book to a small New York press, ignoring the advice of all. My agent told me to; he believed in the book as well.

There is nothing accidental about creating your platform. All successful businesses, speakers, experts, and authors have one. Their survival and success depend on it.

GOT PLATFORM?

If you plan to write a book and use it for marketing your speaking expertise, you need a platform. I had a platform in the eighties; it just wasn't called that back then.

The author's platform consists of three key areas: vision, passion, and commitment. Think of it as a funnel with three balls. Each is connected to the author as they flow through the neck. While within the funnel, they are tossed about as the book is getting ready for birth. The fourth area that comes into play is people—they will find you through your channels of vision, passion, and commitment.

With the Internet, many believe that the platform is all about the people you are connected with. Granted, you've got to have people to buy your books—but the three factors of vision, passion, and commitment are essential. People won't care about you or your book if you don't have them.

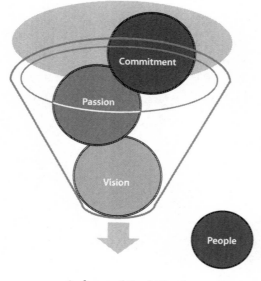

Author and Book Platform

THE VISION FACTOR

It starts with vision—what you as the author visualizes and feels is the big picture. Within your vision, your ideas formulate; they take root and embrace all the "what ifs" that can come your way. Where do you see your book taking you? Where do you see taking your book? What does it look like? Does your book have a "look" to it—for both the cover and interior design?

What and who is your audience? If you think "everyone," you will get lost in the crowd. The niche factor is powerful—narrow your book's audience, where a smaller crowd can find you as you reach out as the expert/go-to person.

When *Woman to Woman: From Sabotage to Support* was initially published in 1987, I thought it was for every working woman. Wrong. No book is for everyone. The belief came from naïveté on my part—it was part of my vision. I knew there was a problem; I understood what the emotional, physical, and financial effects were for working women—I thought that all women would also see my vision. Wrong. And incredibly naïve.

Initially, I firmly believed that the book and the topic were ideal for the general workplace. But corporate America was scared to death of the topic. Women undermining women? You've got to be kidding! I had conducted a national study that included several thousand men and women; interviewed and listened to hundreds of painful stories of betrayal; and discovered that productivity and turnover were directly related . . . surely corporate America wanted the message. Wrong, wrong, wrong. It was a hot potato. Gender harassment topics—women undermining and harassing women—were forbidden. On the other hand, sexual harassment topics—men harassing women—were in.

I thought the mainstream media would embrace it. Right. *Oprah* loved it. So did CNN, *Donahue, Sally, Geraldo,* and every other first-name host, along with the *Wall Street Journal, People* magazine, *Time, Newsweek, USA Today,* local press, radio, and TV across the county. Even the *National Enquirer. Woman to Woman* was a publicist's dream.

After the first *Oprah* appearance, my offices received a call from another Palo Altoan—Tom Peters's personal assistant. She had heard about the book . . . the women in his office were driving him nuts with the backstabbing and gossiping. Could I come in and talk with them and bring a copy of the *Oprah* show? I did. Not surprising, he was leery of the topic—the hot-potato factor—and too hot for the corporate workplace for him to openly endorse. But would I help with his office problem?

It wasn't until several directors of nursing heard me speak on the topic that I found the "right" corporate workplace: health care. Not every woman. Rather, a female-dominated workplace: health care. The field of nursing was a viper's den of undermining and toxicity. The first book specifically for health care, *The Briles Report on Women in Health Care,* was birthed in 2003 and became the main selection for the Nurse's Book Society and a best seller within it. Later books on the topic were specifically written for the health care field with the latest in 2009: *Stabotage! How to Deal with the Pit Bulls, Skunks, Snakes, Scorpions and Slugs in the Health Care Workplace.* I had found my niche. Speaking and book sales skyrocketed.

Niche your book. It is so much easier to be the whale
in the lake versus the sardine in the sea.

Your vision creates the big picture—I saw my book on major shows and covered by the media. It was the first book with a national study of the topic. I saw it used within the corporate workplace, the wrong workplace. The right workplace had to be discovered. And it was. I saw it branding me and my speaking—taking me to the next level. This is what you, as the author and Visionary in Chief, must do as well.

SUCCESSFUL SPEAKERS HAVE VISION

Successful speakers have vision. When Susan RoAne wrote her first book, *How to Work a Room,* she had no idea the journey it would take her on, including landing a coveted first-place spot on the *Book of the Month* best-seller list. Most speakers start their publishing journey via the self-publishing route. Susan chose to publish with New York houses in a mercurial journey with great and not-so-great publishers.

But at all times, Susan had a vision. She knew networking inside and out—her vision even included landing an official federal trademark for "How to Work a Room," which she did. Susan's vision included not selling books in the back of the room, but consciously making bookstores her partners as she crisscrossed the country speaking on networking.

Over thirty years, Susan has created multiple best sellers, all within her vision stream. *The Secrets of Savvy Networking, What Do I Say Next?, RoAne's Rules: How to Make the Right Impression, How to Create Your Own Luck, Networking:*

Beyond the Buzz Word, and her latest, *FACE to FACE*, all have a connection with her original work and vision.

When it comes to books, Elaine Dumler is the first to admit that writing books specifically for the military wasn't in her original vision range. It wasn't her niche. What she was about was helping families stay together when separated. Her writings and speeches were woven through with that message.

Elaine's articles appeared in a variety of publications within the business community that eventually were cross-referenced—other industries took notice, including Uncle Sam. Representatives from the military contacted her directly. In 2002, they had discovered her articles and wanted to know if she could do anything to help military families. Initially, she said no. Why? She didn't know the military. That simple, straightforward response didn't stop them—the military representatives persisted. "You don't need to know the military; we do. You know families. We could give you all the background information you need."

Elaine will tell you that her vision for the work that would so engage her started very softly. She just hadn't envisioned the military family as her primary market. It became a new vision, one that led to the publication of *I'm Already Home*, the first book of three that were published under her own imprint specifically for military families. With the assistance of the military, her new vision became expansive and enthusiastic.

Mark Sanborn, CSP, CPAE, knows that most people today connect him with his international bestseller, *The Fred Factor*, which was published in 2004.

But Mark had a life before *The Fred Factor* was published. As a successful speaker since the mid-eighties, he had made lots of money without being branded as a "content" guy. That changed with *Fred*, which added another piece to his professional persona. He was now a "content" speaker with a clear message, a message that had evolved before *The Fred Factor* was ever published—his vision for the book and its message now put it out to the world, a world that enthusiastically bought more than a million copies. *The Fred Factor* was part of the seeding that would lead to other books in Mark's leadership series, *You Don't Need a Title to Be a Leader*, *The Encore Effect*, and *Up, Down or Sideways*.

As a savvy businessman, Mark knows that you don't put all your eggs in one basket. Visions need to be revisited—expanded and morphed. A lot has happened in the ten years of *The Fred Factor*—ideas that seemed so new a decade ago have become old. *Fred 2.0* will be birthing, taking *The Fred Factor* to a whole new level.

Successful authors who are speakers learn that without the vision factor, their work will merge into the spiral of look-alike authors and speakers. Their visions set them apart . . . visions that rarely come in the middle of the night. Rather, visions that evolve and are developed over a breadth of time. Platforms are not built or executed in a single leap or bound on any given day. Building commences, foundations are formed, structures erected—but as with each of the authors highlighted above, pieces are added through the years.

THE PASSION FACTOR

For a speaker, being passionate about your topic is critical. As it is for your book, passion is essential—you must care about your topic, your book, your writing. The average book is closed on page 18. Is yours engaging? When it is opened, does your reader fall in? When you have passion for your topic, it radiates everywhere: in your conversations with friends, from the stage as you speak, and in media interviews.

My passion was seeded from the embezzlement I experienced—a female partner had withdrawn money for her personal drug usage from a commercial credit line that I had personally guaranteed. The misuse of the funds surfaced only when all the funds were gone, none paid to the many contractors who had provided building services. I had been duped. I'm not dumb, so how did this happen?

Working with the theme of women sabotaging other women—what the problem is; cause, effect, and solution—I've created a career quest that has lasted three decades. With a total of six books on the topic, being identified as a pioneer and conducting nine national studies, I'm still as passionate about the topic as I ever was. It ticks me off when people undermine other people, especially women to women.

For you, the passion factor is as critical as breathing. If you don't have it from the get-go, your book will never develop the roots it needs to survive and thrive. Acquiring passion usually comes from curiosity or an event that triggers a quest, such as what happened to me.

That incident started me on a path that led to multiple books, speaking engagements, consulting contracts, and corporate spokesperson positions over a thirty-year period. I became the "go-to" person if there was toxicity and conflict in the health care workplace.

Susan RoAne's passion was seeded from her years as an educator. She saw the fear that so many experienced when they went to a meeting or an event and they didn't know the other people there. As someone who is known as The Mingling Maven®, it's a fear she doesn't have that fear. What she does have is the ability to show others the tools that will enable them to enter any situation and mingle without heart palpitations. Overcoming being intimidated, fearful, or even frightened of a pending close encounter with someone at a meeting, party, or event was something she knew she could show them in a few steps.

Passion and education go hand in hand for Susan—she wants people to be connected and have a good time doing it. It comes across in her books and when she speaks.

Mark Sanborn has a passion for leaders and for leadership development—a passion that has evolved from his years working with both employees and leadership teams. Mark strongly believes that leadership is not about having power *over* people; it is having power *with* people. When he wrote his breakout book, *The Fred Factor*, he had been speaking for years about extraordinary service—and the extraordinary service that he had received from his postman, Fred.

Mark's books won't be mistaken for doorstops, nor will they be mistaken for fluff. They are woven with the passion that he feels for his topic in a high-content, no-nonsense presentation for the reader. His work is nothing that can be construed as gimmicky, faddy, or in the get-rich, almost snake-oil-like genre that is being espoused by many on the speaking/authoring circuit today. He has put decades into his work—work that has had passion as its genesis. It's what he speaks and writes about and on.

Elaine Dumler dove into what was to become her platform by asking questions. The military was as good as its word—they gave her contacts to start the process of creating *I'm Already Home*. She's the first to admit that what was to become the first in her military family series was not perfect, but as Elaine says, "You go with what you have."

During the process, she interviewed many families, and four months later, she published *I'm Already Home,* with an initial sale of 1,700 copies. As Elaine got to know these families, she realized there was more to the story, and through more research, the next book was created—*I'm Already Home . . . Again.*

With its publication, she was three years into it. "I was speaking on bases, posts—people started coming to me with more ideas. I started asking, 'What do you do to stay connected?'"

Elaine was fully committed to the military families. She saw and felt the stress that they were experiencing. She felt passionate about making things easier and creating more ways for staying connected when families were separated by deployment. With the creation of the Flat Daddy campaign, more than 9,000 of the life-size cardboard cutouts have been donated to families. She came up with the idea to include postcards in any books that were sold and distributing whenever she spoke. On the postcard, she wrote, "Thank you for your service." She then asked one question: "What has worked with your family in staying connected that I can share with others?"

Eleven hundred people responded to her question. Elaine's passion for the families has carried through the three books she created in the series with *The Road Home: Smoothing the Transition Back from Deployment* being her latest. And her commitment and passion have led to more than 80,000 in total book sales.

When authors truly care for their topic, their passion radiates from their work. Their readers feel it in the words that they read and in the speeches they hear.

THE COMMITMENT FACTOR

Ahhh . . . commitment is the "hole" for too many. You can have all the passion and vision, but if you aren't committed, you will fail. Period.

> *Commitment means time, energy, and money. How much time will you put into supporting your book?*

Writing a quality book is just one segment of the commitment triangle. It's also what you do with it as it comes out of the gate. Speakers should aggressively pre-market within the year prior to publication—letting their contacts know that the book is coming and that special speaking discounts will be tied to the launch. My entire speaking year was booked ahead with the announcement of a new book, which meant the calendar was full, many thousands of books would be sold, and that my "brand"—Dr. Judith Briles, expert in female-dominated workplaces—was solid.

This is your work . . . work that will lead to building your brand and your speaking career. The reason I landed a cover story in *People* magazine, on *Oprah*, CNN, the *Wall Street Journal*, and more than 1,000 media-related events was that I made the time for it. Not a publicist—just me working the phones, making the connections, following up, and booking a slot. Just me and the ingredient of time.

How much energy will you put into supporting your book? "Lots" would be an excellent response. No doubt, your vision and passion will be the driving forces. Plus the factor of money—you have an investment that you want to see a return on. The return can come quickly, or it can evolve over a period of time.

Days and evenings will be long. If there ever was a time to take care of you, this is it. Doing any type of media can have you up in the middle of the night being bubbly, insightful, and enthusiastic—yet your body is saying, "Hey, I want to be prone . . ."

Fueling your energy demands that you be selective with where and what you put it into. Two of my long-time keepers are:

Don't do well what you have no business doing.

If you never say no, your yesses are worthless.

Knowing your audience—what your niche is—will help define where your energy should be directed. If it isn't a fit, don't commit to putting your time into it.

How much money will you put into supporting your book? Stories abound about how an author was down to his last $5 on a credit line before the big sale came in. You don't have to live that dream . . . or nightmare. Books take money—the creation will be thousands of dollars.

When Susan RoAne's *How to Work the Room* was published, she committed to supporting her book. It was an integral part of her career strategy. She spent four years supporting *How to Work a Room*—allowing it to grow up, getting it in front of media, in front of meeting planners and bookstore personnel across the country, before she launched her second book.

Susan invested thousands of dollars and thousands of hours in promotional activities supporting her book. It led to best-seller status, a significant fan base, and increased speaking engagements. Her brand is networking. She has stayed in contact with a variety of individuals who have supported her work throughout the years, including reporters she met when she published *How to Work a Room* in the eighties. Susan talks her walk about networking, and she walks her talk. It's her commitment—all fueled by her passion and her vision.

Mark Sanborn's *The Fred Factor* went viral, carrying it to various business best-seller lists for two years, along with sales in multiple countries totaling over

1.4 million copies to date. It didn't happen overnight; he spent years researching leadership issues with his speaking and previous writings.

Mark invested considerable time into building his brand of being a high-content speaker and leadership expert, demonstrating that he wasn't just another speaker who had read a few books. He became the expert, the author. Mark sought continual feedback from his clients and audiences. His expertise was formulated from a commitment to life-long learning.

Elaine Dumler first resisted working and writing within and for the military. She didn't know that once she became involved with the military community and the families within it her commitment would be total. She researched it; she embraced it; she created books and products that would support it; she raised money to help many get her books and Flat Daddy cutouts. Elaine knew the needs of the military families inside and out. On multiple occasions, she was honored for her work with the receipt of more than twenty special military challenge coins, including President Bush's Commander-in-Chief coin.

Lynn Hellerstein did not have the speaking credentials that Mark, Susan, Elaine, or I had as we started on our author journeys. She did, though, have deep-rooted experience in a well-established business. As one of the top optometrists in the country, she finally decided to write her book. *See It. Say It. Do It!* was created and published in 2009, based on her optometric vision therapy practice. Its first book signing brought in the crowds, with more than 900 books sold.

Her vision included speaking nationally on the topic and included the development of programs that professionals in her field could use along with her book with their clients. That has happened. Her vision has led to a coauthored second book, *See It. Say It. Organize It!*, which is a spin-off product providing many of the worksheets used within her first book. She's now at work on a series of books that focus on visualization methods for niche groups.

As Lynn says, "20-20 is not perfect vision." Her passion for working with kids who have been challenged with a variety of sight and perception issues, along with adults, has made her a trendsetter in her field. Her relentless commitment to her work, her clients, and to the public in education about visual challenges has made her a sought-after speaker and media expert.

Today, Lynn Hellerstein's platform has been seeded for a long-term journey.

As the author, you are creating a product—a product that could launch, or re-launch, an amazing journey that can last decades. How much are you willing to invest to get you there? What will your commitment be?

Prepublication costs include editing, design of cover and interior, printing, ISBN numbers—and possibly consulting an expert, such as book shepherd or book/writing coach or even a ghostwriter (you may be the author but writing isn't your skill). Then come warehousing and fulfillment if you plan to reach out to other marketing avenues—avenues outside of back-of-the-room sales. Publicity, marketing, and social media strategists may also be engaged.

All cost money. Be realistic. My books and speaking have grown and fed a family, built a house, and been my primary support for more than thirty years. None of it was done on a penny. No one gave me anything. With the combination of speaking and books, money was always there to add fuel to the expanding book empire. Its growth came from having a book budget and my initial vision.

THE PEOPLE FACTOR

Build it and they will come is the belief of many. Maybe. Maybe not. My first book, *The Woman's Guide to Financial Savvy*, was published in 1981 the old-fashioned way—with a New York publishing house courting me and doing it up big. Three printings in three weeks, national TV appearances including *Good Morning America*—it was exciting and successful.

Mark Sanborn started out self-publishing, and then redirected his publishing efforts with a traditional publisher. It has worked for him.

Elaine Dumler was approached by two different publishers who made offers to buy her books . . . and then, in a candid moment, one of the acquisitions editors advised her not to take the "deal." He told her that she, and her books, would be better off being published by her as an independent small press. She would have the control and make more money. She decided to take his advice.

Susan RoAne has always published her books with traditional publishers. Remember, her vision was to work in a partnering position with the bookstores. She didn't want to sell them; she wanted the stores to. And it has worked well for her over the years.

Times have changed, with the Internet now being a driving force—and that's a good thing. Authors can take control and reach far more people within their niche instantaneously. They don't need the New York houses, and in fact, few care who publishes it. Does your book solve their pain or provide a solution? Does it entertain or amuse? If it is a printed book, is it quality, or does it look tacky (which too many do)? If it is an e-book, has the layout been carefully "laid out" versus just dumped in a Word document?

Authors need a game plan that is directly tied to the marketing of their book to the people whom it is written for.

In 2011, more than 3 million books of all types were created—most likely, 2.7 million shouldn't have been. The Internet can be your best friend in the expansion of your brand and marketing your book. It is also the primary contributor to book pollution. Vision, passion, and commitment will keep you out of the trash heap.

THE PLATFORM ... PUTTING IT ALL TOGETHER

Does building a platform work? Yes. Can it be created in a week or month? No. Platform building is not a short-term investment—it takes time to develop your vision and nurture your passion. Commitment of time, energy, and money can last a lifetime. The numbers will always tell the story. Your book(s) will identify you as an expert. They are part of your brand. Your speeches on the topic of your book add to your expertise and branding. Consulting or coaching that comes from your speaking and your book adds to the branding bucket. Sponsorships from corporations can surface and add to your branding—making you the go-to person in your field.

Yes, a book and author platform creates critical components in your brand. Don't leave the speaking platform without one.

Judith Briles is the author of thirty books, including *Creating and Developing the Author and Book Platforms*, *Show Me About Book Publishing*, *The Tango of Authoring and Publishing*, *The Confidence Factor*, and *Stabotage!* Her platform that started with the publication of *Woman to Woman: From Sabotage to Support* in 1987 has generated $2,674,664 in speaking fees; $1,379,919 in book royalties/direct sales; and $313,800 in corporate spokesperson fees for a total of $4,368,383—more than enough to grow a family and a business. Judith started Mile High Press, Ltd., in 2000 to publish her own work and now publishes others' work as well. Judith is the founder of www.AuthorU.org, a membership organization dedicated to the author who wants to be seriously successful. Visit her at www.TheBookShepherd.com.

NETWORKING AND PUBLIC RELATIONS

NETWORK AS IF YOUR CAREER DEPENDS ON IT . . . BECAUSE IT DOES!

Thom Singer

There is much said about the power of networking to grow a career—and this holds particularly true for those of us in the speaking business. If you ask a dozen speakers to define "networking," however, you may get twelve different answers.

At its essence, networking is the creation of long-term and mutually beneficial relationships between two or more people, in which everyone has more success because of the connections than they would without them. Translation? Networking means getting to know other people and helping them succeed, not finding people who will send you leads. It's about creating ongoing friendships, and being just as happy when one of those friends gets a new client as you would be if you acquired one yourself.

The key point is "mutually beneficial." Too many speakers hope they will meet a well-connected meeting planner or a top-tier speaker who will discover them—and then are surprised when they get no referral business from their celebrity-stalking efforts. It is better to invest your time establishing meaningful connections with others who are at your same level, and then climb the ladder together.

The National Speakers Association provides a great chance for speakers to network with each other. I remember one up-and-coming speaker who told me she couldn't understand why I would invest time and money to hang around with other speakers—she spent time only with people who might hire her. In my humble view, that is shortsighted. The speaking business can get very lonely, and having peers who understand the real experiences that come with this career is priceless. The truth is that friendships with other speakers can result in referrals or opportunities as an add-on presenter to make an event better.

FORGING CONNECTIONS FOR THE LONG HAUL

While joining NSA is a great start, participating at the local and national level is where the real value comes into play. Just like dating relationships, strong connections are not forged by meeting somebody one time. If you are married, you most likely did not propose on the first date—it probably took months or years to establish a long-term commitment.

So, too, meeting a colleague at a conference doesn't make him part of your network; instead he's someone you have met once. It can take seven to 10 interactions with people before they even notice you exist. Being present with people is the best way you can begin to cultivate your contacts.

We live in a world where people want instant results, but networking success does not happen without a significant time investment. Just joining an organization does not create the bond that develops between people who have grown to understand, know, and like each other. You need to invest in each individual to discover the common ground to establish productive relationships.

EMBRACING THE NETWORKING LIFESTYLE

Creating peer groups and other associations with other speakers and meeting professionals is one of the smartest things you can do to find success in this crazy business. Real networking partners share advice, trends, and ideas. Reinventing the wheel on your own is a great way to feel busy, but it is a waste of valuable time.

Networking is a lifestyle. You do not "go networking" when you have free time or need new clients. You have to genuinely care about other people and have an interest in being a referral source and a resource for others. If you are self-focused in your networking efforts, or you try to keep score, you will fail. I hear from people all the time that they met new people, but nobody ever sends them a lead. When pressed about what they do for their new friends, however, they often are at a loss, or have half-hearted and superficial examples. When you honestly work to serve others daily, someone will notice and reciprocate.

If you believe in the idea that all opportunities come from people, then you realize that your network is the way to find future success. The world is full of givers and takers, but when you surround yourself with givers—and act that way yourself—you are recharged, refreshed, and showered in new opportunities to grow your career.

True givers are always watching and know the difference between those who give and those who take. Givers can spot a fraud from a mile away. Givers never waste their time on takers. The only way to be on their radar screen is to be open to helping. This isn't just on the days you are not speaking or have free time. This is all the time.

Many people—perhaps most!—say they want to be givers, but it's just lip service. They are always talking to people about ways to create partnerships or referral relationships, but they rarely do anything to make it happen. Too few have "follow-through DNA." This lifestyle of getting to know people and finding ways to help them cannot be prejudged, prescheduled, or dependent on your ROI calculations.

It goes without saying that networking shouldn't be limited to NSA or other meetings industry groups. Establishing connections happens everywhere. To this day, I get referrals from the network of peers I established in my local business community when I was the marketing director for a law firm. These people are not decision makers in the industries that hire me, but many of them have contacts that can assist me. The people with whom I have cultivated ongoing friendships with are happy to refer me to others. Those I barely knew, and with whom I haven't kept in touch, do not do the same thing.

NETWORKING WHERE YOU SPEAK

A key place to network is at the conferences and meetings where you speak, so it's baffling to know that there are speakers who fly in, speak, and leave. Investing a day or two in participation at conferences is an ideal way to meet people who can refer you more business. Audience members love to talk with speakers after their presentation. If you make yourself visible during breaks and meals, you'll meet amazing people—many of whom are happy to discover how they can refer you. Of course, it's also a matter of learning about them.

The majority of my business comes from those who saw me speak and then met me after the presentation. I am not talking about those who lined up to shake my hand or buy a book, but those who were table mates at dinner or in the lounge. Once you get to have real conversations with people, you can establish a foundation for future conversations.

I sympathize with celebrities who need to get away so they are not mobbed by fans, but most of us aren't at risk of that—and we can find a lot of value in being more engaged in conference activities. One client told me about a keynote speaker who refused to attend the company's board dinner after his talk. (He told them he needed to get work done and ordered room service instead of eating with the decision makers who had hired him.) While they liked his speech, they felt shunned by the declined invitation, and he wasn't asked to speak the following year.

While you may not be famous, you are to the audience for the 24 hours after your presentation. People want to know you, and if you return the interest in knowing them beyond the transaction of a speech for a check, you might create stronger connections that could lead to more business.

Sometimes, of course, you need to head for the airport right after you leave the stage, but this should be the exception, not the rule. The more you give to your audience, the more they will give to you. I think back on the time I shared the stage with a speaker who left immediately. The audience had loved her talk, but by the end of the conference, three days later, they had forgotten her name. Investing the time to be part of the "mini-society" that exists at a conference enables you to create more meaningful relationships with some of the audience members. Sometimes it only takes one referral to make a difference to your bottom line.

GOING ONLINE AND GETTING SOCIAL

No chapter on networking would be complete without talking about the power of social media. Over the past several years we have been overrun with presentations and articles about LinkedIn, Facebook, Twitter, blogging, and other social media tools. All speakers know they should be participating in conversations online, but many still are not using these tools, or employing them effectively.

Social media are not a magic bullet. Just as attending a business event or joining NSA will not automatically create meaningful connections with people, you cannot expect any results from simply creating an account. Interactive tools only work if you are being interactive!

The first word in "social media" is "social." This means that you have to be actively engaged in the dialogue if you expect anyone to care that you are present. You wouldn't attend a business event and stand in the corner shouting at the top of your lungs: "Hire me! I am a great speaker! Read my book!" You can't expect that tactic to work online, either.

While the tools we use to communicate have changed a lot in the past few years, the way we build real bonds with people has not changed. We still want to feel that the other person cares about us and is equally committed to the relationship. This is not something you can outsource. If you are paying your assistant to tweet for you, it is not really you. It is a fake you. People will know the difference. If you are not responding to others, or re-tweeting their valuable content, then it is simply a one-way broadcast.

All online communities and tools are not the same, and people connect with you for different reasons. Some gurus position social media as a quick fix, but noncelebrity results vary widely—and in direct proportion to the effort you put in. While you need to be active, it also can be a time waster. Understanding those whom you are communicating with on the Internet, and knowing what they want from the digital relationship, is paramount to success.

It is not about numbers, but engagement. Assuming that a link to someone has any value is naïve. Just because you post something online does not mean that anyone noticed. The cold, hard fact is that social media contain a lot of noise, and standing out from all the junk is harder now than ever before.

But that's not an excuse to ignore social media. Clients and others are looking you up online, and the lack of a strong presence can be harmful. If the person hiring you is under 45, there's a 99.99 percent chance she's active with social media. Not connecting on that level can send a strong message that you are out of touch.

Finding the right balance of online activity for your business and personality can be difficult. But the online and mobile tools are not a fad. The time to look the other way is long past.

NOT JUST FOR EXTROVERTS!

Be it face-to-face or online, it's easy to shy away from the networking activities that can help you find more success in your careers. But out of sight is also out of mind. Giving a great speech isn't enough.

It's important to note that networking is not just for extroverts. In fact, introverts are often better networkers. They are more prone to ask questions of others and listen to the answers. When you are tuned in to what people are saying, you are more likely to quickly identify ways to help connect them to others. Not being naturally outgoing in social situations is no excuse. Plenty of people, many of them far more shy than you, have learned how to maximize their time networking to create powerful connections that lead to more business.

The overarching message is that it's absolutely essential to take ownership of your networking and work to create powerful relationships. It can be surprising and frustrating to see someone less qualified win a major opportunity, but you may not realize the hard work that went on behind the scenes. People want to do business with those they know, like, and trust—and networking can be your secret strategy for getting noticed in our highly competitive business.

Thom Singer is a professional speaker, sales trainer, and the author of eight books on the power of business relationships, networking, and presentation skills. He has spent more than 20 years in sales, marketing, and business development roles with major corporations and AM LAW 100 law firms. He regularly consults with corporations and individuals on how to cultivate their personal brands and establish professional connections that will lead to more referral business. His speaking includes impactful keynotes, breakout sessions, training programs, and the Conference Catalyst program, which sets the tone for better meetings. Learn more at www.ThomSinger.com.

TAPPING INTO THE POWER OF YOUR "GOLDEN ROLODEX"

Vickie Axford Austin

As a speaker, you have all kinds of marketing strategies available to you, from elevating your visibility on your website to working with a speakers' bureau. No strategy, however, is as powerful as networking. By tapping into the power of your existing network, you leverage the richest source of all—the people who already know you and want you to succeed.

The term networking is often misinterpreted as a frantic rush to collect lots of business cards, the business equivalent of speed dating. Some people think networking is about making new friends versus honoring the people they already know. Nothing could be further from the truth. As a business and career coach, I've developed a networking philosophy which also can help catapult your speaking business. I call it leveraging your "Golden Rolodex."

For those of you under 40, I may need to explain what a Rolodex® is. No, it isn't a fancy watch (that's a Rolex®). A Rolodex is a box or a cylindrical container that holds all your contacts' information. Back in the day, a person's worth often was measured by the bulk of their Rolodex. Super-connected folks boasted of two or three Rolodexes lined up in a row, bulging with contact names, addresses, and phone numbers. We now have computer databases for all that juicy information, but I still love the visual image of a Rolodex as a metaphor for the depth and breadth of our connections.

NEVER UNDERESTIMATE THE POWER OF YOUR NETWORK

One of the biggest surprises I've had as a career coach is how my clients often underestimate their own networks. You've heard the old adage "It isn't *what* you know, it's *who* you know." Sadly, a lot of people don't think they know anybody. In my 15 years of coaching, I've been amazed at how even accomplished, experienced professionals might not realize the value of the network they already have.

Years ago, I had a client named Greg. A talented writer and editor, Greg wanted to make a career transition from editing for an international news service to becoming a freelance writer. The mere thought of taking the plunge made Greg nervous, so he asked me to help him navigate the transition. When I inquired about his network, Greg was sheepish. "I don't really have a network," he said. I nearly fell out of my chair.

"*Au contraire,*" I sputtered. "You not only have a network, you have a... a..." I searched for the right words. I was thinking of all the contacts Greg had from his experience as a financial reporter and editor working at news bureaus in Chicago, New York, and Hong Kong. "You have a 'Golden Rolodex!'" I exclaimed, coining the phrase I've been using ever since.

DEFINITION OF A "GOLDEN ROLODEX"

There are two criteria for the people in *your* Golden Rolodex: (1) They must know you by name (or they know someone who knows you by name) and (2) they must be breathing. That's it. Just think how many people you know who fit that description.

The beauty of the Golden Rolodex principle is that *anyone and everyone can be a resource to you as you build your speaking business.* This is no time to be picky about who can and cannot help you get on the platform as a speaker. Trust me—we all make judgments that limit our marketing impact, judgments that we don't even know we're making. And those judgments will cut you off from your richest resource of all: your own network.

In the world of career coaching, there's an estimate that 80 percent of all job connections are made through face-to-face networking. The same can be said of generating leads for speaking engagements. As with any enterprise, the speaking business is based on trust. People do business with people they know; people do business with people they trust. Referrals are the rocket fuel of your marketing plan, especially with people who have already heard you speak. Bottom line? Start with the people you know.

ANATOMY OF A GOLDEN ROLODEX REFERRAL

In my earlier days as a coach, I used speaking as a tactic to support my marketing strategy, "elevate visibility." The more I spoke, the more I was asked to speak, and suddenly people began asking me, "How much do you charge?" What had once been a marketing strategy became a new source of revenue. I began to think about how I might leverage my own Golden Rolodex to increase the volume of my speaking engagements. I turned to my friend Dan Keck.

Dan is director of information technology for a professional association for financial managers in the health care industry, based in the western suburbs of Chicago. He isn't accountable for their education programs, but he certainly knows the people in his association who are.

One day I ran into Dan, and it occurred to me that he worked for an association—one with which I was familiar because of my background in health care marketing. I told him briefly that I was interested in growing my business as a speaker and asked if he'd be willing to help me. We agreed to follow up with a lunch date.

Let me inject a note here that's an important part of the Golden Rolodex principle. Before asking Dan for any *referrals*, I asked him for his *time* (the lunch date) and during that luncheon I asked for his *ideas, opinions,* and *recommendations*. I call this "IOR." Asking for IOR increases your ROI (return on investment).

Getting Your ROI from Someone's IOR

The best networking approach for building your speaking business is to ask someone for their *ideas, opinions,* and *recommendations* (IOR). People don't like to be mined for their contacts. But if we ask people for their ideas, opinions, and recommendations, we connect on a more strategic level. And people love to be asked for their opinions! Before you earn the right to ask for a referral, you must first ask people for their IOR:

- *Ideas.* Get others involved in your brainstorming sessions. Tell them your mission—to share your message as a speaker. Now, be specific about your ideal audience. Ask for ideas on how you might reach that audience. Where would you find those people? Do they know anything about that industry or profession? What strategies would *they* employ?

- *Opinions.* Everyone loves to share their opinions. Ask directly, "What do you think about my strategy?" (This assumes you have one.) Just asking someone for their opinion is a huge compliment.

- *Recommendations.* Once you've asked for ideas and opinions, you now can ask for their recommendations. This may be a request for resources (websites, books, articles, etc.) or actual referrals. Always ask permission to use the name of the person who refers you to his or her contacts.

When preparing for an IOR interview, write out some questions in advance and feel free to refer to them. Bring a notebook and two pens, just in case one runs out. (This may seem trivial, but there's nothing more embarrassing than asking someone for their time and their IOR . . . and then not having a pen to write things down.) Always write down everything they say, no matter how goofy or outlandish it may sound; never argue or say, "I tried that already." Listen, take notes, and respond with appreciation and gratitude, not just for their IOR but for their time. After all, time is the most precious resource of all.

Before I ask people to help make connections, I ask them for their ideas or "the wisdom of their counsel." Otherwise, it's just hitting people up for their contacts, something I call a drive-by. That's like saying to someone, "I need a job— do you know anybody?" which is disrespectful, abrasive, and ineffective. No one likes to have their Golden Rolodex plundered.

So, after lunch at a nearby restaurant, Dan invited me to his office and introduced me to several of the people who were in charge of programming. Within a few months, I received a call from the director of professional development. Would I be interested in speaking at a preconference workshop at their annual conference in Las Vegas? Would I ever! Thanks to Dan, I was now part of the faculty for the association's huge annual conference. I went to Las Vegas and presented—what else?—"Your Golden Rolodex: How to Network for Results!"

That workshop introduced me to a whole new group of health care financial professionals, including Mike Nichols, who invited me to speak to his local chapter in Illinois. That invitation led to another opportunity to speak to a chapter in southern Illinois, followed by opportunities to present to chapters in Georgia, Arizona, and California. The connections we make through our Golden Rolodex— something we call a spin-off in the speaking world—can be exponential.

A WORD ABOUT GRATITUDE

Gratitude and appreciation make up the social fabric of the Golden Rolodex principle. If you find you have a problem expressing your gratitude or appreciation, I have three words for you: Get over it. When someone opens a door for you as Dan did for me, you owe him or her three things: lunch or dinner (and sometimes a small gift); a handwritten thank-you note; and your undying gratitude. Don't be afraid of being obligated to someone for their contribution to you as a speaker. Indeed, we are all beholden to several someones—our parents, our coaches, our teachers, and our mentors. Acknowledge people for their contribution to you and your success and then, in turn, open doors for others.

PUTTING YOUR GOLDEN ROLODEX TO WORK

Now that you have some perspective on how deep and rich your own Golden Rolodex really is, how can you put it to work? Here are some steps to help you tap into the gold in your own network:

- First, collect the names and contact information of everyone you know. Put it all in one place. Too often we keep names and numbers scattered in different places—on our smartphones, in our computers, stacked as business cards in a dark corner of our office or at the bottom of our briefcases and purses. Whatever method you choose to keep track of your contacts is fine, but the main thing is to consolidate all that content into one place, because this will be the engine of your marketing machine. This may seem like a trivial, clerical function, but in fact it's a critical element of networking. You can't be in contact with people if you can't find them. Many people use LinkedIn as a de facto database, which is OK as long as you have a place to keep notes and track your communications. That's a very important part of maintaining your Golden Rolodex: documenting your conversations and meetings to ensure follow-up and follow-through.

- If you're stumped when it comes to building your Golden Rolodex, think about the various communities you're in. Colleagues past and present, neighbors, old sorority sisters or fraternity brothers, fellow soccer moms or dads, members of the Star Trek Fan Club—all are great connections. And don't forget your family and friends, two categories that are often overlooked. Wherever you've shared a common time, space, or experience with other people, you now have a community. One of the most powerful networks you have is an alumni network. Just by sharing that you went to the same high school, college, or university, you now have a connection on which to build a conversation— and possibly, a relationship that will lead to referrals. Take the time to mine the gold in your Golden Rolodex based on your own communities, and you'll never, ever have to make a cold call.

- Next, create your "30-second commercial." Like networking, the 30-second commercial is often misunderstood. Sometimes it's called an "elevator pitch," because it takes about as much time as you'd have talking to someone in an elevator. Regardless of the label, it gives people context about who you are, what you're up to as a speaker, and ultimately what kind of support you might need from them—and sharing it shouldn't take longer than 30 seconds. Practice with a timer, and pare it down to the essentials. People often try to cram their whole resume into their commercial, so it comes off sounding like, "Me, me, me!" But really it's just the setup for your next objective: to have a more extensive face-to-face (or voice-to-voice) live conversation with that person. Develop something that gives a brief, and I mean *brief*, over-view of your past experience, your current status, and your mission: to grow and learn as a speaker. People are motivated to help you with your mission, to make a difference with your audience—not so much to help you grow your revenue. Share your mission with them, then ask them some really great questions, and they'll be engaged in your mission long after you leave that coffee date.

- Don't judge people by education, experience, or social status. Your nail tech or barber is often the richest resource in your Golden Rolodex. Why? Because they have such amazing networks themselves. And what do people do when they're getting their nails done or their hair cut? They talk. What more could you ask for, right? If they know you and they're breathing, they're gold in your Golden Rolodex.

- Begin generating "Golden Rolodex" conversations with everyone you know. Create a schedule in which you meet with five to 10 people a week to share about your mission to grow your speaking business. That's an ambitious objective, but volume creates momentum and a velocity that nets big results.

- Keep track of your contacts and keep up with them. Whether you do this through an e-newsletter, cards, a series of phone calls and e-mails, coffee dates, or luncheons, you're nurturing those relationships and planting seeds. Take careful notes of your progress and keep them stored in your database.

- Follow up. This is the one that's often hardest for me: I have to remember I promised someone my one-sheet or a copy of my e-book. But without follow-up, the seed that was planted will wither and die. Do what you said you'd do, and do it as soon as possible.

- Express appreciation. I don't think you can ever thank people too much. Young professionals often ask me if an e-mail thank-you is sufficient, to which I reply, "No." A quick e-mail should be followed by a written thank-you note on your own classy business notecard. People get so little real mail these days that thank-you notes stand out as an expression of gratitude and warmth, and notes keep that connection going.

PUTTING THE "SOCIAL" INTO SOCIAL NETWORKING

The Internet provides all kinds of ways to get and stay connected with people. Between e-mail, texting, Facebook, LinkedIn, and Twitter, we can be in communication with people all over the world, 24/7. But remember that social media are like the telephone: They offer ways to communicate and to build and sustain relationships, not the relationship itself. There is tremendous power with social media, but there are also limitations.

Have you ever gotten a request for a connection on LinkedIn and wondered, "Who the heck *is* this person?" Or been asked for a recommendation from someone with whom you've never worked? Social media imply an intimacy that may or may not really exist. Use technology wisely to open doors and conversations with people you know or want to know better. Social media are also a great way to build your visibility as a speaker, positioning yourself as a thought leader or expert in a particular area. Just like face-to-face networking, social networking is about building trust with people over time.

Networking isn't just about receiving. The best networkers are the ones who love to help others with *their* missions, connecting people within their own Golden Rolodexes. Pay it forward, and I promise it will come back to you tenfold.

Vickie Axford Austin is a business and career coach and founder of CHOICES Worldwide. As a coach, she offers strategic planning to people in mid-career transition as well as to business owners in professional services such as accounting, finance, and health care. She speaks to audiences on the topics of business and career success and loves sharing about the power of networking with associations and organizations throughout the world. Vickie is a *magna cum laude* graduate of Arizona State University and has an executive master's degree in international management from Thunderbird School of Global Management. She serves as one of the deans of Speaker University for the National Speakers Association chapter in Illinois and is also a member of the Global Speakers Federation. CHOICES Worldwide is based in Wheaton, IL, with offices in Chicago and Phoenix. You can reach Vickie at vaustin@ChoicesWorldwide.com.

SEVEN STEPS FOR RINGING UP SALES

Kevin Graham

Your message holds the power to change lives . . . but only if people are able to hear it. You may have the patience and bank account balance to wait for all of your inbound marketing efforts to drive business—but if you don't, you'd be well served by picking up the phone.

Go ahead. Heft it in your hand for a moment . . . it actually can be quite sensuous. Yes, my fellow speaker: *The phone is your friend.* It may seem odd at first, but if you have the courage to speak into a microphone in front of a crowd, then you surely have what it takes to make some sales calls. In my experience, there's no better way to market your speaking business—and this chapter will empower you with seven proven sales steps toward a full speaking calendar.

It's been said that when it comes to salespeople and prospecting, there are two types: those who hate it, and those who lie and say they don't. But it doesn't have to be that way. Prospecting is about fitness, just like running on a treadmill or lifting weights. If you're only going to the gym or prospecting for three hours every third Thursday, you'll develop neither fitness nor effectiveness. But if you're willing to make a few phone calls a few times a week, it will reward you handsomely—just like regular exercise provides increased energy levels and vitality.

Granted, not everyone has the demeanor or capacity to cold call. In some quarters, interruption selling is considered as passé as interruption marketing. Nonetheless, the reality is that the most direct path from you to meeting planners or key decision makers is a straight (phone) line. Particularly when you incorporate your various social networks, your "degrees of separation" may be fewer than you think.

7 SALES STEPS TO A FULL CALENDAR

Step 1: The List

In sales, you've got to A-S-K in order to G-E-T. But if you're asking the wrong person, you're unlikely to get what you want. There are many sources for good lists, and the best approach is to overlap your phone calls with your marketing efforts, creating synergy between your brand and message. Identify your target market and leverage your marketing efforts by making the calls.

Step 2: Know Your Value

You know your presentation cold, right? Well, you also need to know why someone should listen to your speech and what effect or outcome it will have. Wordsmith those materials so that the benefits of your talk will be clear and concise. It's important to be able to express your value, and how that relates to your target prospect.

Step 3: Communicate Clearly

Just as your speech needs a strong introduction, your phone call needs to open with compelling material. In fact, studies show that you've got less than eight seconds to answer the listener's WIIFM—"What's In It For Me?" In today's world of multitasking, be clear about how you plan to engage the caller, and make it compelling. If you're fortunate enough to get the decision maker on the phone, don't ramble. State your purpose immediately, succinctly, and clearly.

Step 4: Expect Objections

When you are asking someone for time or money, the first thing most will do is blurt out a reason why it's not a good idea or the right time. You do it. I do it. So don't be surprised or frustrated; simply lead the call to the next phase.

Over the course of time, you'll encounter the whole laundry list:

- "I've got no time."

- "We don't have the money."
- "We don't have an event."
- "We already have a speaker booked."
- "I'm not the right contact."
- "This is a bad week/month/quarter."
- "Can you call me next week?"
- "We don't use outside speakers."
- "We already have a network of speakers."
- "Your topic is not relevant to our business model."
- And the granddaddy of them all: "Send me some literature."

These are not insurmountable objections, no matter how daunting they may sound. Rather than panicking, dropping the call, or caving in to the frivolous request of sending some literature, you just need to relax, take a breath, and lead the call to the next phase.

"No money? Mr. Customer, that's exactly why I'm calling. None of our customers had money budgeted when we were first introduced. I'd like to schedule a brief meeting with you to talk about the positive impact we're having at XYZ Corporation." That simple formula works to overcome just about any objection. The important element is to know your value; keep the conversation moving toward a partnership with your prospect and the potential for a future event.

Step 5: Embrace the "NO" Quota

One of the reasons so many people hate making sales calls is that they don't like rejection. Duh! Who in the world likes to be told "no"? But here's the little secret that true sales professionals know: Regardless of the business model or selling cycle, odds are that the sales professional will face several NOs for each YES. The trick is to embrace the NOs.

Let's put it in monetary terms. Say you make $5,000 for each booking, and typically face ten NOs for each YES. What you need to do is convince yourself that each of those ten NOs is actually worth $500—because that's what it'll take to get the $5,000 YES.

To get there, you're also going to have to drink the Kool-Aid. If you are not passionate about what you are selling, how can you expect a prospect to get excited enough to take action? On the other hand, if you are convinced of the value and likely outcomes from your presentation, your enthusiasm will win the prospect over—and you will find it easier to lead the call forward.

In the sales profession, there are two things that separate the superstars from the also-rans. (1) They have the diligence to prospect on a regular basis, always feeding the top of the sales funnel. (2) They've been hit by so many busses that they refuse to get hit by any particular bus again. If at one point, for example, they lost a deal because a meeting planner or key executive took a day off—rest assured, they'll start tracking the upcoming holidays of key decision makers.

Don't hide from rejection. Many people don't *succeed* enough simply because they are not willing to *fail* enough. Start that process by embracing the NO Quota, and you'll find that you succeed more frequently.

Step 6: Avoid Common Mistakes

As with all sales processes, there are common pitfalls to phone pitches. Here are a few tips for avoiding them:

People respond in kind. If your approach is underhanded or overbearing, you'll likely get the same in return. If you're upbeat and energetic, you're increasing the odds of an attentive partner.

Be in the moment. Forget about your to-do list and other customers and prospects, and turn off your e-mail and web browser. Focus exclusively on the decision maker you've got on the phone.

Mirror the prospect. The power of mirroring has been debated over the years. While some professionals take it to an extreme, most sales representatives barely take the time to pace their dialogue to that of the other person, let alone adopt other simple mirroring techniques. You need to match your prospect's energy and pace of conversation before you start to inspire or otherwise move it to a new level. Prospects and customers want things on their terms, and that includes human interaction.

Have a specific objective. Are you trying to source information on their upcoming events? Do you wish to compel them toward creating an event for your specific topic? Know what your specific objective is with each call, and stay focused toward that end.

Ask good questions. Are your questions simple, yet thoughtful? Do they allow the other person to speak on areas that will feed your sales process? Do the questions expose pain points or the opportunity for improvement? Armed with high-quality questions, you'll discover that it is fairly simple to lead the conversation and uncover the information that you need to sell effectively. But really, you shouldn't even think of it as selling; think of it as investigative work. After all, qualifying is the most important step in the sales process.

Listen well. When asking those good questions, remember that you've got two ears and one mouth; use them in that proportion. We've all experienced that overbearing caller who talks too much. Become a good listener and you'll find that prospects actually enjoy talking with you.

Speak their language. Be sure that your dialogue and questions reflect the customer's world, not yours. There's an old adage in marketing: "Talk about my lawn, not your grass seed." By demonstrating an affinity for their market, you'll quickly be seen as an expert, and your odds of getting the gig will increase dramatically.

Step 7: ABC (Always Be Closing)

It would be hard for any sales expert to talk about closing without coming right out and saying: ABC, Always Be Closing. It's important, so I'm going to repeat it. Always Be Closing.

But you know what? Most people misinterpret what that mantra is all about. It's not about lambasting your prospect with an endless barrage of closing questions. It's about maintaining momentum toward the close.

If you know your objective and are truly engaged with the decision maker on the phone, then stay on course. Regardless of the temperament of the other party, or the actual objections you may face, continue to press toward your stated objective. You will likely find that you have more ability to lead the call than you thought you had . . . so lead the call in the direction of your objective.

These seven steps can empower you to successfully promote your speaking business by the tried-and-true way of the telephone. Just as writing regularly allows you to develop and hone your message, regular phone work will allow you to be limber and flexible in demonstrating the value of your message. That vitality will come through as you deliver your speech on the platform. More important, you'll drive some bookings while you're waiting for your inbound marketing to take hold.

The phone is your friend. Don't be afraid of it. Speak, my fellow speaker, into the telephone!

Kevin Graham is an author, speaker, and expert on sales and leadership. He's "been there/done that" when it comes to sales success, having qualified for President's Club status in three Fortune 500 companies in the ultracompetitive technology sector, led teams of more than 100 hundred associates, and successfully achieved annual revenue objectives in excess of $1 billion. Kevin serves as managing director of Empowered Sales Training, which offers custom programs to empower sales success. Visit www.EmpoweredSalesTraining.com to take the Empowered Sales Quiz or to download free sales guides such as *Book More Meetings* and *Get The Decision Maker on the Phone*. The Empowered Sales YouTube channel offers dozens of free sales videos. Contact Kevin directly at graham@empoweredsalestraining.com, or by phone at (888) 402-1117.

HOW TO PREPARE FOR AND GET MEDIA INTERVIEWS

Patti Wood, MA, CSP

Your phone rings. You answer it and someone says, "This is ABC News, and we would like you to be on our show tomorrow morning." Does that sound like a phone call you would like to receive? I was lucky enough to get that call from ABC News and participate in an interview. Since that call back in 2001, I have given an average of two national media interviews a week—interviews with outlets like *Forbes, The Wall Street Journal, Good Morning America*, CNN, Fox News, and hundreds more. My NSA friends tease me and say, "Yep, after twenty years in the speaking business, you were an overnight success."

With technology today, if you're a credible expert in your field, you don't have to wait twenty years to get your first media interview. Just like getting speeches, if you are willing to put in the work, you can make it happen.

WHAT THE MEDIA WANTS

Here is what the media wants in an expert:

- A true credible expert.
- Someone who can answer questions quickly and clearly.
- Someone who can cite the most current academic research on his or her topic.
- Someone who knows all the latest books as well as other media sources and information on his or her topic.

- Someone who can relate his or her topic to current events, politicians, business leaders, Fortune 500 companies, and famous people who are currently in the media spotlight.

- Someone who responds immediately. Get a smartphone and check it often. I have lost big opportunities because I didn't check my e-mail or texts for just a few hours.

- Someone who is ready NOW! The media are full of extremely hard-working people. Their deadlines are tremendously tight, and they are under enormous pressure to find a good source quickly. Print and online media typically need an immediate answer, and the broadcast media typically will give you a few hours' notice before your interview.

The media world is very small, and just as in your speaking career, word on the street can make you or break you. To give you an idea of how small the media world is, just one publisher, The Hearst Corporation, publishes seventeen magazines, including *O, The Oprah Magazine*; *Good Housekeeping*; *Esquire;* and *Cosmopolitan*, as well as more than seventeen newspapers. My experience in the last 10 years is that media contacts are very kind and amazingly generous. If they love you, you are in.

A speaker did an interview with *US Weekly*, and it went so well that the next day a writer for *First for Women* called saying she was at dinner and the speaker's name came up as the "go-to expert" for that topic; the following week, that writer's roommate called the speaker for an article she was writing for her magazine.

If they don't like you, however, you are out. An expert I know was about to do a TV interview, and while in the hallway overheard someone telling the host of another show, "Yes, we got the word you didn't want [expert's name deleted] ever on the show again." The host replied, "Thanks, I have never seen anything like it. That guy was full of himself and couldn't answer the questions!"

HOW TO BE A TRUE EXPERT

Make sure you can, in one or two sentences, honestly and clearly, answer the question: "What makes you an expert on _____?" In fact, if you can, do it now right here. _____

NSA member Richard Weylman, CSP, CPAE, said at a Georgia Speakers Chapter meeting years ago, "If you read for one hour a day on your topic area every day for a year you will know more than 90 percent of the people do on that topic." Start now, Google every book, buy them, and read them. Google your topic, and research it every week. Find out who the leaders, movers, and shakers are in your area, read everything they have said, and study RRS feeds.

If you are an academically accredited expert on your topic, you have more credibility with hard news outlets. If you can do academic-level research in your field, do it. If you can write a great book on the topic, go for it. Experts in their field like Barbara Glanz, CSP, CPAE, The Employee Motivation Expert; Laura Stack, MBA, CSP, 2011–2012 NSA President, Time Management Expert; and Shep Hyken, CSP, CPAE, Customer Service Expert, have done the work to become credible experts in their fields. Study them and other expert speakers like them.

OTHER WAYS TO GROW YOUR EXPERTISE

As a speaker, you have access to your audience's knowledge and opinions. Listen to them, and write about what you learn from them. You can start taking courses related to your topic and go learn from leaders and experts in your field. Taking a weekend class doesn't make you an expert, but it can build your expertise!

Ask yourself, "Can I easily talk all day on my topic?" If you can, great! The media loves that preparation! If you can't, here is what I challenge you to do: Prepare a full-day program on your topic that is all YOUR material.

GET READY FOR A TV INTERVIEW

Being a speaker is a good start to being great on TV, but a media interview has different challenges. Practice giving short pithy answers, ideally with a media coach.

On TV, your physical impression is critical. Have you ever seen someone on TV and said, "She looks awful," or "Can you believe his hair?" Look at the experts on the TV shows you want to appear on. What do they look like? Be honest with yourself; look in the mirror and see if you're a match. Most TV shows are looking for someone who is energetic, attractive, and composed and talks quickly, giving pithy comments. They want to see you give interesting sound bites in less than a minute and half. A TV interview takes three to four minutes, tops. You can't tell a 3-minute story and you can't be slow!

Here are a few exercises to help you prepare:

Exercise 1: Pick a show you would like to be on.

- Research the show and its audience.
- Tape a week of shows, and study all the expert interviews.
- Look at the experts.
- Ask yourself:
    What does the average expert of your gender look like?
    Do you fit that same physical profile of an expert?
    How do they dress?
    What did they do right? What did they do wrong?
- Study the interviewers, and ask yourself:
    What is their style, pacing, and viewpoint?
    How do they ask questions?
    What creates a good interview on that show?

Exercise 2: Make up questions the host could ask you, and answer your questions.

Exercise 3: Get a professional image makeover. Whether you're male or female, have a professional consultant look at your clothing and hairstyle—and for women, make-up. Have a "looks-great-on-TV" outfit ready to go.

Record yourself, and watch and critique yourself over and over.

GET READY FOR PRINT AND ONLINE MEDIA

Do you have a print or online publication you would like to be quoted in? Study the media outlet to find the perfect place for your expertise. Perhaps it is in a column in the *Wall Street Journal* or the financial business section of the *Huffington Post*. Study that media's content, review and study the advertisements, and understand the audience. Then see if what you know is a good match for that market.

GET YOUR WEBSITE AND OTHER AVENUES MEDIA READY

Have the words "media interview" and your expertise in the HTML code of your website, on your home pages, and in other content of your website, your blog, your YouTube channel, and all your other online and print materials. Upload a good video of you being interviewed to your home page.

TV media outlets—even local ones—want to see how you look on camera. If you don't have videos, create them. Ideally, you'd film this in a studio with a professional videographer and an interviewer asking you questions that you quickly and brilliantly answer. Every new TV media source who calls me has looked at the TV interviews on my website and/or my YouTube channel before calling me. They can't risk a newbie.

Put a Media/Press button and section on your site with your bio, talking points, insightful things you could say on the air, etc.

I got all my first media interviews because my website ranks high in search engines for my area of expertise. Producers and journalists will Google the topic they need and expect the best experts to be on the first page. To take advantage of this tactic, follow these tips:

1. Brainstorm a list of all the words the media would use to find someone who is an expert on your topic. Then put all those words in your code and on your website.

2. Write on your topic. Tim Richardson, MS, CSP, talks about the richest people being those who give back through service, create charities, and volunteer. Before he sent his first press release suggesting he be a guest on the day that Forbes listed the 100 financially wealthiest people, he read and watched the media outlets that have news about wealthy people. He saw who was interviewed by Fox News, MSNBC, and *The Wall Street Journal*, and he started commenting about them on his blog.

Exercise 1: Watch and read the media you want to be featured on, and comment on what they are saying on your blog, YouTube channel, and website, ideally every day!

My biggest and simplest recommendation is to tie your expertise to current events. If you want more details on how to do that, you may want to read my chapter in Elsom Eldridge Jr. and Mark Eldridge's book, *How to Position Yourself as the Obvious Expert.*

Exercise 2: Every day, research the hot topics in the news. Ask yourself, "What can I say about this topic that relates to my field?" If you talk about customer service and a hot topic is Walmart's new vests for their customer greeters, what is something interesting and new you can say about it? What are three changes small businesses can make to their greeting process? If you're an expert on ethics and a CEO is arrested for misdeeds, what opinion do you have on it, or what seven important rules can you give for business leaders to avoid ethics violations? If people are talking about job loss and you are an interviewing expert, what success stories can you share? What are three things most job seekers don't know about finding a job? Then write about it.

Put your own video on your website, your YouTube channel, and your blog. Remember, the media wants to see how you are in stressful interviews being questioned. Create your own videos tied to hot stories in the media, and use keywords to link to your videos, such as the topic and your name.

Subscribe to services that send you a daily list of topics and media contacts seeking experts. There are many available. You have to read all the leads to see if there is a match to your expertise. It is time-consuming but worth it.

CONTACT THE MEDIA

Don't take the following actions until you have done your homework in the exercises. You need to be a true expert, be media-ready, know the media outlets and their audiences, and how your topic relates to their lives. You can also pay a PR or media relations professional to secure media interviews for you. If you are a true expert, are media-ready, and have the money, paying for PR services is an option. You can contact the media in several ways.

One way is to send them press releases related to the news of the day. If you are doing a speech that is open to the public on a newsworthy topic, you can send a press release to all the local media announcing it and offering to do an interview. In any press release, make sure you send them great interview ideas and/or send five great bullet "talking points" that you could discuss.

One particular TV interview that I put on my home page has gotten me not only many more media interviews but many speaking engagements, a job as a national spokesperson, and a book deal. I had done hundreds of TV interviews before this one, but it was a biggie. I was lucky I got the call a week before I had to fly to New York to do the interview. I prepared for more than forty hours for those six minutes on camera. That meant writing content, including four "talking points." I help clients prepare for media interviews, and I used every tool I teach, including thinking of all the questions and comments that the host might come up with and what I could say in response. I worked with two comedy coaches to loosen up my funny bone. I didn't use any of the funny material that I prepared, but knowing I had it helped me be confident enough to ad lib on live TV. The show was on a subtopic in my field of body language, and I had written a chapter in one of my books on it. I had also blogged about it. A journalist at *Health Magazine* had searched for the keywords, found my blog entry, and called me for the interview. The magazine pitched it to the TV show producer along with my name and the other expert quoted in the article. The other expert did not have video on their website. I was lucky I did.

I clock my hours on each task in my workday. I spend at least six hours a week working to get media interviews and approximately seventeen hours a week prepping for or doing those interviews. It is hard work, but it can get you business and make the business you have more lucrative.

Being interviewed by the media will challenge you, motivate you to be at the top of your game, and allow you to have even more fun than taking a barrel of monkeys on a rollercoaster ride. Now you know what the media wants in an expert, how to work on your expertise and draw media to your website, how to prepare for a media interview, and the action steps to make you the go-to media expert in your field. Enjoy the thrilling ride.

Patti Wood is called "the gold standard of body language experts" by *The Washington Post* and credited in *The New York Times* with bringing the topic into the national consciousness. Patti has degrees with a specialization in nonverbal communication and was a university instructor in body language, nonverbal communication, and other communication topics for eleven years. Her areas of research are First Impressions, Deception Detection, and Sales Presentation Body Language. She is the author of seven books, including the forthcoming *SNAP: Making the Most of First Impressions, Body Language, and Charisma* with New World Library. Patti is a speaker and consultant for Fortune 100 companies as well as hundreds of national associations. She speaks on *Good Morning America*, PBS, the BBC, CNN, Fox News, Headline News, The History Channel, *Nancy Grace*, *Dr. Drew*, *Inside Edition*, The Discovery Channel, and more. She appears regularly in hundreds of newspapers and magazines around the world. To book Patti, go to www.PattiWood.net.

ORDINARY MARKETING STRATEGIES, EXTRAORDINARY RESULTS

Vincent Kituku, CSP

A while back, I received an e-mail from one of my great NSA friends that read, "Hello, Vincent, Please share with me, if you would, how you open some doors. I have been 99 percent bureau-driven. I can't afford to do that; it doesn't support my dreams. I'm at the top of my game, but I think I remain hidden in my local market. Locally I am an unknown in a big way. I can't help people if they don't know that I am here, Vincent, and worse, I can't prosper."

Because I was determined to be home as our children were growing, I was motivated to develop sustainable marketing strategies in southwest Idaho and the surrounding areas. Those marketing efforts made it possible for me to attend more than 95 percent of our children's parent-teacher conferences and sports activities and to enjoy the comfort of my bed 300 nights a year.

There are some benefits to joining chambers of commerce or service-oriented clubs such as Kiwanis, Lions, or Rotary and serving as a board member for non-profit organizations. However, to develop ongoing marketing momentum, you need more than that. Your marketing efforts have to be a combination of different strategies because one approach would soon saturate the local market and become boring.

BECOME A COMMUNITY ENCOURAGER

I follow local news, including recognition for professional achievements. An individual's contribution to the Boise community is factored into the annual selection of Women of the Year, presented by the *Idaho Business Review* to about fifty women. The Tribute to Women and Industry (TWIN), presented by the Women's and Children's Alliance (WCA), honors about thirty women for similar achievements.

Winners' names and photos along with their organization are printed in the recognition event's program. We search for their addresses and mail a congratulatory letter and a gift—most often a copy of *Overcoming Buffaloes at Work & in Life* and the Top 45 Must-Know Lessons for Top Achievers poster. Sometimes I include a carved wooden letter opener from the Kamba community (my people) of Kenya. The letter I write is simple:

> Dear Martha,
>
> Congratulations for winning the 2011 _____ Award. This recognition by the (name of award-giving organization) is a result of your leadership, hard work, and focus on what matters.
>
> Please allow me to join others who are inspired by your achievement and congratulate you for your efforts. The enclosed (names of the gifts) are small tokens of Kituku & Associates' deep appreciation for being a positive role model.
>
> Martha, your success is an inspiration for many people to believe in themselves, especially women and girls. I have long known and believed that when a woman succeeds, a community moves forward. You are the reason someone will have a better tomorrow. Keep moving forward!

When I first mailed gifts to strangers, a leading mortgage expert whose work I had read about received one of those congratulatory letters. She sent a thank-you note that read, "Vincent, I have admired your work for years. My husband and I would love to take you out for lunch." The expert became the main financial sponsor of many of my seminars, introduced me to other sponsors, and buys hundreds of my books to give to clients.

Here is an actual e-mail (names of writer and her company changed) from another stranger:

> Good morning, I received your congratulations package related to the TWIN award program and wanted to let you know that I really appreciated it. I receive unrequested mail daily, and as I opened the package I thought this might be the same. I was moved immediately as I read a portion of the "9 Must-Know Lessons . . ." booklet. I loaded the CD and listened all the way through as I looked up your website online. Obviously I was very affected and wanted to let you know right away.
>
> In an effort to help others feel similarly impressed, I wonder what your options for keynotes or short motivational seminars might be. I am the manager of a training unit for Maximum Producers of Idaho's Member Service Department and would like to see if a program you offer could fit into our training plans for this year. We are located in Boise, Idaho.

She had no idea her office was less than five minutes from mine. This "gift" has led to ten different business projects in three years.

CREATE WELL-TIMED EVENTS WITH MAXIMUM IMPACT

Celebrate your business's anniversaries with maximum impact utilizing 100 percent free publicity and gaining huge monetary returns. If well planned, a single event has the potential to create immediate benefits. As I am writing this, I am working on a project that I expect to bring a minimum of 2,000 participants to celebrate my fifteen years in business. I have invited a beloved former Boise State University football star to be the keynote speaker. This will be his first public event after leaving college. His participation is being covered by all the local media outlets, as well as social groups and professional associations. I have invited and received sponsorship from several large organizations that want to be associated with this young man who is well-known in our community and beyond.

There are expected and unexpected positive results from events like this. In addition to the publicity, organizations learn about and become interested in your topic. Instead of registering their employees for the event, they contract you for their own customized in-house program. Further, when you develop handouts and workbooks for the event, you have the opportunity to include the services and products that you offer. At the event, you will sell your products (CDs, books, manuals, etc.); you will encourage people to register and pay for your next workshop session, seminar, or customized program; and you will create awareness of and donors for your nonprofit organization.

Here is your homework: Follow the news on people in your community who have new and inspiring stories. It can be a current Olympic gold medal winner or a coach with an inspiring successful season or a person who recently transformed his life from homelessness to living like a king through hard work and determination. Try to find one that is covered by both local and national news. It helps if you knew that person before his or her success or have a mutual friend who can introduce you. But, even if you do not, contact them and congratulate them on their accomplishment, and invite them to share their story as the keynote speaker for your event. Be ready to compensate them for their time. If it is a personal friend, he or she may not need you to pay.

TIPS FOR MARKETING IN YOUR LOCAL MARKET

Be seen, read, and heard often. The key is to hear, "I see you on TV," or "I read your articles," or "I listen to you on the radio," every week, if not daily. Here is how to do that. You write a weekly column that will be published by numerous newspapers and share the same message/information with your TV and radio audiences. Adjust the message to the intended audience as needed.

Let me add that a regular electronic newsletter (in which, by the way, you can reuse the newspaper column) is the cheapest form of marketing I have ever used to promote seminars and books. There are also opportunities in blogs and social media, but I have not yet seen their benefits in my business.

Take advantage of zero competition. You are likely to sell more books and CDs in your local businesses that *don't* sell books and CDs than in any bookstore or on Amazon.com. How many sandwich shops have you seen display (and sell) a speaker's books or seminars? Can you imagine conducting a book-signing event outside your favorite deli? Have you ever gone to a hardware store to purchase motivational books and CDs? When have you taken your clothes to an alteration shop and left with a book written by a speaker or trainer or life coach?

In a customer's mind, the business is endorsing your works. Further, because customers don't have a gazillion choices, they can spend a few minutes reading your book jacket or CD case while waiting for their sandwich. An offhand statement such as, "Oh, have you read that book?" from their waitress can prompt the customer to purchase it.

Write an article featuring your client. Have the article printed in the local newspaper of your client's hometown. Fortunately, I am a weekly columnist and regular writer for several newspapers. This is huge. Here is what one of my clients wrote:

> What a perfect article. I cannot thank you enough for this gift of encouragement and recognition. You are an incredibly gifted writer, and you did a tremendous job of capturing the spirit and heart of our company. We are blessed by your support in so many ways . . . Thanks for all that you are doing for us! With much appreciation and respect, K. Henderson, Executive Director, Community Progress of Idaho, Inc.
>
> (Note: The strangest thing happened. The client doubled what we had agreed on and then became a sponsor of my weekly radio program.)

Be part of something bigger than you and/or your business. I wrote motivational articles for a coach I had never met and volunteered to speak to the Boise State University (BSU) football team before I had seen an entire American football game. Within a short time, the coaches started talking about me and my stories in public.

In 2003, I was selected as the school's Homecoming Grand Marshal. In addition to the exposure through the events leading up to game day, I was introduced to all the fans at half-time as I was given an award of appreciation.

In the 2007 Fiesta Bowl, the Boise Broncos played and defeated the heavily favored Oklahoma Sooners. A few days later, Idaho's largest newspaper had the following headline: "Motivational speaker gets credit for part of Broncos' success."

The article noted my lack of football knowledge but highlighted what current and former coaches said about my presentations to the team. That coverage led to numerous contracts. Further, when a BSU coach gets a job at another university, that becomes a business opportunity.

Sponsor events your clients are attracted to. Children's and women's programs, generally speaking, have special appeal. People want to do business with those who care about the programs they are concerned about. Can you imagine seeing a football team's gear with your name or business on it such as Kituku Buffalo Fighters or Kituku Warriors?

Update your community. Most newspapers have a business section that dedicates space for press releases to announce not only public seminars but also news about professional awards (and recognition), a move to a new location, new training programs, or a major new contract with a well-known organization. In each press release, include the services you provide and how you can be reached. This is free and keeps your name and business in front of newspaper readers.

Forget doing what everyone else is doing. Just before Mother's Day, handwrite a good note to your female clients who have children, recognizing them for being exemplary mothers. You may include a moving poem or an article about your own mother. Do the same for male clients prior to Father's Day (customized for men).

Fresh food, straight from your garden to your clients' tables, has its magic. From July to early October, I deliver fresh tomatoes, onions, bell peppers, cabbages, carrots, collard greens, and cucumbers to my Boise, Idaho, clients without booking an appointment. I have never been told to come back tomorrow. Within a few days after I deliver tomatoes, I usually get a call to discuss my availability for next spring.

Your interest in people matters. Nothing proves more to clients that your relationship goes beyond business transactions than your genuine interest in their well-being. Visit or call a client when he/she or a loved one is sick. Send a congratulatory card or gift when someone gets a new certification or graduates from college. Clients never forget this thoughtfulness. You can never overestimate the healing power of your presence.

Give a memorable gift. My community, Kamba, in Kenya, is well-known for woodcarving. When I present wooden letter openers to clients with a simple description of how it's carved, from what tree, and what it symbolizes, doors of opportunity open. Unique items are kept as a constant reminder to clients of good deeds.

PRESENCE PAYS OFF

There are sustainable benefits when the local market is aware of your services. The local market will still use your services despite unpredictable events such as

September 11, 2001, tsunamis, or a bad economy. Your work is known, and they don't have to use meager resources for travel expenses. From an intangible perspective, you become both successful and fulfilled because your business (which is you) is making a difference. And your dominating local presence soon gets recognized beyond your community because your local clients have relatives, colleagues, and former schoolmates in other parts of the world.

Dr. Vincent Muli Wa Kituku, CSP, international speaker, columnist, and author of *Overcoming Buffaloes at Work & in Life*, works with organizations and individuals who want to increase productivity and stay focused and motivated. He is the founder of Northwest Speakers Forum, based in Idaho, and cofounder of Platinum Speakers Bureau in Kenya. Both programs provide aspiring and established speakers opportunities to develop their skills and learn speaking business practices as well as a platform to showcase their abilities. Dr. Kituku is the founder and executive director of Caring Hearts and Hands of Hope (www.caringheartsandhandsofhope.org), a nonprofit organization that provides high school tuition and fees for orphans and other needy students in Kenya. His e-mail address is vincent@kituku.com, and his website is www.kituku.com.

GO GLOBAL WITH YOUR MESSAGE

Dr. Taira Koybaeva

Globalization has become synonymous with borderless markets. Richard N. Haass, the president of the Council on Foreign Relations, described it as "the increasing volume, speed, and importance of flows across borders of people, ideas, greenhouse gases, manufactured goods, dollars, euros, television and radio signals, drugs, germs, e-mails, weapons, and a good deal else" in his Jan. 8, 2006, article in *The Washington Post*. Potentially, your marketplace can be the whole globe. In addition, because more virtual and real inroads are being built to facilitate this flow, it is becoming easier to reach that market.

HOW HAS GLOBALIZATION AFFECTED YOUR MARKET?

It is no great surprise that U.S. companies have been outsourcing many jobs. According to the International Association of Outsourcing Professionals, in just one year, the number of companies that expect to expand outsourcing has increased by 20 percent, with the trend being toward highly skilled labor. That same year, according to the United Nations Conference on Trade and Development (UNCTAD), foreign direct investment into the services sector increased by $54 billion. Training these workers will no longer be about assembly lines and paint-by-numbers job descriptions. Programs that increase innovation, motivation, and efficiency are going to be in high demand.

In fact, this is already happening at formal educational institutions. The majority of foreign students choose business as their major, and countries whose economies are rapidly developing are investing billions into colleges and universities. King Abdullah University of Science and Technology opened in Saudi Arabia with a $10 billion endowment. In India, the Education Ministry intends to build fourteen world-class universities. From 1998 to 2009 the number of institutions of higher education in China more than doubled.

They understand education is key to prosperity, and they don't want to be left behind. And if history is anything to go by, after formal institutions are set up, coaching and speaking are next in demand for increasing human capital. So, if you have heard news of a declining speaking and coaching market, don't listen—your market is not declining; you might be in the wrong country!

IS THERE MONEY IN DEVELOPING COUNTRIES FOR ME?

These are rapidly developing countries, but, you say, Can they afford me? At least 100 million people are considered middle class in China, about 95 million in Brazil, 58 million in India, with more and more residual income to spend. For many of the families in these countries, investment in education of their children is considered more important than retirement savings. Culturally, they see their children's future income as retirement; therefore, no money is spared for their children's education. Case in point, with China's one-child policy, there are two parents and four grandparents per child. That is six people's disposable income that will be put toward the education of one child.

According to World Bank and International Monetary Fund estimates for 2011, per capita income of United Arab Emirates is more than $65,000, more than $97,000 for Qatar, and about $50,000 for Singapore, compared with $48,000 in the United States. I will let you do the rest of the math on the so-called declining market with "decreasing" residual income.

I DON'T REPRESENT A UNIVERSITY.
CAN I STILL BE A PART OF AN ACADEMIC NETWORK?

The United States is one of the few countries where you can get an education from formal and informal educational institutions. In other countries, especially emerging markets, this distinction does not exist. The difference between a certificate and a diploma is marginal. The major dissimilarity is that formal institutions' content is much more regulated. Your content has to be high quality. In addition, coaches and speakers belong to associations that can be leveraged in formal educational institutions.

BEFORE YOU GO GLOBAL, WHERE IN THE WORLD DO YOU WANT TO GO?

You have decided that you want to go global. Now what? The first step is to identify what markets you want to target. There are three ways to do this:

1. Do you already speak language(s) other than those of the country you are from? If so, this might be a good place to start. Most likely, you also have contacts with people from countries who speak that language.

2. Do you have a particular pull toward a country or culture? Many people dismiss this inclination, but a built-in fondness for a culture may prove to be the best asset in finding contacts and creating a network.

3. Who is hungry for your message? Following global trends may be one of the best investments of time in your business you will ever make. I am not talking about just political trends, but what people are thinking, wearing, buying, reading. You can get an overview of trends on sites such as Goglobalfast.com, Globaltrends.com, Worldpress.org, or by reading magazines and newspapers published in other countries. Just glancing through a Spanish version of *People* magazine can give you clues to differences in trends.

Once you have chosen the market(s) and acquainted yourself with the cultural trends of the chosen market, you are ready for the next step—making your content global-friendly.

ARE YOU GLOBAL-FRIENDLY?

Making your message, marketing, and content global-friendly is not just a matter of making sure your company name doesn't translate into an offensive word in another language. It is a matter of making sure your message doesn't get lost in cultural translation. In North America, we have become so accustomed to certain cultural underpinnings in our content that we take it for granted. According to research by leading cultural analysts, Americans assume that, in general, people want:

- The right to mold their own destiny
- Equality among people
- Efficiency, because "time is money"
- Freedom to express their individuality
- Control of themselves and their environment
- To believe that change equals progress

Review your materials to see if any of this is implicit in your content. Often, you will not be able to identify these messages due to your deeply ingrained cultural habits. I highly recommend you have your message reviewed by a cultural analyst, or a professional from that culture. This does not necessarily mean you need to remove these ideas. Many foreign markets are hungry for these messages. You will either need to leave them, make them explicit, modify them, or remove them altogether.

ADJUSTING YOUR CONTENT

Your first question is: What are the assumptions of the culture I'm marketing to? There are three ways to get acquainted with a culture's values and assumptions. Depending on availability of time and money, you can choose from the following:

1. High expenditure of time/low expenditure of money: Volumes of academic research have been dedicated to the topic of cultural analysis. They will give you a theoretical and thorough understanding of any particular culture. Hofstede and Trompenaars are two of my favorite authors, as their works are most related to business. A quick overview of many cultures can be found on geert-hofstede.com. There are numerous books written about specific cultures and countries as well.

2. Medium expenditure of time/low expenditure of money: Read popular books about cultures. The *Culture Shock!* series, published by Graphic Arts Books, is a very easy read. These books will give you some insight into any given country. Short and relatable, although not as thorough, they will give you an awareness of basic differences. The limitation of this series is that it addresses specific countries, rather than broad markets. It also leaves you clueless as to which of your messages will be received in a

hostile manner and which with open arms. The cultural intelligence quotient (CQ) is a concept that addresses the need to deal with multiple cultures and countries. You can read about CQ by various authors, but this information doesn't provide specifics on content modification.

3. Low expenditure of time/high expenditure of money: Hire a cultural consultant. This option may end up being the most expensive, but may very well prove to be most cost efficient. Good cultural consultants are worth their weight in gold. You will not need to do any analysis; they will do it for you. Cultural analysts can help you decide what markets are a good fit for your content and how to modify it without losing its essence. Cultural consultants can specialize in specific cultures or can cover multiple ones.

The next step is identifying differing and matching values and assumptions between your content and any given culture. For example, if a culture assumes freedom of individual expression is a good thing, such as Australia, then leave it. If change is not always seen as progress, such as in many European countries, you will either need to explain explicitly why changes you are suggesting are going to lead to progress, remove the message if it isn't key to your content, or modify it. Modification is possible if there is a universal belief that can be distilled from the message.

Books have been written about superficial taboos in each culture, so I will not elaborate on them here. Suffice it to say, if you properly understand fundamental cultural differences, you will automatically learn about taboos. Reviewing your content for relevance to the market is a crucial step. Often, this is the reason so many speakers and coaches fail when they try to go global. Going through this process will also prepare you for international networking.

GOING GLOBAL

You have identified your market(s) and modified your content. Now you are ready to go global. The rule of "It isn't what you know, but who you know" applies to almost all of the emerging and developing markets. Creating connections and building relationships, or what we call "networking," is where you need to invest most of your efforts if you are to get anywhere with your global expansion.

CONNECTING ACROSS BORDERS

The cultures of most emerging markets are what is termed *collectivist*. "The group is more important than the individual" is the defining characteristic that has huge implications in how you approach people, develop relationships, and even market your business. In such cultures you do not "network"; you build relationships. The very word *networking* can be offensive, as it has implications of seeing people as "useful functions" and "how can this person benefit my business."

To make things more complicated, Americans are stereotyped as very utilitarian and ethnocentric in their approaches. However, they are also considered the leading experts in business topics. You will be seen as an expert just because of your place of origin. You might be frustrated at the length of time it takes to build relationships, but it is well worth the effort, as in collectivist societies it takes only one or two to accept your message before the rest will follow.

GETTING INTO THE CIRCLE OF TRUST

The first step is to make a contact with someone in that country. This is much easier than you might think. You can do so in several ways:

1. Think of any people you know who are either from that country or know of people in that country. Ask them to connect you with a business or organization that your topic might be beneficial to.

2. Research academic programs in that country that are related to your topic. Find any contact available on their website.

3. Search social media sites for foreign groups or organizations related to your topic. I prefer sites that are more professionally related, such as LinkedIn. Join these groups and monitor the posts by the group's members. Once you see something of interest, start a dialog. Do not market your business—at this stage you are just connecting.

4. Search online for coaching or speaking organizations in those countries and look for ways you can collaborate with these organizations.

Once you identify contacts, you can connect with them by e-mail, phone, or Skype. Use a neutral, so-called international version of English, which is more formal than you are accustomed to in the United States. In your communication, introduce yourself, state your expertise, and describe the organization you represent (it can be your own company). Inquire about what programs/initiatives related to your expertise exist in the organization. Ask to be given the telephone number or e-mail address of the director of that program or at least his/her secretary.

Once you have the information of a person directly related to your field, you are able to make a more direct connection. Collaboration is your intent. Make sure to express interest in how they implement and view the subject matter of your expertise. You need to come across as someone who wants to listen and learn. This seems counterintuitive, when you are trying to position yourself as an expert, but it works. At that point you start a dialog that will last anywhere from a month to a whole year before you are invited. Your goal is to be invited to speak, train, or collaborate.

ONCE YOU ARE THERE

Once you are in a foreign country, do three things: listen, listen, listen. This will put you into an observational mode that is crucial for gathering information. This information will be later used in your marketing and content development. It will also set you apart as a nontypical American who doesn't just want to impose his or her views but wants to learn, thereby expressing respect to others' way of life. This is the sure way to not only be invited back, but to be invited into the homes of your hosts. Your hosts might then be able to connect you to other organizations. Once you are back home, you will be able to leverage your new knowledge in your domestic business.

Going global can be easy; you just have to follow certain steps. Make sure you understand your market and modify your content to fit it. While networking, take time to build relationships, as they are key to your global strategy. Position yourself as a receptive and respectful expert. Who knows, maybe next time I am flying across the ocean, you will be sitting next to me.

Educated in Russia, Germany, Switzerland, and the United States, Dr. Koybaeva has worked with various domestic and international agencies such as the U.S. Congress, Canadian Ministry of Foreign Affairs, the Norwegian Embassy in the United States, the Russian Duma, Ukrainian Department of Defense, and the Tajik government. She has facilitated multimillion-dollar international R&D projects, including documentation for the International Space Station, and taken a $1 million annual budget to $50 million in less than five years.

Dr. Koybaeva founded Go Global Fast, LLC. It enables companies and people to achieve global expansion through Dr. Koybaeva's proprietary methods, strategies, and processes that have been solidly supported through years of rigorous research and practice. She can be reached at tk@goglobalfast.com, or www.goglobalfast.com. You can also learn more about what she does at her personal website at www.tairakoybaeva.com.

SOCIAL MEDIA AND TECHNOLOGY

A SPEAKER'S GUIDE TO SOCIAL MEDIA: BECOME A GEEK IN ONE HOUR A WEEK

Corey Perlman

If paid speaking gigs are what you're after, the following is a step-by-step guide to getting results and maximizing your efforts. I came up with this approach after hearing the two biggest challenges speakers have with social media:

1. I don't have time.
2. If I had the time, I'm not sure how or where to spend it.

Fair enough.

I then posed a question to the responders: If they could significantly ramp up their number of quality speaking gigs, could they—and would they—spare one hour a week?

Almost every speaker I spoke with said, "Yes!"

Challenge No. 1 solved.

The rest of this chapter is dedicated to the second challenge of helping my fellow speakers know where they should spend their time online to increase their speaking business.

Note: If starting from scratch, some of these strategies may take more than one hour to complete. Over time, you should be able to see a result within the one-hour time frame.

FISH WHERE THE FISH ARE

Don't be a jack of all social media sites, master of none. Focus on the few sites that give you the biggest bang for your time. It's been my experience that LinkedIn is an obvious place where our customers and prospects are spending time. Meeting organizers, event coordinators, training directors, etc., are all on LinkedIn, and most have active profiles.

So, where should you spend your time on LinkedIn?

Begin with building a profile you're proud of. If you haven't reached 500+ connections, stop everything else you're doing and get connected with your network. When someone visits your profile, LinkedIn shows only the number of connections up to 500. After 500, they just add the + sign. So, whether you have 501 or 5001, your profile will show 500+.

Make no mistake about it—numbers matter. Almost every meeting planner I've spoken with has said they check out a speaker's LinkedIn profile prior to booking him or her. What message do you convey with just 112 connections?

Planners answered that question with: "small," "disconnected," "out of touch," and "fly-by-night." These perceptions won't help you get hired as a speaker. So start connecting with your colleagues, customers, and prospects on LinkedIn, and don't stop until you hit 500+.

Ask for recommendations from past speaking events. At a recent conference, I was chitchatting with the event coordinator, and I asked her how she decided on me to deliver the keynote over the other speakers. She quickly responded, "A LinkedIn recommendation." In fact, she recited pieces of the recommendation that she had read. I was blown away.

You see, when it comes to recommendations, it's quality over quantity. If you ask the right people to recommend you on LinkedIn, they will spend time crafting an endorsement worthy of the exceptional performance you gave at their event. Recommendations matter.

No, scratch that.

Quality recommendations matter—recommendations that come from people who booked you and loved your performance.

Update your profile daily. This takes little to no time at all, but could result in significantly more booked gigs. Go check out your LinkedIn profile. You'll notice some updates from a few of your contacts. These are people who have posted an update to their profile and did it right around the time of your visit. If you're in "buy mode" for their products or services at the time of their posting, this could be the friendly reminder that earns them your business.

The same goes for your prospects. They could be in need of a speaker, and you may have fallen off their radar for one reason or another. But during a visit to LinkedIn, they see a status update from you referencing a great *Harvard Business Review* article on leadership. Whether they read the article is irrelevant. The point is you jumped back on their radar at precisely the right time, and a speaker inquiry could result.

Here are a couple other tips for posting to LinkedIn (and any other social media site you update):

Make it about them. It's okay to occasionally promote yourself or talk about yourself, but try to talk about your network's interests. Ask yourself, "Is this valuable to my audience?" If the answer is "no," consider a different update.

Vary your updates. Do some in the morning, some in the evening. Do some during the week, and maybe a few on the weekends. People frequent social media sites at different times, so you'll reach a wider audience by mixing up the timing of your posts.

Don't sell; softly promote. "Book me now. I'm available!" is not going to go over well on LinkedIn. A shady man selling watches from his trench coat comes to mind. Instead of the blatant sell, remind people of the great places you've been visiting or how great it was to work with ABC Organization. Last year, I had the chance to speak at the Fargo Dome. It was, by far, the biggest venue at which I'd ever spoken, so I had someone take a picture of me jumping in the air in front of the massive facility. I posted it to my social media sites with the caption, "Look, Mom, I made it!" Even though this post was about me, people seemed to get a kick out of it, and I received some great responses.

There are great resources out there to find valuable articles to share with your network. If you have an iPad, check out these great apps: Flipboard, Newsrack, and Pulse.

MIX BUSINESS AND PLEASURE

Think of your largest client. (Hint: It's probably the person or company who paid you the most money last year.) The client I'm thinking of is Mary Johnson (yes, that's a fake name). Mary paid me well over five figures last year for two speaking engagements and a private consulting session.

Her birthday is May 11th. I had my assistant send her this unbelievable chocolate bark from my hometown of Sarasota, Florida. She loved it, and so did her kids.

She just celebrated her tenth anniversary of being smoke-free. So I sent her an e-mail and shared my personal story of my mom's battle with smoking and how impressed I was that she'd overcome such a powerful addiction.

I also know that Mary went to the University of Alabama, so I congratulated her on the Crimson Tide football team recently being crowned national champions. She told me she went to the game and it was amazing.

And most important, Mary just became a grandmother for the first time, and her granddaughter's name is Morgan. My daughter was born close to the same time, and we share many pictures and funny stories.

What's the point of it all? Three words: Relationships, relationships, relationships!

Harvey Mackay, author of *Swim with the Sharks*, shared in his book the power of building true relationships with our clients, but he never could have imagined how easy it would become to do so with the proliferation of social media. Yet, why are so many people afraid to connect with their clients on Facebook?

Oh, right, we're afraid they might see something unprofessional or—dare I say—personal? The horror! (Cue the blood-curdling scream.)

In all seriousness, we do have to filter a bit if we decide to open our personal Facebook profile to our business contacts. However, I believe the advantages far outweigh the disadvantages. In a very casual, organic way, I'm able to stay top of mind with my clients and prospects just by engaging with them on Facebook. Sometimes it's a simple "like" of one of their posts, and other times it's someone interacting with something I posted.

If I told you I had a room full of all of your prospects and customers and you could interact with them in a meaningful way, you'd pay good money to get in that room, right? Well, why not connect with them on Facebook and enter the room for free?

You might be wondering if this will replace your business's Facebook page. The answer is no. Ideally, you should have both: Your organization should have a business page, and you should have a personal page. The business page is for fans and others who are interested in you. This is why people connect to your business by "liking" this page. It acts completely differently from your personal page. For example, it's okay to have others participate in keeping the page updated. It's your company page, and if other employees are posting to it, that's acceptable.

The number of "likes" you have on your business page matters. Believe me, if a meeting planner Googles your company name and lands on your Facebook business page and sees 36 likes, it looks pretty insignificant. So make a conscious effort to grow this number. Invite the attendees at your events to join your page and provide an incentive for them to do so. Send an e-mail blast to your list and give them five compelling reasons to connect with your Facebook page. You'll be up above 1,000 fans in no time.

IT'S A GOOGLE WORLD; WE JUST LIVE IN IT

I know, I know, I just finished telling you not to be a jack of all social media sites, and now I want you to focus on yet another social networking site?

Yes, and here's why:

I believe Google+ can compete for market share over goliaths like Facebook and LinkedIn. Why? Well, for starters, it's GOOGLE! They've built one of the most successful companies in the world because of their willingness to grow and innovate. But more than anything else, it's their powerful search engine that's currently scaring the pocket protectors off the nerds in Silicon Valley.

Let me explain.

In early 2012, Google changed its search algorithm to share posts from Google+ connections in search results. Say someone does a Google search for presentation tips. If they're connected with you on Google+ and you've posted an article on this subject, Google could share your article in their search results. That's HUGE.

Google also did a really good job improving on exactly what we don't like about Facebook. They make it really easy to draw a clear line between our personal and professional lives. If you add me to your Google+ network, you can put me in a "business circle" and keep me out of any of your personal circles like "family" or "friends." I won't know what circle you put me in and when you post something on Google+, you can choose which circles the post goes out to.

So, will Google+ overtake Facebook, LinkedIn, or Twitter? Only time will tell. But I recommend you spend a little time planting your flag on this new frontier so you're prepared.

LET'S RECAP

Here's a breakdown of your hour a week:

1. **Build a LinkedIn profile you're proud of.** A nice, short bio, 500+ connections, more than ten recommendations, links to your blog and other social assets, etc. Time: 15 minutes

2. **Update your profiles daily.** Whichever social media sites you've decided to focus on, they must be updated consistently to be effective. But it doesn't need to take a lot of time. The bulk of your time is coming up with quality posts. So bookmark great articles you read throughout the week and jot down ideas that can help others, and soon you'll have plenty to pull from. Time: 5 minutes a day (five times a week)

3. **Engage your best clients on Facebook.** Don't be offended if they ignore your request; they may have decided to keep their Facebook page strictly personal. For those who accept your request, just interact with them as you do your friends. You'll build stronger relationships and stay on their radar. Time: 10 minutes

4. **Play with Google+.** No one knows where it's going to go, but I think it's worth having a profile. So I suggest building a profile, creating a few Circles, and adding some colleagues, customers, and prospects. If it starts rivaling Facebook or LinkedIn, you'll have a huge leg up on your competition. Time: 10 minutes

There you have it—a guide to what I believe are the most important areas in which to spend your time while using social media. Of course, these times are just estimates, and they will fluctuate week to week. But if you stay consistent and focused on just the activities outlined above, I believe you'll be rewarded for your efforts.

Corey Perlman, founder and CEO of eBoot Camp, is an entrepreneur, best-selling author, and nationally recognized social media expert. His book, *eBoot Camp* (Wiley), became an Amazon.com best seller and received global attention, with distribution rights deals in both China and India. Corey's company also manages the social media marketing for more than twenty businesses around the world. He's a member of the National Speakers Association and presents to about twenty-five audiences per year. Corey and his wife, Jessica, reside in beautiful Royal Oak, Michigan, and recently welcomed their first child, Talia, into the world. In her first year, Talia has already tweeted and posted a YouTube video and loves her new iPhone. She's currently working on building a following on Google+. To learn more, visit www.eBootCamp.com.

THE (REAL) IDIOTS GUIDE TO SOCIAL MEDIA MARKETING FOR SPEAKERS, CONSULTANTS, AND THOUGHT-LEADING PROFESSIONALS

David Newman

Too many speakers, consultants, and thought-leading professionals want to get involved in social media but—sadly—do not understand the intent, ideas, or influence factors that make social media an effective tactic in their overall marketing arsenal.

How can I put this? Ummm . . . well, *they're IDIOTS.*

Relax . . . **IDIOTS** is an acronym that stands for the six key misconceptions, faulty assumptions, and pillars of goofy thinking that prevent most thought-leading professionals (*you,* perhaps?) from generating maximum results from their social media marketing efforts.

Let's break it down and give you some strategies, pointers, and tactics to make sure you don't make the same mistakes. Namely . . .

I: "I, Me, My" syndrome

D: Dumbing it down

I: Information without invitation

O: Overselling

T: Talk without action

S: Short-term focus

Now let's examine each of these six mistakes in a bit more detail—and discuss how to do social media marketing the right way:

I: "I, Me, My Syndrome."

No, your social media postings do not need to be all about you. In fact, if all you do is talk about your company, your book, your speeches, your brand, your articles, your resources, your tools, your programs, your products, your services . . . *people will ignore you, tune you out, and dismiss you for the self-centered IDIOT that you are.* (Please remember, IDIOT is an acronym—don't take it personally!)

How to do it right: Experts promote other experts. Experts aren't insecure about shining the spotlight on others. Experts are curators and pointers-out-of-cool-things. Experts link to book reviews by other experts for yet-other-experts' books. Experts invite other experts to post guest blogs on their websites (and they, in turn, get invited to do the same!). Experts share, collaborate, and cross-promote with other experts with a genuine abundance mind-set and not a scarcity mind-set. The mantra goes even beyond *"give to get"*—rather, it is *"give to give."*

As long as *you* can be counted on to share interesting, relevant, valuable, maybe even edgy content, guide your followers to the "good stuff" online, and position yourself as a reliable guide and sherpa in your area of expertise, you'll get plenty of attention, love, and respect . . . even more if you're not forever focused on hyping only yourself.

Grow up. Step up. Be a real expert and learn once and for all: It's not just about *you.*

Action Question: When's the last time you promoted a fellow speaker, consultant, or thought-leader in any of your marketing communications?

D: Dumbing It Down.

This mistake comes from the fear that if you give away your very best ideas, strategies, tools, tactics, insights, and other secret sauce—yes, the very same ideas you get paid big bucks from your paying clients!—that you will somehow diminish the demand for your paid products and services.

So you "dumb it down." You post that second-rate article. You remove critical details from that tip sheet, because you want people to buy your consulting services and not do it themselves. You post the video that contains only three of your ten key ideas, because heck, if you gave out all ten ideas, they'd never hire you to keynote at the big industry conference. You've already "spilled the candy in the lobby."

Yep, you guessed it: That's IDIOT thinking rearing its ugly head.

How to do it right: The reality is . . . it works 180 degrees the other way. The only way folks are going to pay you the big bucks is if they have a firsthand experience of your genius—if they feel it, taste it, touch it, and fully experience it. Only then will they want more. Only then will they share it with their colleagues. Only then will they call their boss over to look at your website or—better still—e-mail your link to a key decision-maker.

The Rolling Stones fill their concerts with fans paying $300 per seat for a stadium show, making tens of millions of dollars in the process. But now, imagine that they pursued that goal by forbidding radio stations to play their songs for free. Imagine if they pulled their music from online sites like Amazon and iTunes because, gosh, if people can listen to the very same songs for 99 cents in the comfort of their own home, they would never pay $300 to come see them live. When we put this scarcity thinking in the context of the music industry, we see exactly how ridiculously faulty this argument is!

Do you want to be *shared* . . . or do you want to be *scared?* Your call, but you probably already know which will make you more money. Unless you're an IDIOT.

Action Question: When's the last time you shared something for free that's so valuable that people have paid you good money for it in your speeches or coaching or consulting work?

I: Information Without Invitation.

Social media sites and your blog should not be a dumping ground for your old, outdated, second-rate content from books you wrote in the 1990s or articles that you could never get published. Even rock-solid, current, highly relevant information is *necessary but not sufficient* to fuel your thought-leadership platform and build your empire as an expert.

Here's a secret: The Internet actually does *not* need more information posted on it. Not from you. Not from me. Not from anyone.

How to do it right: An effective social media campaign shares information of stand-alone value and then invites a two-way (or five-way or 17-way) conversation around that information. How? Simple: Ask questions, seek engagement, invite involvement. Ask the most powerful question in sales, leadership, and relationships: "What do you think?" . . . and then deliver the value you know you can.

Action Question: When's the last time you invited a two-way conversation on your blog or your social media accounts, inviting others to post their ideas, opinions, and feedback?

O: Overselling.

I recall one particularly IDIOT-ic individual bragging proudly that all of his social media posts have a hyperlink. Every. Single. One.

Hyperlink to where, you ask?

To his online store, his products, his books on Amazon, his speaking page, his consulting page, his services overview. "If you're not linking every post to a selling opportunity," he told me, "you're just putting a lot of dead-end junk out there and you'll never make any money."

Now that is pure, unadulterated, bona fide IDIOT thinking. And the sad news is that it's also the number-one complaint that most buyers have about the way many speakers and professional services firms market themselves: namely, that it's all self-promotional hype with zero relevance to buyers or their organizations (and zero relevance to helping them solve their urgent, expensive, pervasive problems)!

Social media sites are not about posting "Here's how to buy my stuff." They're not about creating an extra dozen or so sales pages for your products, services or programs.

If your goals are . . . Sell on Twitter. Sell on Facebook. Sell on LinkedIn. Sell on YouTube . . .

Your results will be . . . Unfollow. Unfriend. Un-network. Unsubscribe. You're done. Buh-bye.

How to do it right: Content comes before commerce. Offer solutions, answers, strategies, templates, tools, and ideas—not sales messages.

Why? Because we're living in an environment of *voluntary attention*. The age of old-school outbound selling (random cold calling, batch-and-blast direct mail, buying ads and working hard to interrupt strangers) is broken. The new reality is this: *First, you earn their attention. Then, you earn their money.*

Action Question: How can you turn your next sales message into a value message? How can you solve, fix, advise, and guide, instead of hitting your prospects over the head with yet another blunt "buy my stuff" message? And which one do you think they will keep, share, forward, and remember you for?

T: Talk Without Action.

Too many speakers, consultants, and thought-leading professionals do *almost* everything right . . . but then leave their fans, followers, and subscribers wondering what to do next.

See how many of the following statements sound familiar:

- "I've been blogging for two years and haven't gotten a single call or e-mail about hiring me."
- "I work for hours and hours on my e-zine, and although I get compliments about how good the articles are, I've never gotten business from it."
- "I post all the time on Twitter, Facebook, and LinkedIn, but I've never gotten a single phone call from any of my social media efforts."

How to do it right: People need to be told what to do next, in the form of a call to action (often abbreviated as CTA). If you want people to e-mail you, explicitly invite them to do so AND give them a compelling reason AND provide your e-mail address. Here are two examples to get your creative juices flowing:

CTA EXAMPLE #1

My friend Scott Ginsberg always ends each blog post with an invitation similar to this one:

LET ME SUGGEST THIS . . .

For a list called, "9 Things Every Writer Needs to Do Every Day," send an e-mail to me, and you win the list for free!

* * * *

Scott Ginsberg

That Guy with the Nametag

Author, Speaker, Publisher, Artist, Mentor

Scott@HelloMyNameIsScott.com

CTA EXAMPLE #2

My friend Gerard Braud is a media training and crisis communications expert who introduces himself to hand-selected high-probability prospects on LinkedIn, and ends his message this way:

> If a brief conversation about your team's media-readiness and/or crisis communication plans would be valuable, please call me or drop me a line.
>
> Wishing you continued success,
>
> Gerard Braud (pronounced Jared Bro) 985-555-1212

Action Question: Are you using value-first CTAs in your e-mail, blogs, and social media postings? Are you giving people a compelling reason to engage further with you in meaningful ways, such as subscribing to your e-zine, calling you, or e-mailing you?

S: Short-term Focus.

The final mistake is to think of social media in the same way that you might think of outbound sales activity. Cold calls. E-mail blasts. Direct mail. Use these tactics, and the natural question to ask is: "OK, how much did we sell today?"

You made 100 dials, you connected with 20 humans, you had 14 conversations, you qualified 5 serious prospects. So, how much did you SELL TODAY?

You sent 10,000 postcards. Requests came back for 300 quotes. So, how many widgets did you SELL TODAY?

Social media marketing doesn't work that way. Social media are . . . well, social. They're about relationships and trust. Relationships and trust don't have an on/off switch. They develop over time.

Transactions happen today from relationships you built last week, last month, and last year. The benefit of that, and the reason it's worth the "wait," is that social media develop a permanent asset: trust.

How to do it right: *Blog entries are forever.* They continue to sell your expertise, your company, and your value day after day, week after week, year after year. *LinkedIn recommendations are forever.* People who wrote glowingly of you in 2002 are still selling for you and your reputation today. But a voice mail? Beep.

Gone. An e-mail? Zap. Gone. A face-to-face meeting? Done. Bye! Those happen today, and they're gone today.

Sure, you have to sell today. You have to make your quota today. You have to feed your family today. But social media marketing ensures that what you create once today works and lasts and brings customers and clients to you for many years to come.

Not because you sold them like an IDIOT—but because you built the trust and relationships that encouraged them to buy . . . today, tomorrow, and beyond!

Action Question: What *permanent assets* are you building today so that your best-fit buyers will seek you out for your expertise, ideas, and solutions, at the precise moment they are ready to spend money on outside help? Are you putting *irresistible bait* on *enough hooks* in the *right ponds* so you won't go hungry next week, next month, and next year?

David Newman is a marketing speaker and founder of Do It! Marketing, a marketing strategy and "done-for-you" services firm dedicated to making thought-leading professionals more successful. He served as president of NSA Philadelphia during 2010–11 and was named Member of the Year in 2009 and 2011. Free resources, including his 97-page *Strategic Marketing* e-book, are available online at www.DoItMarketing.com. Contact David directly at David@DoItMarketing.com, or call (610) 716-5984.

TUNE IN TO OPPORTUNITY: MARKETING WITH YOUR OWN RADIO SHOW

Brett Clay, MBA

In today's market, online content is the gasoline of your marketing engine—and audio and video content is like adding rocket fuel.

When I was doing the radio show tour for the launch of my book, I asked my publicist, "Hey, how can I have my own radio show?" Two years and more than seventy episodes later, it's more important than ever in marketing my business.

CONTENT AND INBOUND MARKETING

First, let's put things in context. We are several years into the new era of "inbound marketing," a phrase coined by Brian Halligan and Dharmesh Shah, founders of Hubspot and coauthors of the book *Inbound Marketing*. The premise of inbound marketing is that buyers are now empowered by the Internet to find and procure the solutions to their problems. In other words, you don't find clients, they'll find you. Therefore, as a seller, you must be findable.

In the past, being findable by Internet search engines involved publishing a high volume of keyword-laden content. Thus, we had the era of blogging. In 2011, Google sent shockwaves through the marketing world by changing how it ranks search results. The algorithm now looks for content, especially multimedia content, that it believes people have found most useful. How Google determines that is the new subject of debate and speculation. Nevertheless, it means you must produce a constant stream of content that people will comment about and share with friends and colleagues. Hubspot marketer and search engine optimization (SEO) scientist Dan Zarrella says, "Don't worry about SEO. Just publish mountains and mountains of remarkable content!" In fact, many corporate marketing organizations are starting to look like publishers—and even video production houses.

How about you? Are you producing mountains of content?
What is your content marketing strategy?

As a marketer, you have no end of places and ways to invest your finite resources. Should you invest in video, newsletters, blogging, microblogging, or article publishing? Here is the most important principle to follow: *You must have a presence in all of the marketing mediums, so you can leverage them together.* For example, a Twitter account with no blog content would offer little value; and a blog without thousands of Twitter followers to whom to publish would also be useless. Thus, an optimal content marketing system has multiple forms of content that fuel multiple publishing mediums, all feeding each other. I call that a Social Synergy System˙.

We still have the questions, however, of where to begin and where to invest. The strategy that I and a number of other NSA colleagues have chosen is to have a presence in all the forms of content, and then focus on one or two to do really well. So, why should you focus on a radio show instead of, say, your YouTube channel? By the end of this chapter, you will be better informed to answer that question for your own business.

WHAT IS A RADIO SHOW?

My publicist (yes, the very same one I'd paid to arrange the radio tour) said that traditional terrestrial radio, given the associated demographics and overall decline of traditional media, wasn't a good way to reach my target audience. He strongly advised against pursuing the path of a local AM or FM station. The Internet, he said, would provide a much bigger, worldwide reach. It quickly became clear that I was going to have an "Internet Radio Show."

What is the difference between Internet radio and podcasting? There's no clear black-and-white definition, though here are some typical associations:

Radio:

- Interviews with guests
- Callers who ask questions, though many shows don't have callers
- "Radio-style" intros and outros
- Commercials
- Timely content on current events

Radio channel:

- "Always on," 24/7 streaming content

Podcast:

- A single speaker
- Content similar to a blog, e.g., an audio version of a blog
- How-to content in a specific area, such as fly fishing, home improvement, or cars

When you get right down to it, there really are no rules. I ran across a website, for example, that called itself a radio station, complete with a full schedule of radio shows. But then, in their rock-and-roll intro, the booming voiceover said, "Podcasting around the world from . . ." Conversely, terrestrial AM and FM radio stations are increasingly building their audiences and delivering their shows on the Internet. So, the difference between a podcast and a radio show is becoming less important.

An important advantage of an Internet radio show, despite the name, is that you can also include video content. Several years ago, I attended a how-to session at the NSA Convention on YouTube video recording. The speaker was Terry Brock, MBA, CSP, CPAE, who speaks on technology. He extolled the concept of interviewing interesting people and publishing the video interviews as episodes of your "radio show." I now take my "Terry Brock video interviewing kit" with me whenever I speak or attend conferences.

WHY HOST A RADIO SHOW?

So, why make hosting a radio show your activity focus, rather than activities such as video production or blogging?

1. **Extend your voice.** Hosting a radio show enables your voice to extend from the stage to the Internet cloud. We all know the value of staying in constant contact to build an audience and retain its attention. Whether you are an established, popular speaker with a large following or are just getting started, enabling your followers to tune in to your "voice" on a regular basis is a great way to feed their desire long after you've left the stage.

2. **Create currency.** A radio show provides currency for cooperative marketing. When I offered to start my radio show, my publicist was overjoyed. Previously, he'd been in the position of having to beg, "Could you please write about my client? I promise that his content would be much better for your audience than the hundred other authors who are knocking on your door." In contrast, with my radio show in hand, he could say, "Would you be interested in being a guest on my client's radio show to promote your work to his audience? And would you be interested in reciprocating by publishing a review of my client's book to your audience?" For example, speakers Jill Konrath; Mary Kelly, PhD; Avish Parashar; and others have published reviews of my book in their newsletters after I promoted them on my show. I have found this to be the most rewarding aspect of the radio show.

3. **Build your network.** Being a radio show host makes you a member of the press, which is invaluable for networking. When I go to trade shows and conferences and meet a speaker or expert I want to build a connection with, I say, "Hi, would you have 15 minutes to be a guest on my radio show?" Before attending one event, for example, I sent a LinkedIn invitation to a panelist, a chief marketing officer for a large insurance company, asking if he'd be interested in being a guest on my show. Then, while speaking on the panel at the event, he stated that he only accepts LinkedIn connection invitations from people in his personal network. So, I thought, "Well, I guess he didn't accept." When I met him at the reception afterward, he said, "Yes,

of course, I accepted your invitation. Send me an e-mail, and my assistant will schedule the interview." After four months of scheduling and rescheduling, we finally did the interview. Since then, we've worked together on articles and we regularly promote each other's blogs and other content.

4. **Leverage OPK (Other People's Knowledge).** Interviewing experts in your field not only has a halo effect of authority, but it really does help you maintain and grow your expertise. Every guest brings a different perspective and has done research that you have not. Each interview offers the opportunity to learn from world-class experts, literally from around the world. One of my recent guests was a management professor at the London School of Business, whom I found in a *CNN Money* article. Another was a marketing consultant in Sweden, whom I discovered while browsing Internet radio shows.

   Another important benefit of these experts is that you are leveraging their own efforts to provide valuable content—to fuel your own content marketing system. Recently, one of my followers tweeted me: "Hey, could you re-post the link to that great interview with the LinkedIn author? I'd like to share it." That's a win-win-win: Your audience wins, your guest wins, and you win.

5. **Best ROI.** Producing a radio show is less expensive and more convenient than producing video. Sure, all you need to post a video is a smartphone with a camera, but according to *FastCompany* magazine, there are more than 500 million YouTube channels. So, how do you stand out? Furthermore, as the cost of producing high-quality video content continues to decline, the need to be "outstanding" goes up. When your peers are producing CNN-quality video content, do you really want your brand to be associated with grainy video and barely audible audio? Entry-level professional video production equipment starts at around $10,000 and requires a dedicated room for the studio—not to mention either a steep learning curve or paying for expensive video editing and production services. In contrast, a state-of-the art, professional audio recording and production setup runs about $3,000, and you can get started without any equipment at all, other than a phone. Interviewing someone from London in your video studio is rarely possible. On the radio, they're just a phone call away.

3 WAYS TO GET YOUR RADIO SHOW UP AND RUNNING

Option 1: Done-for-You (DFY)

The easiest way to get started is to contract with a DFY radio production company, such as Contact Talk Radio. For a monthly fee, the company will:

- Create your intros, outros, and commercials
- Record and produce your show
- Broadcast your show on their online radio station
- Host your radio shows on their web servers
- Publish your shows to iTunes
- Coach you on how to host your show

All you need to get started with a DFY service is a telephone, so that you can call into the studio and host your show. This option is attractive if you don't have the time or inclination to take on these tasks yourself.

Option 2: On-the-Cheap (OTC)

If you are not sure you are ready to make a $300–$700 per month (depending on the number of shows) commitment, another way to get started is to buy a $50 USB microphone, interview your guests using Skype, and record the shows to your computer. You can then publish your shows on your website and to iTunes using a service such as Blubrry.com. The OTC option seems like a no-brainer. But be forewarned: I have spent countless hours and many panicked moments trying to get the PC-based system to work. During an interview with Mark Sanborn, CSP, CPAE, the radio station's computer crashed and we had to reschedule the interview. Another time, after an interview with Joachim de Posada, CSP, I discovered that the computer had garbled my voice, almost rendering the recording unsalvageable. After two years of computer travails and embarrassments, I have moved to the DIY option below.

Option 3: Do-It-Yourself (DIY)

A third option is to acquire professional audio recording equipment (see "Assembling Your DIY Kit" sidebar) to produce and publish the show yourself. This option is particularly attractive if you have other needs for recording audio and hosting a website. For example, I have produced one short audio book, and plan to record my entire printed book and release it as a full-length audio book. I also have a virtual dedicated server with a web hosting company for my four websites, including the radio show website. As a result, there is no additional cost for me to host the audio files for my show. Another attractive aspect of DIY is that I can record and publish shows whenever I have time in my schedule, rather than adhering to the published show schedule of a DFY radio station.

ASSEMBLING YOUR DIY KIT

I recently upgraded to this fully professional setup after hearing the great sound quality of Jon Buscall's show, "Online Marketing and Communications." This system builds on his recommendation and eliminates the use of a computer during recording. It also allows you to take live calls from listeners if you have a talk-show format. For more information, check out Buscall's new, how-to guidebook called "Launch a Podcast," available at http://jontusmedia.com/launch-podcast.

- Heil PR 40 microphone
- Soundcraft M4 mixer
- DBX 166XS gate/compressor/limiter
- DBX 131S graphic equalizer
- Zoom H4N audio recorder
- JK Audio Innkeeper PBX telephone-audio interface
- Cisco SPA303 IP phone
- RingCentral business IP telephone service
- Adobe Audition editing software
- Blubrry podcast publishing and tracking service
- Live 365 Internet radio broadcasting service

CHOOSING YOUR SHOW'S STYLE AND FORMAT

There is no right or wrong style and format for a show. There are a number of formats and they all work. However, there is only one right style for your show—your style. Larry Winget, CPAE, and Jeffrey Gitomer, CSP, CPAE, like to be edgy and pushy, so they can jolt the audience into action. Glenna Salsbury, CSP, CPAE, and Lou Heckler, CSP, CPAE, influence their audiences with well-crafted stories that might even draw tears. The style and format of your show should be consistent with your brand.

Here are some considerations.

- How much will the show be centered around you as a personality?
- Will you have guests? If so, who will they be, and how will you split the airtime between you and your guest?
- Will your show be recorded, or will you commit to a regular schedule and broadcast live?
- If you broadcast live, will you encourage listeners to call in to ask questions and chat?
- What will be the primary theme of the show? This should be 100 percent consistent with your speaker brand and target audience.
- How much of your own content will be in the show? There are many options here. The entire show could be dedicated to your own material, such as an audio version of your blog. Or, you could dedicate a small segment of your show to your own content. For example, I recently added a 3-minute segment at the beginning of each show during which I discuss one principle from my book.

RIDE THE (AIR)WAVES

Hosting a radio show can be a fun and rewarding way to create content for your marketing system. Whether you choose to focus on audio, video, or text, the most important thing to do is make a daily effort to create content and interact with your audience online. Measure your success with these two questions:

1. What have I created today?
2. Who connected and benefited from it?

When you produce a constant stream of multimedia content, your audience will remain connected long after you've left the stage. More importantly, the search engines will help you drive more business, as new clients discover your message and talents. So, get started, today . . . and use a radio show to put some rocket fuel in your marketing engine.

Brett Clay is the founder of Change Leadership Group. He brings more than 20 years of sales and marketing experience, most recently with Microsoft Corporation, to the stage. He is the creator of the award-winning Social Synergy System® for marketing and is the author of the book *Selling Change, 101+ Secrets for Growing Sales by Leading Change*, named the best sales book of 2010 and 2011 (USA Book News and Axiom Business Book Awards). Brett is also the host of *The Actuation Zone® Radio Show* (www.ActuationZone.com), where he and his guests share ways listeners can grow in their businesses and in their lives. He can be reached at (800) 351-LEAD (5323) or Brett@ChangeLeadershipGroup.com.

DIY VIDEO MARKETING

Jonathan Halls

Anyone can create marketing video for the web, right? Sure. Just whip out your Flip camera and start shooting. But how easy is it to create *great* video that doesn't turn people off—and instead compels potential clients to hire you or buy your products? That's a little trickier.

Online video has emerged as a key tool for marketing. Studies show that e-commerce sites using video to showcase their products and services make more sales. So, it stands to reason that speaker sites should make video a key part of their conversion strategy.

Search engine optimization specialists point to the power of video, because it boosts your chance of scoring a page-one ranking in Google. Just think about YouTube, which has morphed into one of the world's most powerful search engines. Speakers who don't have a video marketing strategy are neglecting all sorts of opportunities.

BUT IS IT AS EASY AS IT SOUNDS?

According to the most recent statistics, 48 hours worth of video is uploaded to YouTube every minute. Think about that: You would need almost eight years to watch every video that was uploaded yesterday. Want to watch every video uploaded last week? It would take your entire career.

So, while video is crucial for speakers, how do you know people will choose to watch your videos when there are so many other people competing for eyeballs? More video is *not watched* than watched. The answer is, people love to watch *good* video. And most of what they see is boring.

If you plan to create a video marketing strategy, you need to create compelling video that people want to see and share. As well as conforming to your SEO (search engine optimization) strategy and carrying your marketing message, it must be produced well and do what video does best. That is, tell a visual story.

You Can Do It

The fact is, you can accomplish that in natural lighting conditions using consumer cameras such as the $400 Vixia. No need for expensive cameras or lighting rigs. Following these techniques will enable you to quickly and inexpensively populate your website with engaging video that looks as professional as possible.

But first, let's look at the three most common mistakes made by amateur videographers—and the techniques used by professionals to make videos that stand out from the unwatched, unwatchable crowd.

Three Big Video Bloopers

The three biggest mistakes people make with video is they don't:

- Create content driven by pictures
- Shoot enough pictures
- Record good-quality sound

Rule 1: People Watch First

Video is image-driven. People watch before they listen. They remember the pictures, and often forget what was said. Think back to the last time you watched the weather forecast on TV. Do you remember what the forecaster said? Or do you remember what you saw? Like the satellite maps with ominous storm clouds looming over your city.

Smart videographers don't think in terms of the script they are going to write. They think in terms of what pictures they will shoot, and how those pictures will tell their story. If you speak on the subject of peak performance, you need to find pictures that show peak performance in action. For example, don't stand in front of a camera and talk about how athletes improve their performance. Show a picture of a runner in training.

The secret to making pictures the driving force of your video is to draw a storyboard before you shoot anything. A storyboard sets out each part of your story, picture by picture. A storyboard consists of quick, rough sketches, like the one shown below that accompanies the "Peak Performance" script.

Wide shot of hand with stop watch

Wide Shot Athlete at start line

Wide shot, athlete running

Close-up of stop watch at 15 seconds

Close-up - expression of grim determination

Wide shot - after race doing stretch

Peak Performance Script
By Fred Smith
Location: Athletics Field, Johnsonville
Actor: Hillary Jones
Camera: Fred Smith

1. Mid-shot of stopwatch in coach's hand. Running track in background.
   Narrator: Improving your game is critical in today's workplace.
2. Wide-shot of athlete at starting line. Takes off.
   Sound Effects: Starting Gun

3. Wide-shot of athlete as she runs along track.
   Narrator: Some people make it look easy . . .

4. Close-up of stopwatch as second hand turns to the 15-second mark.Narrator: . . . as they work against all odds.

5. Close-up of athlete. Expression of grim determination on face.
   Narrator: But the reality is, it's hard work.

Rule 2: Change It Up

Because video is image-driven, viewers are constantly looking for more pictures. And if we don't change the frame regularly, our viewers will lose interest and look away. This is why lecture videos never work well. You've usually lost your viewer within 30 seconds if you just talk directly to the camera and haven't changed the shot. It turns people off.

Pro videographers do not create video with only one shot, and they rarely shoot video that features one person talking to the camera for more than 15 seconds. They change the shot size, angle, and position regularly to keep their viewer's interest. And they find extra shots to illustrate their point.

To go back to the example of a video about peak performance, you wouldn't just show a picture of an athlete running on a track. Show some close-ups of her face as she is running, highlighting the grim determination that is needed to achieve peak performance. Take your viewer into her world with some shots of her at the start line, someone holding a stopwatch, or performing some stretches at the end of the race.

Rule 3: Avoid "Can You Hear Me Now?" Syndrome

Pictures must lead the narrative, but that doesn't mean you can get away with subpar audio. In fact, viewers notice lousy audio more than lousy pictures.

The key to good sounding audio is to use an external microphone. The microphones built into consumer-grade cameras are rarely any good. They usually pick up noise you don't want on your recording—hands brushing against the camera, loud air conditioning, and background noise. Often the speaker sounds distant, with annoying echoes.

To get the best sound, buy a clip-on microphone for interviews and a shotgun microphone for multi-person formats or testimonials. If your camera does not have a plug for an internal microphone (and many consumer cameras don't), you have to work with what you have. In that case, position your camera as close as possible to the person speaking.

CRAFTING YOUR VIDEO

You'll probably hear that making effective marketing videos means hiring a professional. In my experience, 80 percent of the people who will tell you this just happen to run their own production company. Now, I won't begrudge them their business pitch, because good professionals are the right call for complex, high-profile projects such as your speaker demo. But there's nothing stopping you from developing the basic skills to shoot good-looking video for testimonials, short messages, or content embedded in your weekly e-zine.

I work in the "people enabling profession," and have spent the last twenty years teaching media to people in radio stations, television stations, newspapers, and the corporate world. I have seen that good techniques can be learned. And I've seen great results in workshops from people who had never touched a camera. So don't get put off by the naysayers. You can learn to make great-looking video with consumer cameras.

Ah, but now you're scratching your head, thinking I have contradicted myself. I just suggested you can make your own video, but if it's a speaker demo, hire a pro. The reason for this is that consumer cameras aren't good enough to get speakers in action. You need professional equipment to capture wide-shots and close-ups of you on the platform from a distance. Add to that the difficulties of lighting and audio in an auditorium, and you can understand why it's best to leave this type of content to the pros who specialize in such environments.

So to create great video, what do you need to learn? First, some editorial skills. Second, some basic production skills.

EDITORIAL 101

Before you press "record," it's essential to clarify your objective and identify your audience. You will never know if your video is successful if you don't have a clear vision of what you're trying to achieve. And you won't know how effective it is if you don't consider what the best approach might be for your audience.

Aim for a single objective. Perhaps that objective is to get people to hire you. Maybe it's to convince them to sign up for your e-zine. It might be getting clients to change their thinking about the science of peak performance. Whatever you do, don't try to achieve more than one objective per video, because your message will become watered down. You want strength in your message.

Once you are clear about your objective, brainstorm how your video will achieve it. How long should it be? What does your audience want? What pictures will achieve your purpose?

Plan your pictures first. Using our previous example to get the message across that achieving peak performance is hard work, we could show a wide shot of the athlete running on the track, and then do a close-up of her face where we would see an expression of grim determination. The first shot tells us that we are talking about peak performance. The second shot tells us that peak performance takes a lot of work.

What pictures do you need to tell your story, and in what order will you need these shots to convey your message in the most powerful way? The best way to think it through is to draw a storyboard. It doesn't need to be a piece of art—it can be stick figures. But you'll find the very act of drawing one will save you time and focus your mind.

Write your script. After you have worked out what pictures you want, you need to write a script. Good scripts reinforce the pictures rather than repeat them. So, if the picture shows the athlete running, don't write a voiceover that says, "This woman is an athlete who is striving for peak performance." Instead write something like, "We all strive for peak performance." Then for the close-up of the woman's face you might write, "But it's not easy."

The key to good scripts is to choose simple words that are easy to pronounce. Avoid long sentences, and write in a conversational tone. Professional media practitioners look at every part of their message, from phrases and words to pictures and sound effects. They ask how they can make it simple. The simpler it is, the quicker and easier it is for the viewer to understand. Consider following the standard, two-column format used in documentary scripts. In the left column you describe what the viewer will see, and in the right column you include audio such as spoken word content, music, and any sound effects. (Visualize script and storyboard on p.171–2 in two columns to see the close relationship.) The narration does not repeat what is obvious in the picture—rather, it enhances the message.

Repetition. When you draw your storyboard and write your script, repeat your key point with both pictures and commentary. Repetition is one of the keys to marketing, which is why radio and television ads always repeat telephone numbers and other key points several times.

With the storyboard drawn and script written, it's time to shoot—yeah!

PRODUCTION

The first trick to looking professional is to shoot your video using a tripod. Even if you're on a Flip cam, buy a small tabletop tripod or a fully extendable tripod. A shaky cam undermines your credibility and turns your video into amateur hour. I've lost track of how many students and trainees have handed in well-conceptualized videos that were spoiled because they were shot without a tripod.

When you set up your shot, look at your background and make sure it supports your message. If you are doing a short video about the importance of working out to develop good mental stamina, don't shoot yourself standing with a blank wall as your backdrop. A better choice would be in a gym with some equipment behind you or people working out. Your background is as important a part of your message as your close-ups on the athlete with her look of grim determination. Likewise, make sure there is nothing in your shot that undermines or distracts from your message.

Reinforce the message. Consider other factors that can help tell your story. For example, if the person in your video is a scientist, you will probably shoot him in a laboratory. But also ask him to wear a lab coat. Yes, this is cheesy and plays to stereotypes, but that's what media are about—whether you like it or not. And it beats having to use a clunky voiceover along the lines of "This man is a scientist."

Bright ideas. One of the technical limitations of consumer cameras is that they don't work well in low-light conditions. But it's not enough just to have lots of light. Make sure the main source of light, which is referred to as the key light by professionals, is aimed on your subject or object. If you want it to look classy, aim the light at a slight angle rather than directly on your subject.

Never shoot a subject inside a building standing in front of a window, unless you're striving for a silhouette. If you're shooting outside, position your subject so that the sun is shining on her from the front, or again, you'll also end up with a silhouette. By the way, the best time to shoot outdoors is in the morning and afternoon. That's because the sun is at such an angle that the light is softer. If you shoot at high noon, your subject's skin will look dry and harsh.

Blair Witch Projects Anonymous. Finally, some tips to prevent your video from looking unprofessional—or like a horror flick. Avoid camera movements. Constantly zooming in and out of a shot, panning the camera, and tilting it makes viewers seasick, and your video will look like a home movie shot by Uncle Abe. Camera movements look even worse when streamed on the web, since they'll appear jerky and heavily pixilated. Use camera movements sparingly, and only when they have a narrative purpose. Fancy transitions and special effects are a constant temptation, but the reality is that they draw attention away from your message.

EQUIPMENT 101

If you haven't already purchased a camera, you may be wondering what will work best. One of the first criteria is the capacity to take an external microphone, which will give you great sound if you use a shotgun or clip-on microphone. Buy a camera that has as many manual functions as possible. That way, you can focus your shot, set the exposure, and manage the audio yourself. Auto functions are never as good and can look flaky.

Software considerations. Once you have shot your video, you will need to edit it together, which means using video-editing software. The professionals use software such as Final Cut, Premier, Avid, and Sony Vegas, but Windows Live Movie Maker and Apple iMovie are the usual DIY solutions. The benefit of these two packages is you can easily learn to use them in under an hour, whereas the fancier programs will take days or weeks if you've never encountered them before. At the end of the day, your choice of software is less important than your decisions about how to cut the pictures together.

Teleprompters, DIY style. If you want to look natural when speaking on camera and don't want to memorize your script, you can buy a professional teleprompter from $900 to $10,000. But if you have a smartphone or tablet, download a teleprompter app from Apple's App Store or the Droid Marketplace. There are many inexpensive brackets, priced from $50 to $500, that will hold smartphones and tablets on your camera to give you a cheap teleprompter.

DIY MARKETING VIDEO

If you need video fast and want to do it on your own, today's user-friendly electronics make it possible. Craft your message so it's focused for your audience, with one clear marketing objective. Adopt the habits of professionals by planning your pictures first. And avoid the novice traps—minimize camera movements, avoid fancy transitions, and shoot on a tripod.

Research tells us that the average web surfer in America views more than 150 videos every month. More than three quarters of surfers have watched online video ads, and a significant number actually forwarded them on. This has business implications, because we know that a high proportion of people who watch videos go on to buy a product or service. Make sure you make video that people want to watch ... and you'll put your speaking business and talents into sharp, professional focus.

Video Brainstorm Template

Message

- What's the purpose of your video?
- Who is going to watch your video?
- What is the core message you want them to remember?

Video

- What are the best pictures to convey your message to your viewer?
- How long is your viewer likely to spend watching your video?
- What can you do to repeat your core message?

Jonathan Halls speaks and runs workshops on multimedia communication and leadership communication. He formerly ran the BBC's prestigious, multimillion-dollar television, radio ops, and new-media training department in London. Jonathan is the author of *Rapid Video for Trainers* (ASTD Press 2012). He is principal of Jonathan Halls & Associates and an adjunct professor at George Washington University. Based in Washington, DC, Jonathan has spoken in more than 20 countries and taught people from more than 30 nationalities. His website is www.JonathanHalls.com and he can be reached at jgh@JonathanHalls.com.

ADD A NEW DIMENSION TO YOUR MOBILE MARKETING WITH 2D CODES

Jeff Korhan, MBA

Mobile technologies are among the top influences on consumer behaviors today. They're being embraced for a variety of reasons, with convenience and social interaction being two of the key drivers.

What is convenient is typically used more frequently, and when it is also mobile, it can be used in a variety of contexts, including conferences and events. Speakers who want to be more relevant to meeting planners and the audiences they serve should consider using mobile to meet them where they are, when they are most receptive, and in a manner that is congruent with the increasingly social business environment.

More than a trend, mobile is a transformative shift that is well under way. Already, more than 50 percent of all local web searches are accomplished with mobile devices. In the most recent quarter, Apple Computer sold three times as many iPads as all Macs combined, with iPhone sales more than doubling from the previous quarter. Facebook, too, is going all-in on mobile. Their chief technology officer recently stated that within the next three years, nearly every Facebook employee will be working on some aspect of mobile.

Mobile is a revolution that promises to integrate the digital world with what we experience every day—effectively blurring the lines between virtual and real experiences, communities, and events. Among the triggers responsible for making this integration faster and more seamless are two-dimensional (2D) codes, such as the QR (Quick Response) code shown below that links to the speaking page of my website. These digital barcodes instantly connect the real and digital worlds via mobile devices, creating multiple opportunities for social sharing, communicating, and, of course, marketing.

2D CODE APPLICATIONS AND USES FOR SPEAKERS

QR codes are the most familiar of the current 2D technologies. Although they are similar to the barcodes used by retailers to track inventory at the point of sale, the key difference is that linear one-dimensional barcodes hold only about 20 numerical digits of data—whereas QR and other 2D codes can hold approximately 7,000 alphanumeric characters of information! This capability, and the fact that the QR code technology is both free and open source, creates practically unlimited opportunities for their use as digital marketing triggers.

All 2D codes are easily generated for free using online code generators, such as the Microsoft Tag Manager, or native apps on mobile devices, such as Qrafter and i-Nigma. The data within these codes are then captured with a code reader, sometimes referred to as a scanner, which works on any camera-enabled mobile device. These readers are mostly free, with special features incurring incidental charges. Choosing whether to use QR codes or MS tags is a personal choice, but the key is to use them to accomplish specific business objectives—not just as technology for technology's sake. 2D codes are simply triggers for digitally linking to the mobile devices of your audience. The versatility of 2D codes lets speakers engage directly with potential buyers, meeting planners, and audiences in ways that showcase their presentation skills.

2D Code Applications

Using 2D codes to trigger mobile responses will require careful planning, considering the objectives of your business, and the needs of your ideal customers.

Social sharing. Speakers can enhance their opportunities for getting hired by sharing their ideas and expertise online, and encouraging further sharing with friends of friends. 2D codes can be used to share links to online content, such as videos, documents, and e-books. The 2D code itself can also be shared as a distinct digital object that can deliver different types of content, depending upon where it is scanned, and how many times by the same device.

Community. Sharing is how you build community online, and arguably the most popular arena for doing this is Facebook. Speakers can use Likify.net to create a QR code that links the mobile device of their user to a fully functioning LIKE button for their Facebook page. This is valuable for instantly engaging event attendees with your Facebook community. The code displays the signature "thumbs-up" icon that clearly suggests the purpose of the code. PingTags.com is a similar QR code-generating service that makes connecting on LinkedIn as easy as scanning a QR code.

Calls to action. As profit-minded small businesses, the time comes when speakers want to mobilize their online communities to take action. What are you trying to accomplish? As one example, you can alternate special offers by linking your 2D codes to unique landing pages, while also encouraging concurrent actions, such as opting into your e-mail list.

Search optimization. In addition to your relationships with people, search engines are examining your relationship with shared online content—known as social objects. If you want to enhance your web marketing presence, you need to create and share social objects: images, music clips, and videos that add valuable content to your social graph. Your social graphs are digital maps that search engines use to make you and your business more findable by your ideal buyers. The more content you create and share, the more enhanced your social graphs. 2D codes enhance your search optimization by encouraging more sharing of your unique message—one that better aligns you with your ideal clients.

Social proof. To help build your offline community, and otherwise create opportunities for more bookings, it is helpful to use your vibrant online communities as social proof of your influence and expertise. As one example, you can use 2D codes to link to specific blog posts that have earned an abundance of activity—the social proof of comments, social shares, and inbound links.

Tracking. If you use 2D codes to link to website addresses, you may want to consider using one of the link-shortening services such as bit.ly and goo.gl to generate a clean QR code. Shorter addresses (technically known as URLs) create higher-quality codes with a much lower failure rate. The additional benefit is that they will track how many times the code is scanned by date and location. This is especially useful for assessing which types of audiences are more receptive to scanning your codes.

Practical Uses of 2D Codes

Here are some ways speakers, consultants, and trainers are using 2D codes now, as well as some suggested uses that you may wish to consider.

Where 2D codes can be used:

- The back (or front and back) of your business card
- Program handouts—both digital and hard copies
- Brochures and other marketing materials
- Speaking proposals
- On presentation slides in front of a live audience
- Within printed or digital books, or on the outside cover
- Event nametags, kiosks, and booths

What 2D codes can link to:

- The process for hiring your professional services
- Your demo video, bio, or introduction
- Access to download your presentation slides
- Download your mobile app
- Connect with your LinkedIn profile
- Like your Facebook page
- Updates to your book
- Special offers and up-sell opportunities
- Free MP3 or e-book downloads
- Digital surveys and customer feedback

5 MOBILE MARKETING BEST PRACTICES WITH 2D CODES

To enhance the results of your mobile marketing with 2D codes, you will want to become familiar with these essential best practices.

1. Plan Your Mobile Strategy

Success with mobile marketing starts with understanding your audience, then implementing an appropriate strategy to engage them, ultimately delivering a favorable user experience. There are a number of factors to consider, beginning with understanding the needs of your business, and those of your audience, buyers, and influencers.

Understand Your Target Audience

- Do they need instructions regarding the use of 2D codes?
- Should they be using a specific type of reader?
- Do you want them to activate geo-location to enable tracking?
- Will the codes be scanned indoors or outside, and from what distance?

Have Clear Objectives

- Are you trying to grow your e-mail list?
- Should you consider split-testing, i.e., using different codes to measure response rates to any number of variable conditions?
- Will your codes offer choices to accommodate user preferences?

Provide Useful and Valuable Incentives

- Download a free e-book
- Get VIP access to gated content
- Provide discounts on products and services

Planning your mobile marketing strategy should consider every relevant variable, from before, during, and after you engage with your audience. While all of this may appear fairly simple, when technology and human behavior are involved, it is always best to be certain. Even major brands have made embarrassing mistakes with 2D code marketing campaigns because they overlooked minor details.

NSA speaker Mellanie True Hills developed a unique strategy for using QR to brand her expertise in atrial fibrillation. Melanie distributes stacks of non-promotional cards to physicians that contain a QR code linking to a mobile website with videos and other educational content on atrial fibrillation. The cards serve as a valuable resource for their patients, while also keeping her top of mind as a speaker for conferences and community events.

2. Create Quality Codes

The widespread use of QR technology has attracted lots of developers who want to cash in on the trend. However, with open technologies such as QR, there is always the risk that generally accepted standards will not be followed. QR code generators and readers are only as good as the developers creating them, so you have to do your due diligence.

MS tag technology is proprietary, allowing for complete control over the entire user experience of generating, reading, and tracking the tags. In contrast to QR codes, MS tags are easily customized and branded with images and logos using Microsoft PowerPoint. (Check out a quick demo video at http://bit.ly/ yiYWZM.) QR codes can also be customized, but that is best left to experienced digital designers to ensure the integrity of your codes. One thing to consider is that while customization may help branding, the common black-and-white QR code is most familiar to the general public, making it more likely to be scanned by a larger audience.

What happens if your QR codes do not function properly? For one thing, your reputation and brand are tarnished—just as they would be if a visitor to your website discovers broken links. The message is clear: Test your codes.

The following practices will maximize your effectiveness with 2D code technology:

- Use link shorteners such as bit.ly to create clean codes. Longer URLs require more complex codes that incur a higher failure rate.

- Avoid using colors that do not provide sufficient contrast—a potential problem with both QR codes and customized MS tags.

- Make your codes at least 1″ x 1″ for standard print materials. Increase the size of your codes 1″ for every foot of distance from which they will be scanned. For example, a 10″ diameter size is the minimum recommended for reading from a distance of 10 feet.

- Provide a sufficient quiet zone around the code. This is the necessary white buffer around your code that enables it to function properly. (For additional tips, view the video here: http://bit.ly/zfbqRu.)

- Avoid using 2D codes on highly reflective surfaces.

- Test your codes with multiple readers and devices.

- Consider where your codes will be scanned. Codes can be scanned when there is no Internet signal and then bookmarked for later access to the web.

- Use a quality QR code generator. Kerem Erkan, i-Nigma, and MS Tag Manager all have solid reputations.

- Use a quality scanner or reader. Qrafter, i-Nigma, and Tag Reader all work well with iPhone. i-Nigma also works with BlackBerry. Tag Reader and QR Droid work well with Android phones. i-Nigma and Qrafter are unique, as apps that are both QR code generators and readers.

3. Link to Mobile-Optimized or -Friendly Sites

The most common mistake marketers make with 2D codes is having them resolve to a standard web page that is not optimized for mobile. Worse yet is to have a code connect to a site with Flash video, which is not currently supported by iOS devices (iPhones and iPads). As a minimum, the web page your code connects to should be mobile friendly. For example, one of my codes resolves to the speaking page on my WordPress site. A couple of taps on a mobile device enlarges it to fit nicely to the screen.

Mobile optimized is better than mobile friendly. Mobile sites are websites optimized specifically for smartphones by developers. It is suggested you host your mobile site on a subdomain or subdirectory of your main website, thereby taking advantage of the traffic they bring to enhance the search engine optimization of your primary site.

Here are additional considerations for building a mobile site:

- Build your site around the desired user experience.

- Smaller images and solid colors load more quickly.

- Size your links and buttons to be touch friendly.

- Use concise copy—sentences rather than paragraphs.

- Use "fluid width" for horizontal and vertical orientation.

- Test, test, and test again—on iPhone, Android, and BlackBerry platforms.

The primary benefit of 2D codes for speakers is encouraging action, and this will vary according to your business and business model. Some speakers will prefer to receive a phone call, some may wish to filter leads by having a web form completed, and still others will want to direct prospects to their best multimedia content, such as live video that shows them in action.

Regardless of the features you choose for your mobile site, you may find this list of the most requested features for mobile-optimized sites helpful.

- Tap to call links
- Tap to e-mail links
- Tap to SMS (text)
- Social sharing links
- Links to YouTube and Vimeo (both are mobile optimized)

The cost of building a mobile-optimized site is comparable to a professionally designed and built WordPress site. If you are not ready to make that investment, there are several services that allow you to create mobile sites hosted on their platforms. However, the risk is they have full control of your intellectual property.

4. Track and Measure with Code Management Systems

QR codes and MS tags can presently track basic actions, such as the number of scans. Codes generated with services such as bit.ly offer these capabilities. However, if you use a robust QR code management system, you can gather even richer data, such as scans by location and time.

Using the Microsoft Tag Manager, you can create MS tags and QR codes that will track a number of mobile actions. For example, you can track the location of your user by ZIP code, or by longitude and latitude, as long as the user device has geo-location activated. Additionally, the user must be using the MS Tag Reader when scanning the code. You can easily accomplish all of these capabilities on your own. However, if you are willing to enlist the help of a developer, you can also track more specific real-time actions, such as scans by the type of mobile device.

To be clear, gathering data on the actions of buyers and influencers with 2D codes requires generating that code with a service that offers code management capabilities. Thus, you have to entrust your codes to someone, and this is one reason why an established company like Microsoft has a shot at building a platform that becomes a destination for mobile marketers.

5. Deliver a Favorable User Experience

Will QR codes and MS tags gain more widespread use? When it comes to technology, there will always be naysayers. What is most important is that you, as the marketer, are the one who gives your codes value when you use them to create favorable experiences.

Each and every one of us is the center of our own universe—wherever we happen to be. The opportunity for marketers is earning permission to have access to that moving target: what is central, relevant, and essential to the lives of their buyers and influencers. Mobile marketing makes that possible.

2D codes are an opportunity for speakers to start learning the nuances of mobile marketing, though whether these codes will find widespread use remains to be seen. Yet, regardless of whether your speaking business uses 2D codes now, or waits for the more advanced technology triggers that are on the horizon, it will more than likely be using some form of mobile marketing. One thing is certain: The intersection of social networking, location-based marketing, and mobile technologies will prove to be a marketing sweet spot.

Jeff Korhan, MBA, is an authentic, informative, and inspiring speaker who helps mainstream small businesses use social media and Internet marketing to increase their influence, enhance customer relationships, and accelerate growth. He is an author, syndicated publisher, and regular content contributor to leading business publications and websites. Jeff's popular *Digital Media and Small Business Marketing* site has ranked among the Top 100 Small Business blogs in the world by Technorati Media. In addition to his business experience and authentic style, Jeff's audiences especially value his special skill for simplifying technology and complex business ideas to make them practical and useful. His website is JeffKorhan.com and he can be reached via e-mail at speaker@JeffKorhan.com.

BUSINESS
OPERATIONS

FASCINATE THE AUDIENCE
BEFORE THE AUDIENCE

Sally Hogshead

Want to increase your speaking fee?

The traditional route is very slow, probably uncertain, and all-but-certainly labor intensive. Here's how it goes: Gradually build your platform. Spend a few years developing your content and reputation. Cross your fingers that people notice. Schmooze your butt off. Release a *New York Times* best seller. Repeat.

You can go through these steps to raise your fee.

Or, you can take the shortcut.

In 2011, I doubled my speaking fee in six months. More important, I earned the chance to speak at better events, for larger groups, and for bigger opportunities. And you can do this, too. Here's how.

Fascinate the audience *before* the audience.

You already know that you need to grip the attention of the audience sitting in front of you during a speech. This audience, however, is not the only audience that you need to captivate. And, I'd like to suggest, they're not even the most critical one.

First, you must fascinate a different group: the audience *before* the audience.

As speakers, we're so busy trying to communicate to the crowd sitting in conferences and meetings that we fail to communicate effectively with the people who play a role in the speaker selection process.

If you want to be more sought-after, commanding a higher fee and greater respect and more prestigious schedule, here are the audiences before the audience:

- Prospective clients
- Event planners
- Speaking bureaus
- Committees
- Convention organizers
- Anyone else in charge of finding and select speakers

These are the influencers and decision-makers. If you fail to fascinate them, it's unlikely your career can reach its potential. You're not going to get booked at the best events, with the best fees, and the best opportunities.

Giving a great speech is easy . . . compared to getting booked for a great event.

Before you can share your work with hundreds or thousands or millions of people, you need to get in front of those people in the first place.

It doesn't matter how good you are if nobody knows about you. It's not enough to finesse your presentation skills if nobody sees you present. It doesn't matter how hard you work if that hard work doesn't lead to leads.

You could be the world's most talented speaker, able to mesmerize participants and change their lives, but that talent is wasted if you're not getting booked. This isn't about only losing revenue . . . it's losing the opportunity to spread our message.

GIVING THE SPEECH VS. *GETTING* THE SPEECH

Most speakers focus on giving the speech: the content and delivery, with a special focus on that critical first impression when they're introduced and walk onstage. Yet few speakers work to create as strong an impression when introducing themselves to potential clients.

Think of your marketing materials as your representative, selling you out in the world, championing you like an agent. You have complete control over these materials and the impression they create, and it's your job to make sure they embody the best of what you offer.

Until a year ago, I didn't fully understand this. I assumed (incorrectly) that clients would recognize the value in my delivery and content. It's not that I was passive: I worked with one of the top speaking coaches in the country, published a book with HarperCollins, and worked hard on my skills. I just couldn't seem to push to the next level, and I started getting discouraged. The truth was, I was putting so much effort into my content and delivery that I didn't make the time to create a speaking video.

Until this point, I'd only concentrated on *giving* the speech instead of *getting* the speech.

We might get an hour during a speech to share our message. Yet with decision-makers, it might be just a few seconds. How will you create materials that can break through immediately?

THE (GULP!) 9-SECOND ATTENTION SPAN

According to the BBC, the average attention span might only be nine seconds long. Nine seconds. (Scary, right?) Every time you walk onstage, your audience might be distracted before you've even opened your mouth to begin. This has huge implications.

First, the bad news: Not only does the nine-second attention span makes it more difficult to keep an audience focused throughout a speech, but it also makes it far tougher to keep potential clients focused long enough to view your materials.

Now, the good news: You can use the nine-second attention span to your competitive advantage. That's because, used wisely, fascination—*an intense emotional focus*—can become your shortcut to persuasion.

My company researches exactly what makes one person more persuasive and influential than another. After testing 100,000 people and publishing studies around the globe, I've discovered specific patterns. When you fascinate a prospect, they stop thinking about e-mail and meetings and start completely focusing on you.

Fascinate them, and they're hooked.

In fact, when you fascinate someone, they're more likely to *trust* you, *respect* you, *buy from* you, and *like* you.

Of course, if your content isn't great and your skills aren't up to par, those nine seconds won't help you or the client. But let's say you're good. Even great. How can you leverage those first nine seconds?

7 TIPS FOR THE FIRST 9 SECONDS

When doing any sort of marketing for yourself, such as a video, one-sheet, or social media, you have a challenge: You must convince a prospective client that

YOU are more compelling than all the other options. And you must do it before they become distracted by the next speaker.

If you're not the most <u>famous</u> speaker, or the most <u>respected</u> speaker, you must find one way in which you are the most <u>fascinating</u>.

This actually isn't as hard as it sounds. For starters, here's a secret: Many people are great at speaking, but not so great at creating speaking materials. Most use the same words as everyone else, without actually saying much of anything.

Here's where you can create your competitive edge. If you can be just a *little* more fascinating—drawing upon your natural personality advantages—you can get to the next steps, in which you can start a long-term relationship. The following seven tips can help:

1. Understand Every Step in the Decision-Making Process.

How, exactly, is one speaker chosen over another? What's the hidden engine driving demand? Which is more important: word of mouth around a speaker, or a great agent selling that speaker? Are speaking fees a result of tangible measurements, such as experience or awards or public relations? For example, just how much does a *New York Times* best seller boost a speaker's fee?

As speakers, we are the "product" being sold in the marketplace. We should understand how the marketplace places value on us. It's a murky, underground world of long-standing relationships and complex protocols. I've researched events from TEDTalks (Technology, Entertainment, Design) to the Million-Dollar Round Table, reviewed websites (both good and bad), and compared fees listed on bureau websites (from overpriced to underpaid).

It comes down to just a few factors:

Who is the key decision maker? Is it the bureau, the event planner, a committee, a CEO, or some other audience?

How is the decision usually made to book a certain speaker? Does the client reach a decision by polling attendees? Or is just one person in charge? Or does it have to do with the name recognition of the speaker?

What factors shape their decision? Are they seeking an established reputation (in which case they'll probably go for a safe choice)? Or are they looking for a fresh interpretation (in which case reputation is less important than content)?

And then, there's the most important question of all:

Exactly what can you—the speaker—do to influence the decision?

Your opportunities might be different from someone else's, depending on your unique combination of strengths. Which points in the process can you capitalize upon?

If you want to create fresh energy around your brand, those first 9 seconds are your best friend.

2. Understand Your Disadvantages, But Harness Your Advantages.

Overcoming your weaknesses begins with understanding them. I stood back and took a long, hard evaluation of my obstacles:

- I didn't have relationships with bureaus or event planners.
- I wasn't an international best-selling author.
- I wasn't a household name with audiences.

Here's what I did have. I knew how to create an instantly fascinating "wow" experience. For instance, I developed a different kind of speaking package: "The Fascination Emporium." It's just about guaranteed to produce that "wow" from the client or agent receiving it.

How can you introduce yourself to give the client your *signature experience*?

3. Invest As Much in Your Speaking Video As the Fee You Are Trying to Reach.

I cannot overemphasize the importance of your speaking demo video. For clients who have not seen you live (which is probably 99.3 percent of them), it's their main yardstick for evaluating your value.

If you want to earn a $5,000 fee, plan to spend at least $5,000 on the video. If you want to reach a $40,000 fee, be ready to invest that much in your materials.

Your video doesn't have to be that expensive, of course. Yet the reality is, as speakers, we're selling an impression. If we can't make an outstanding first impression with our video, we're unlikely to convince others that we can do so with an audience.

Our price tag is not just defined by the speech we can give—it's also a result of reputation, network, endorsements, training, online presence, and other factors.

As you budget your costs, pick your priorities. Personally, I prioritize these three:

- Skillfully captured pieces of content
- Stage presence that lives up to the live presentation
- Connection with the audience

Does your video instantly convey to the viewer exactly the same message and emotion that you are trying to convey to your audience? Mine didn't. So I changed it. Within six months of posting this new video to my site, it had more than 10,000 views, and I'd signed $300,000 in new contracts.

4. Don't Make Your Speaking Materials Look Like . . . Speaking Materials.

Many speaker materials incorporate the same old format, standardized graphics, and cliché stock music. But consider this: The person viewing your materials—whether an agent, an event planner, or a CEO—has been charged with finding the perfect speaker. That person is making a recommendation. At some level, that means putting his or her own reputation on the line, along with yours.

While you're at it, don't overlook one key detail: The person evaluating you wants to see participants responding to your messages and connecting with you as you speak. This costs more to shoot, because you'll need at least two cameras (one to capture you, one to get the audience) and a good editor to put it all together.

Simple and understated is fine. Cheesy is not. If you don't have the experience to know the difference, look around and hire someone who does. Your video should capture the experience of watching you present live. This is 100 percent within your control.

We cannot control all the things that determine our perceived value. But we can control most of them, which brings us to . . .

5. Identify Your Winning Advantage.

Advantages become ways in which you add value. How can you add value to your program, beyond just the speech? I created a personality assessment that reveals exactly what others find most fascinating about you. It's similar to Myers-Briggs or StrengthsFinder®, but with a crucial difference: Those two tests show how you see the world. This is about *how the world sees you*. That research is a critical difference in selling my program, because I observed that higher-end clients want researched credibility.

Some of the patterns I observed when researching the market included:
Less-established speakers can stand out if they're willing to:

- Over-deliver in specific areas (such as proprietary research or brilliantly in-depth handouts)
- Become the most well-known speaker in one very specific niche (such as a very specific aspect of health care content, or type of event, or an audience)
- Wildly exceed expectations on a particular point in the process (such as the prep time before a speech, or level of service for the event planner)

Highly paid and sought-after speakers often have Achilles' heels:

- They are usually less likely to take risks or experiment
- They are often less "hungry" in exploring untraditional fee structures
- They can get into ruts with content and be less willing to customize and go that extra mile

Okay, so *you* have disadvantages. *They* have disadvantages. How can your advantages beat their disadvantages, so you can spread your message?

6. Outsmart the Market.

When you position yourself, don't just think in terms of generic categories or clients. If you speak to leaders, for instance, you might automatically assume your topic should be leadership. But not so fast. Is the market not glutted with speakers on that topic? Is there more opportunity in a niche?

Ask yourself: What topics are increasingly in demand at a high fee, but are *not* overwhelmed with speakers?

A few anecdotal observations on categories in which I speak: "Creativity" and "Innovation" are very similar topics, but "Innovation" has much higher perceived value. "Branding" is smaller than "Marketing," but less competitive and more prestigious. "Personal Branding" is having a resurgence for leaders. The "Sales" category is overwhelmed by people willing to speak for low fees, which drives down the overall price point of the inventory. Speakers on "Social Media" make up to 30 percent more than equivalent speakers, because the topic is so in demand, with few experts.

Look at your own content, and the market. Which topics pay more, yet have less competition? Identify a topic with greater demand, higher price point, and lower competition.

7. Remember: It Doesn't Matter If You're the Best Speaker, If Nobody Knows or Cares Who You Are.

There will always be other speakers who are more established, more famous, or more connected. But those speakers can't be you. They can't capture your personality, your energy, your ideas, and your gloriously unique way of expressing yourself.

Nothing will make you more valuable as a speaker than becoming more of who you already are. And nothing is more important when it comes to fascinating the audience *before* the audience.

Sally Hogshead teaches how to instantly persuade and captivate in a world with a 9-second attention span. She is the author of *FASCINATE,* and creator of The Fascination Advantage™—the world's first test to measure not how you see the world, but how the world sees you. Sally is an international keynote speaker, with research on 100,000 participants and studies translated into 14 languages. Her websites are www.HowToFascinate.com and www.SallyHogshead.com, and she can be reached at Fascinate@SallyHogshead.com.

THE SELF-EATING WATERMELON: THE SECRETS FOR MORE MONEY AND HAPPIER CLIENTS

Kent Cummins, MBA, CMCE

What is The Self-Eating Watermelon?

I can tell you this much right away: It's one of the ways I was able to earn a six-figure income as a magician. And it can help *you* make more money through marketing that achieves everyone's goals.

"The Self-Eating Watermelon" is a catchphrase that some friends and I started using while we were attending Louisiana State University in the early 1960s. Our basic idea was to create projects in which everybody wins. We felt that part of our job was to help the client find the money to pay our fees . . . and *we* are in control of the possibilities.

Maybe the best way to understand the concept is with a few examples.

1. Fund-raising Can Be Fun.

I was contacted by the band director of a school in Hamlin, Texas. She wanted me to consult with them to provide magic for their competition against other high school bands. But she didn't have the budget for a reasonable consulting fee.

That would have been the end of the call, if I hadn't suggested The Self-Eating Watermelon: "What if we produce a family magic show for your school, sponsored by the band? We can split the proceeds 50/50, so if we don't have great ticket sales, you won't have to pay the normal performing fee. But if we can sell a lot of tickets, we can both make some money."

I have been a magician for sixty years (yes, since I was a kid), so I know how to put on a magic show. But I also have learned the logistics behind the show: printing, promotion, ticket sales, marketing—the things that matter the most when the goal is fund-raising.

I helped Hamlin High School create a souvenir program in which they sold ads that paid for the costs of printing the program, tickets, and posters. The school provided the auditorium. The Band Boosters and students sold tickets and program ads. My company, Magic Hotline, organized the event and produced the show.

I also suggested that the band sell refreshments during the show and that they could keep all of those proceeds, in addition to their 50 percent of the net ticket sales. We sold magic books, tricks, and autographed photos, and kept those proceeds.

The show was a big success, and Magic Hotline made money from putting on the show. But the client, Hamlin High School, also made money—nearly half of which they spent to hire Magic Hotline for consulting. And the band won their competition with an amazing show! That's what I call a win-win.

2. Success Through Sponsorship

The Lung Association wanted to hire "The Fantastic Kent Cummins" to be master of ceremonies and auctioneer for its magic-themed gala. (They had gotten my name and contact information from an agent.) But they didn't have enough in their budget to pay my fee. They called the agent back and said they would need to find someone less expensive. The agent told them, "You need Kent! Go find someone to sponsor his fee." They did!

I received my full fee, the agent got her 20 percent, and the Lung Association didn't have to pay my fee. The gala was a fabulous success, and I made sure the sponsor received extensive recognition, which is what they wanted. That's a win-win-win.

3. Fair-Trade Barter

"I'll give you a copy of my book in exchange for a copy of your book."

Barter involves trading products and services to which we have profitable access for those products and services that we need (or at least want). It means that virtually anything—not just money—can be a medium of exchange.

Probably everyone uses barter to some degree. "You don't have to pay me for editing your manuscript; just let me have a signed copy of the finished product." Or "I'd like to pick your brain for some marketing ideas. When can I buy you lunch?"

One of my proudest barter projects involved a new spa company opening up in our part of town. They knew how to sell and repair spas and hot tubs, but they knew nothing about marketing their new business. I was experienced in marketing, and my wife and I wanted a hot tub on our deck. No money had to change hands.

That was in 1991, and we still enjoy the hot tub. Win-win for sure!

IT'S ALL ABOUT CONTEXT

My wife calls me "Too Much Context Man." I *think* it means I'm a super hero because I relish the details and background that create successful projects. Herewith, courtesy of Too Much Context Man, is more information than you may want or need about how the concept of The Self-Eating Watermelon got started.

- John Schexnaydre (a magician who also loves tech stuff), Reggie Keogh (he became an attorney), Rhett McMahon (his recording studio behind his house was called "Elite Productions"), and I developed the concept.

- Inspired by Heinlein's *We Also Walk Dogs,* the four of us were committed to making money in a variety of interesting ways. We called ourselves "Entrepreneurs Incorporated," although we were not actually incorporated back then.

- As college students, we didn't have any investment capital. So, we looked for projects that had the seeds of their own financing within the project itself. None of us can remember why, but we started calling such a project "The Self-Eating Watermelon."

- Today, the phrase is listed in the Urban Dictionary, but with a negative connotation:

  "Any undertaking that exists only to justify its own existence rather than to serve a productive purpose."

  The dictionary credits Luther Setzer, 11/21/08. But we were using the term in 1961! And that is by no means the way that we have used the phrase for the past half a century.

- We use the term in a positive rather than pejorative sense. Specifically, we use it to embrace any project that has the seeds of its own success within the limits of the project. Often, we use it to define projects in which we help the client find the money to pay our fees. All of our youthful projects seemed inextricably interwoven, and we loved the concept.
- I still do.

PUTTING THE FUN IN FUND-RAISING!

Whether you are an entertainer, speaker, trainer, consultant, coach, or whatever, you have products and services that could form the basis of a fund-raising opportunity. If you can't imagine how, just shoot me an e-mail, and let's talk about it. Maybe you have something to barter . . .

Fund-raising could include providing a portion of the sales from your speaking engagement or book sales to a favorite nonprofit. Or you might create a speaking opportunity that creates its own fee.

Take the National Speakers Association and this book. The authors wrote chapters without asking for an author's stipend, saving the association significant costs. NSA sells the book and earns revenue, which it uses to provide benefits to the authors, who are members of NSA. The authors' names and bios are seen around the world. And everyone who reads the book learns how to improve their marketing. Wouldn't you call that a win-win-win?

AND NOW, A WORD FROM OUR SPONSOR

Commercial sponsorship is a world unto itself, with its own organizations, publications, and conventions. The basic idea is simple: Get some big corporation to donate money to your cause. You see it in the names of sports stadiums and the backs of T-shirts at local fun runs.

Here's the main secret: *You must appeal to the sponsor's needs rather than your own!*

It may sound simple—even obvious—but I can't begin to tell you how many speakers and entertainers have told me they couldn't convince a sponsor how wonderful they were. But that isn't the point. The secret to obtaining sponsorship is to convince the sponsor how well your product or service will help them achieve *their* goals.

There used to be an event called "Great Tastes of Austin," which was an outdoor festival on Auditorium Shores that attracted families throughout the area. It had music on several stages, in keeping with Austin's slogan, "The Live Music Capital of the World." It also had lots of local food and drink, plus a large children's entertainment area.

Magic Hotline had been hired to provide all of the children's entertainment for several years. But one year, I was told they had lost one of their commercial sponsors, so they would have to significantly reduce the budget for the children's entertainment area. Of course, that meant a considerable reduction in my fees, and I'm married to a bookkeeper!

What to do? I called on The Self-Eating Watermelon, of course. I sold the sponsorship idea to a small local mall with which I was already doing business. They agreed to become the new sponsor. They put their name in front of Austin families. The event promoter loved me, and even brought me in for "Great Tastes of Houston." My budget was restored.

Win-win-win.

I'LL TRADE YOU WHAT I HAVE FOR WHAT YOU HAVE!

The barter concept was institutionalized in the late 1970s and 1980s, as barter exchanges sprouted up to monitor (and profit from) tricks of the trade. Some of these exchanges didn't last long, probably because they represented a segment looking for "something for nothing" rather than a mutual exchange of value.

The reason for a barter exchange is to provide a way to trade indirectly. For example, you need a new computer but the computer store isn't interested in your keynote speech. No problem when you use an exchange; you receive "barter credits" when you do your keynote for a different client, and you can spend those credits at the participating computer store.

That's right; barter exchanges reinvented the concept of money! Of course, they take a percentage of each trade, and that percentage typically has to be paid in cash. There was also the periodic problem of businesses raising their prices for barter transactions, not honoring their normal sales prices.

Another problem with barter is that the transactions *are* taxable, and the IRS got very interested in those who were trying to avoid paying taxes on items received in trade. However, there are still reputable barter exchanges available, including both local and Internet-based exchanges.

But you don't necessarily need an exchange to benefit from barter.

Last year, I served as executive director of a military nonprofit organization, the International Military Club Executives Association (IMCEA). We didn't have the budget to send our staff to the National Restaurant Association Show in Chicago. We couldn't afford a booth. So we traded them a training session, "Selling to the Military," for a booth in the Partnership Pavilion. Yes, there was watermelon at the food show!

The Self-Eating Watermelon.

It's a funny phrase, but it may help you remember some ways to increase your business. Get your full fee whenever you can, but when you can't, consider (1) fund-raising, (2) sponsorship, and/or (3) barter. The secret is to look for projects that are win-win-win.

"The Fantastic Kent Cummins," owner of Magic Hotline, is an author, speaker, and entertainer who makes his home in Austin, Texas, but speaks and performs all over the world. Kent loves to hear from readers at kent@KentCummins.com. Learn more about Magic Hotline at www.KentCummins.com. Kent lives the proof of his slogan: *"Sometimes, it takes a Magician!"™* Kent can be reached at kent@kentcummins. com or visit www.MagicHotline.com.

25

HOW TO TURN YOUR EXPERTISE INTO MULTIPLE STREAMS OF INCOME

Ford Saeks

In today's overstimulated world, your prospects and clients are bombarded with marketing messages, influenced by social proof, and impacted by industry and economic conditions. That means it's more important than ever to position yourself as an expert; understand your value propositions and revenue model; improve your product offerings; engage, connect, and convert your prospects and clients; leverage your website; expand your digital footprint; and use video marketing effectively to get more bookings, sell more products, attract new clients, and make money.

POSITION YOURSELF AS AN EXPERT

As a professional speaker, author, or consultant, you no doubt think of yourself and refer to yourself as exactly that—a professional speaker, author, or consultant. But you couldn't be more wrong when communicating to your target market! Thinking of your expertise in terms of *how* you do what you do means you're focused on the features and not the *benefit solutions* you provide.

Your expertise in a topic area or your ability to speak, write, or consult is a feature. The benefit is the value your clients get from your products and services. Ask yourself, "What problems do I solve, or what solutions do I provide that other people will *pay* to make go away?"

The key is to position yourself (and your company) as an expert in a specific area and focus first on the benefits you offer. Always lead with benefits and substantiate your claims with features and social proof. Benefits stand out from the competition and cause people to pay attention.

If you're speaking to a meeting planner who is looking to hire a professional speaker for a conference, of course, you're going to refer to your expertise as a speaker. But remember—they don't want a speaker just to speak—they want an expert to deliver value.

Whatever your unique expertise, you must keep that focus at the forefront and position yourself accordingly. After all, with today's information overloaded society, high competition, and fast-changing economy, it's more critical than ever that you be positioned as the ultimate resource and solutions provider in your niche.

So remember: Speakers, authors, and trainers don't get paid to speak, write, and train; they get paid to deliver value, entertain, educate, and inspire performance improvement.

UNDERSTAND YOUR VALUE PROPOSITIONS AND REVENUE MODEL

Have you ever wondered what marketing really *means*? Quite simply, it's giving people enough information so they can make an informed buying decision; it's getting the right message in front of the right market using the right methods. To do so, you must understand your value propositions and revenue model.

Understanding your value propositions, also known as Unique Selling Propositions (USPs), means figuring out the unique benefits you offer and communicating them to your marketplace in your promotional and sales efforts. In other words, why should people do business with you instead of someone else? What value and benefits do you offer that make you unique in the delivery and results of your products and services?

But what about your revenue model?

A revenue model includes the avenues or categories you use to deliver value and generate sales. For example, in my company, Prime Concepts Group Inc., we have a revenue model that consists of five streams of income:

1. Speaking/Training (keynotes, workshops, and public seminars)
2. Coaching/Consulting (one-on-one, small groups, and inner-circle masterminds)

3. Products (physical and digital)

4. Professional Services (Internet marketing, website design, and website development)

5. Joint Ventures (strategic partnerships)

These streams represent "how" we deliver our value propositions, not "why."

We know professional speakers who make the majority of their income from keynote speaking with some back-of-room sales, while others speak for free and upsell their audience members into mid-tier and high-tier consulting deals or product packages. You have to define what is best for you and where you are in your career. In other words, is your revenue model congruent with your current lifestyle or the lifestyle you desire? For example, if 75 percent of your revenue is from presenting keynotes all over the country but you want to travel only a few weeks out of the year, your revenue model needs to shift to accommodate your desired lifestyle.

On the other side of the coin, if you're spending 80 percent of your time consulting, but 80 percent of your revenue is actually derived from your speaking, it would only make sense to increase the amount of time you're speaking and decrease the amount of time you're consulting or figure out ways to leverage your efforts.

IMPROVE YOUR PRODUCT PYRAMID

Whether you have a plethora of products and services, or you just focus on a few main services, it's important to have a variety of price points from low to high; otherwise, you may be leaving money on the table.

Let me explain what I mean with some pricing examples. The following are not meant to be absolute as every market, industry, and business is unique.

Most information marketers, which is what you are when you're a thought leader or expert, create a product pipeline that resembles a pyramid. At the bottom are introductory products or services that are free or at lower price points. These may be $10 to $20 books or $20 to $100 special reports, individual audios, or videos. From there, products or services gradually go up to the midrange. These could be $150 to $5,000 physical products, digital products, public seminars, or coaching programs. Finally, you have the higher-end products or services. These may be $5,000 to $100,000 (or even higher) multimedia information products, coaching, or consulting packages.

Does this mean you need to cover every single price point? No—the object is to have at least one product or service for each of the main price ranges that fits your specific target market's needs. This way, you're allowing your prospects to engage with you at the level at which they are comfortable. Additionally, the higher price points also help to position all of your other price points.

For example, we have several free videos, audios, and special reports on business growth, innovation, and success that we use as "lead magnets" to use in exchange for prospects giving us their contact information. This helps us build a qualified marketing list. We produce monthly webinars for a fee, record them, and use them as products and product bundle bonuses. In our webinars we deliver 95 percent value-added, action-oriented content and spend 5 percent on promoting the next item or action step in the pyramid.

HAVE A CONVERSATION WITH YOUR CUSTOMERS

You don't need to have the mind of a marketing master to implement changes and tweaks that will help you grow your business. Nevertheless, many people we've worked with make the same mistakes related to their marketing efforts. They create a website, a demo video, or a blog and sit back, waiting for the phone to ring. They assume that having the latest in technology or making dismal outbound efforts will automatically capture "top-of-mind awareness" with their prospects.

Effective marketing is not about technology or having the latest flashy tool; it all boils down to communication . . . and communicating value. Successful communication, as it relates to marketing, includes three main areas; consider these areas as they relate to your business.

You first *engage* by pushing out information with promotional marketing methods like your website, social media, direct mail, or sales calls. From there, your goal is to encourage the other person to *connect* with you and your business. And, in the end, you want them to *convert* by taking some sort of action step.

Keeping these areas fresh in mind, let's look at some specific marketing examples.

USE YOUR WEBSITE AS THE DIGITAL FACE OF YOUR BUSINESS

Think about your website as the digital face of your business. Common sense tells you that your prospects are going to Google you or visit your website before hiring you. So, your website visitors are most likely made up of meeting planners looking for a speaker, business executives or staff looking for a solutions provider, audience members looking to connect or purchase a product, or the media wanting to interview you as a thought leader.

This means your website must effectively communicate who you are, what your area of expertise is, who else you've worked with and, most importantly, what problems you can solve for them. It's the digital face of your business, and it's the social proof that your customers are looking for.

Before prospects visit your website, you're just a name among thousands of others. After they visit your website, ideally, you've communicated why they should do business with you. In many cases, professional speakers' websites are so ineffective that they're actually "sales prevention" tools rather than tools to connect, engage, and convert.

Let's start with a few brief thoughts on graphic design. Clearly, you need a website that is visually appealing and congruent with your style. If you have a disorganized, confusing, or ugly website, your visitors will instantly be turned off and you'll lose business because of it.

But, as much as graphics grab attention, it's compelling copy that actually sells. The visuals and the copy must be in alignment to communicate effectively. Like I mentioned before, if you don't communicate your benefit message with a clear call to action, it won't matter how pretty your site looks.

You also need to consider your *findability*. Simply put, how easy is it for people to find you online? Do you know what specific keyword phrases your prospects would type into a search engine to find you? Is your website search engine optimized with the proper keyword themes and sections? Do you have your keyword phrases identified and included throughout your social media profiles and your blog?

Speaking of which, you have a blog, don't you? If you're a thought leader, speaker, author, or consultant, a blog is an integral part of adding fresh, relevant, keyword-rich content to your website. Blog posts with keywords related to the problems facing your marketplace, as well as the solutions, are essential to generate traffic.

Now that customers can find you, evaluate the *usability* of your website. Most people online are like wandering monkeys on crack looking for the banana. They scan, jump around, and are easily distracted. It's your job to help guide them into your sales funnels and capture them as qualified leads. Is it easy for visitors on your website to find the information they want? Are important areas of your business buried under countless pages?

Beyond the navigation, usability also touches upon the different versions of your website. The number of people using mobile phones to access websites online is growing exponentially. Do you have a mobile version of your website? What does your website look like on a smartphone or tablet? Is it easy to navigate? Your customers use different devices, so you need to consider how your website displays on all of them.

Most importantly, you need to look at your site through the eyes of a prospect. If you were visiting your site for the first time, would it make you want to click further, subscribe, read more, or contact you? Would it engage you to take action? Would you know where to click to get the information you're looking for?

These are all questions that need to be answered from a client's perspective. Clearly, if you don't like what you see, neither will your potential customers, and before you know it, they will be on to the next website and company.

Next, you need to measure the profitability of your website. Do you have a conversion strategy to build customer lists? Are you using specific sales funnels, and are they effective? Do you know what your visitor-to-lead conversion rates are? In the end, you want your business to produce better results and make more money, but you need to know where you're starting from to measure your success.

By reviewing your current website analytics, you'll be able to evaluate whether the changes you make are affecting your results and making you more money. When was the last time you reviewed your website's statistics? Ask your website provider for the analytics access. Most likely you're using the free service Google Analytics, but you need to know how much traffic you're getting, what pages visitors are viewing, and how many leads and sales you're getting from your website.

USE SOCIAL MEDIA TO EXPAND YOUR DIGITAL FOOTPRINT

Social media websites are important marketing channels, and as a thought leader, you need to have a strong social media presence. But if you're not leveraging social media correctly, you can easily spend countless hours and produce lackluster results. Your goal should be to build relationships and add value first, not to sell.

Once you have established that relationship, the benefits will continue to grow. Consumers will seek you out for additional information, and you'll be able to create trust, improve communications, get higher rankings in the search engines, and create more links and traffic back to your website. In the end, you'll expand your digital footprint, reach more customers, and produce better results.

Keep in mind that using your keywords on your LinkedIn profile, YouTube video titles and descriptions, Facebook pages, Google+ pages, and Twitter tweets will also help attract new prospects.

While we're on the subject, are you using video effectively? You're going to continue to see an overwhelming use of video for much more than just speaking demos: video sales letters, product demos, online and on-demand learning courses, learning management systems, new video products, personality web-TV shows, webcasts, video blog posts, virtual replays, and video sharing websites like YouTube. To see an example of a video sales letter, visit www.GetPaidtoSpeak.com. It's a short video message using an audio narrative track with graphics to keep the viewer engaged.

In the end, when leveraged correctly, an increased social media and video presence will expand your digital footprint, reach more customers, and help you grow your speaking business.

As you leverage your social media presence, however, you need to proceed with some caution. With so many people pegging themselves as social media experts, "speaker parasites" continue to pop up. These people specifically prey on new speakers and try to sell services they may not need.

The point is that you need to be careful about who you hire to help you leverage social media for your business. There is no way for anyone to claim to know everything about social media networking. Do the wrong things and you could easily create a social media marketing or identity theft nightmare. Do nothing and you'll be left in the Dark Ages.

NOW WHAT?

Your marketing plan should never be stagnant. It needs to be a living, breathing document that you go back to and refresh on a consistent basis. New distribution channels open up every day, new opportunities are created, the markets continue to shift, and trends come and go, as do your competitors. As these changes occur, continually evaluate your marketing performance. If you think of your marketing as an afterthought, you will continue to miss opportunities and experience dismal results.

But if you are actively engaged in effectively positioning yourself as an expert; understanding your value propositions and revenue model; improving your product offerings; engaging, connecting, and converting your prospects and clients; leveraging your website; expanding your digital footprint with social media; and using video marketing effectively, you'll continue to successfully grow your business.

Ford Saeks, president and CEO of Prime Concepts Group Inc., is the publisher and mastermind behind Randy Gage's multimillion-dollar business and a host of other well-known Internet marketing efforts for CSPs, CPAEs, authors and consultants, websites, and public events. He is a national director on the board of NSA and a member of the prestigious Speakers Roundtable. He speaks to thousands each year on business growth strategies and Internet marketing. Ford not only talks about information and Internet marketing solutions; he lives them daily. He has helped thousands of people dramatically improve their search rankings, digital footprint, lead generation, and sales conversions. Learn more at www.PrimeConcepts.com, or contact Ford directly at FordSpeaks@PrimeConcepts.com.

26

THE POWER OF SYSTEMS: TAKE YOUR SPEAKING BUSINESS TO THE NEXT LEVEL

Patrick Donadio, MBA, CSP, MCC

In 1991, while in Japan as a Goodwill Ambassador, I became aware of something that changed the way I operate my business to this day. After a week of enjoying the Japanese cuisine, I was craving some American food. My host family graciously agreed to take me to McDonald's®. As I was eating my "Biga Macu" and fries, it dawned on me. This food tasted exactly as it did in my hometown of Columbus, Ohio. That is when I realized the secret to McDonald's success—systemization. By having quality controls, recipes, and systems in place, no matter where you go in the world, McDonald's hamburgers and fries are going to taste exactly the same.

SYSTEMIZE YOUR BUSINESS

In his book *The E-Myth*, Michael Gerber proposes that we look at our business like a franchise, such as McDonald's. He suggests we act as if we were going to franchise our business someday. Gerber recommends we systematize each aspect of the business so we could hand it over to someone else and they could run it for us. The Japan experience and reading this book prompted me to integrate systems into my own business. I began to systemize my speaking and training business to help take it to the next level.

WHAT IS THE NEXT LEVEL?

The *next level* is the natural progression for you and your business. It could be growth in income, more engagements, gaining work/life balance, etc. It is all about competing with yourself, analyzing where you are now, and comparing that with where you want to be in the future (the next level). For me, the next level was working less, making more, and finding a way to spend more time with my family. So I set goals to increase my income, minimize the amount of travel, and be more efficient at the business side of speaking. This was a lofty goal, but one worth pursuing.

What is *your* next level? Get a clear vision for what the next level looks like. Then arrange your business in such a way to make this happen.

WRITTEN GOALS: PRACTICE WHAT WE PREACH

Most of us at some point in our careers have encouraged our audiences to set written goals. I preach it because of the amazing impact written goals have had on my personal and business lives. However, sometimes we forget what got us to where we are.

One day Winnie Ary, CSP, challenged me to write down what I would like to be making in two years and to keep it in my wallet where I could see it. So I did. I would see it occasionally when I pulled out money to buy a cappuccino, while waiting at the airport. In two years, not only had I met my written net income goal, but I'd exceeded it by 30 percent. That's the power of written goals!

Written goals are a key ingredient to taking your speaking business to the next level. Write out your vision, and set specific goals and deadlines to make it a reality.

WORK BACKWARD TO RECREATE SYSTEMS

As my Italian grandmother approached 80, my mom and I attempted to get her recipes. However, we found one problem: Grandma could not read or write English very well, and thus she had no written recipes. So, one day we went over to Grandma's house. While she cooked, we interrupted her to measure everything she did. We took notes and recreated her recipes. I subscribe to the philosophy of starting at the end and working backward. Find out what has been working and dissect it to recreate the system. Then discover the components that make it work, so you can replicate the process to get similar results.

I suggest you try the same approach with your business. Get a clear idea of what you want, and then by working backward, figure out what you need to do to make it happen.

SYSTEMS YOU'LL NEED

Here are a couple of systems that you will need to grow your business:

Financial Systems. Achieving revenue and expense goals is essential to reaching the next level financially. The best way to manage all this is with a budget and a good accounting system. Budgeting is a systematic way to help your business get to where you want it to go. Your budget is an extension of your written goals. I break down the income side of my budget by categories, setting dollar targets for each. Here are a few examples of my revenue categories:

- Keynotes
- Keynotes—Bureau
- Training
- Training—Bureau
- Coaching
- Consulting
- Products

You can further break products down by specific product types—books, CD/MP3, videos, and more.

Next, use a good accounting system to help you streamline this process. There are many accounting programs available; I happen to use Quicken®. It is not only great for your bookkeeping/budgeting but also for your retirement planning. The system will tell you at any point in time how well you are achieving your financial goals.

Sales/Marketing System. Another area I found critical to systemize was the sales/marketing process. Here's how. First, choose your top 20 to 30 best clients for the past three years. Then, dissect how you obtained them and what you did to help them make this list. Try asking these three questions:

1. What did you do to get them? (Before)

2. What did you do while you were servicing them to make them love you? (During)

3. What did you do after the sale to keep them, sell more to them, or get referrals? (After)

Now try to uncover all the steps you took for each client. By analyzing each, you will begin to notice certain things you are doing over and over again—common denominators. Write these common denominators on a master sheet, listing each in one of the three areas: (1) Before, (2) During, and (3) After.

You will also notice some activities you are doing only occasionally. Look at the occasional activities. Are you seeing these activities with more successful clients? What if you did these occasional activities more often? What might happen? If the answers are positive, write them down as well.

Are you consistently applying your best to each client and potential client? Now you have recreated a sales/marketing recipe that will help you do just that. Your system consists of a list of activities to do for each phase—before, during, and after. Begin applying this system to every client and potential client. Continue to fine-tune it, add to it, and subtract from it. In about six months you will have generated a system that not only creates great clients, but also will yield more repeat business from that client. This approach will help you make sure you (or your staff) more consistently perform.

LEVERAGE TECHNOLOGY

The next phase is to take these new systems and use technology to make them work even better and faster and with less effort. Just like Quicken® made my accounting/bookkeeping run smoother, I wanted to find software that could do the same for the rest of my business. That's when I discovered contact management software. This software combines a database, a word processor, and a calendar in one program. (I use ACT!™, but there are many other similar contact management programs out there: Outlook®, Maximizer®, Infusionsoft®, and E-speaker®, for example.)

I took a look at my new Sales/Marketing System (see page 219) and began to discover that there were certain activities I could computerize using ACT!. The first level was to create merge documents/templates for any documents I used in my system. This would speed up the process, increase consistencies, and improve my chances of doing these steps. Here are a few examples of templates I created:

- Sales letters
- Program outlines
- Letters of agreement (for speaking/training and coaching)
- References
- Audience analysis questionnaire
- Handout cover letter (permission to reproduce copyrighted handouts)
- Invoices
- Customer satisfaction survey
- Thank-you letters (thanks for choosing me, thanks for the referral)
- E-mail sales/marketing templates to respond to requests for information, etc.

The second level is to preschedule these sales/marketing activities. For example, in the "during" stage, I know that for every engagement I am going to conduct an audience analysis, send a letter of agreement, and send a tailored handout. Or in the "after" stage, I will send a satisfaction survey. So when I book the date for this engagement on the ACT! calendar, I also schedule a reminder notice for each of activities in my sales/marketing system. Now when those dates come up, a reminder notice pops up on my computer screen to remind me to do that specific activity; for example: "Call the meeting planner to schedule the audience analysis conference call." By computerizing the system, you will see tremendous results. In my case, I doubled my net income in just three years.

THINK STRATEGICALLY

After applying the system with some success, I began to explore the next level for me—how to make more, work less, and have more family time. I discovered two concepts that were very powerful. One I call "deep and narrow"; the other I call "maximizing downtime."

Deep and Narrow. After a speech, I used to think: "Next!" Now I think: "How else I can help this client before I move onto the next client?" Repeat business has become more a part of my business in the last ten years. For each stage of my "system," I built in components to help me get more repeat business.

For example, in the "before" stage, I built in some questions to uncover future speaking/training/coaching opportunities. I use these questions when I am talking with the meeting planner and/or interviewing audience members. In the "during" stage, from the platform, I strategically and subtly plant seeds (using a story, quick reference, or example) of other services I can offer. Finally, in the "after" stage I send out a customer satisfaction survey that also specifically asks my customers what other topics I offer that they might be interested in having me present. It is easier to sell to a current client than trying to sell a new client.

Maximizing Downtime. The area that jumped out at me for maximizing my downtime was coaching. Once a date is booked for a speech/workshop I've lost the inventory. That is, if another client calls for the same date I have to say no. Coaching allowed me to have the flexibility to use my downtime (non-platform time) to make money. I could schedule my coaching sessions around my speaking engagements, and if I had to, I could move a coaching session more easily than a speaking engagement. Coaching was also a way to increase my income without having to leave home (more family time, time to go to my children's sporting events, and so on).

The first year I introduced coaching, it accounted for less than 10 percent of my income. Last year it was 50 percent. My overall income went up by making my downtime more profitable. For some speakers, their consulting, mentoring programs, products, etc., can achieve the same results. Coaching is also a way to generate new material for the platform while giving you a product to cross-sell. It can even open doors to clients who may have never hired you as a speaker.

FINE-TUNE YOUR SYSTEMS

While touring a Nissan automotive factory in Japan, I noticed this sign on the wall: "Kaizen." I asked our tour guide what it meant. He informed me it meant "continuous improvement."

"How do you do that?"

"By continuously learning from your mistakes."

So, when I returned to the States, I began to apply this concept to my business as well. I encourage you to do the same. The "systems" I discussed above work. They will work even better once you have fine-tuned them. Your system should be constantly evolving. You do this by developing systems, by implementing them, and by making mistakes. The fine-tuning comes after the mistakes. Here's my "continuous improvement process (system)" to help you fine-tune your systems. After each mistake, simply ask yourself these two questions:

1. What did I do well?
2. What can I do differently the next time?

These systems and concepts have helped me take my business to the next level, and I know they can do the same for you.

Sales/Marketing System

Here is a simple template to help you get started on your Before, During, and After list:

BEFORE—What do you need to do before you get a client?

_____

_____

_____

_____

DURING—What should you do while you are servicing a client?

_____

_____

_____

_____

AFTER—What do you need to do after the service to keep them and obtain other clients?

_____

_____

_____

_____

© 2012 Patrick Donadio, MBA, Certified Speaking Professional (CSP) and Master Certified Coach (MCC)

Since 1986, Patrick Donadio, MBA, CSP, MCC, has guided leaders and their organizations with powerful presentations and one-on-one business communications coaching. From the boardroom to the frontlines, he teaches and coaches people how to increase profits, improve communications and presentation skills, enhance their credibility, deepen relationships, and boost performance—in less time. Patrick has taught at The Weatherhead School of Management, The John Glenn School of Public Affairs, and the University of Notre Dame. Patrick also served two terms as president of the National Speakers Association's Ohio Chapter. Contact Patrick at 614-488-9164 or Patrick@PatrickDonadio.com, or visit www.PatrickDonadio.com.

POTPOURRI OF PROVEN PRACTICES

TURN HEADS AND CLOSE DEALS: TIPS FOR CREATING A POWERFUL IMAGE

Sandy Dumont, CTIC

Want to wow potential clients? These days powerful content is more essential than ever, but that might not be enough to get your foot in the door. You need to look good, too. We do judge a book by its cover, so it's time to take a good hard look at this oft-underrated component of the speaking industry.

Is style as important as substance these days? It's very likely that speakers with a strong academic background would give substance greater weight, but a number of popular keynote speakers would argue otherwise. These dazzling speakers keep their audiences entertained and spellbound for an hour with a minimum of substance, and you can be sure they pay attention to how they look, because they are seasoned professionals.

Whether you're an aspiring speaker or one who has achieved monumental success, in these financial times, you can't afford to play Wardrobe Roulette® with your image. While you need both style and substance, my experience has shown that style trumps substance any day. Even the most learned and esteemed experts will have less credibility with a poor image. Your message without words—your image—conveys a message more powerful than words.

Social psychologist Robert Cialdini, PhD, author of the best-selling book, *Influences: The Psychology of Persuasion*, demonstrated that if you look good, it is assumed that you *are* good at what you do. And, of course, the converse is true.

Looking good doesn't have anything to do with Hollywood glamour. Top speakers look classy, not flashy. Their appearance is polished and professional at all times.

There's yet another important element to consider—your perceived status. According to social psychologist Kevin Hogan, PhD, when you meet people you put them into one of three categories: Yes, No, or Maybe. He asserts that most people are in the No category and are dismissed entirely. Hogan says it is difficult to get out of the Maybe category and that only a few are in the Yes category. He contends that those in the Yes category have a high-status look.

So what is a high-status look? Here are the basics:

- A high-quality, well-tailored suit
- Well-made shoes that are elegant but don't stand out too much
- High-quality, fashionable accessories, such as brooches for women and elegant ties and watches for men
- Good grooming from head to toe
- Stylish, healthy-looking hair or an artfully shaved head
- Professional and refined makeup for women

You must captivate your audience in the first few minutes if you want them to follow you. If you look ordinary, you'll lose them.

As a speaker, you are a brand, and quality brands aren't packaged in plain brown paper. Exclusive brands permeate because they have a recognizable image that comes easily to mind.

SPEAKERS MUST LOOK LIKE THE EXPERTS THEY ARE

Expertise is one of the four tenets of an NSA speaker, along with eloquence, enterprises, and ethics. As NSA speakers know, it takes years of experience before you become an expert in your field. *Deliberate practice* is the term *Fortune Magazine* gave to a phenomenon that Malcolm Gladwell also wrote about in his bestselling book *Outliers*.

Both publications took their cue from a 1993 assertion by Anders Ericsson that it takes ten years or 10,000 hours of practice in one's field to lay claim to the title *expert*.

Ericsson cited Bill Gates, who spent thousands of hours in 1968 programming a state-of-the-art school computer at the age of 13, giving him an enormous advantage. In terms of branding, he was the only dot-com "geek" who habitually wore a suit, perhaps giving him an edge when he bargained successfully with IBM.

The Beatles performed live in Hamburg, Germany, more than 1,200 times from 1960 to 1964, amassing more than 10,000 hours of playing time. By the time they returned to England, they were not only experts, they also had a distinctive look, which is one of the most important tenets of branding.

NSA speaker and neuroscientist Scott Halford, CSP, has done extensive research in the arena of expertise, and he contends that it requires 1,000 repetitions (that's about three years) to become an expert. Ultimately, all experts on the subject agree that you can't be an overnight success when it comes to expertise.

Obviously, a powerful brand requires a professional image, but it can be taken a step further.

The most important ingredient is the "uniform," and it turns out that a business suit is among the most powerful of uniforms. In Cialdini's mock setup, casually clad jaywalkers were criticized sharply by onlookers, while jaywalkers clad in powerful business suits were not. In fact, they even "inspired" others to do the same.

You didn't gain your expertise overnight, so don't tarnish your brand's image by looking like a novice who isn't clued in about professional image. When you know you look good, you stand taller and look people straight in the eye. You convey an air of confidence that cannot be overlooked.

A lot has been written about power dressing, but a man's "power dressing" look is nearly the opposite of a woman's. A *fashion look* for men greatly diminishes credibility and power, but a *high-fashion* look for women dramatically magnifies those qualities.

Fashion looks for men include dark shirts with ties in any color, perfectly matched shirt/tie boxed sets, and ultra slim-fit suits that look more suggestive than professional.

Women have been told that a "classic" look is best for speakers. This is dated information from the 1980s. A "classic" look for women usually connotes a safe or conservative look that ends up looking androgynous or robot-like, because it consists of the ubiquitous tailored suit with few or no accessories. Female speakers need a high-fashion wardrobe, because it signifies success. It should be worn with polished and professional makeup, plus power accessories to increase credibility and power.

Conversely, a classic look for men is derived from the British high-end tailor shops, where "old money" looks reign supreme. In this "mover-shaker" arena, fashion looks are seen as being for dandies, gamblers, or ladies' men.

You're a brand. The question is, are you an eye-popping, memorable brand that turns heads when you enter a room? The same principles of branding apply for both products and people:

1. **Be distinctive.** You must look head-and-shoulders above the rest of the crowd, so you stand out as a mover and shaker.

2. **Maintain a professional look**. Never compromise your professionalism by giving in to "business casual" attire. Casual attire suggests a casual attitude. It also shouts mediocrity instead of star quality.

3. **Convey an air of trust.** Unkempt hair, dirty nails, scruffy shoes, and un-ironed shirts suggest carelessness. Designer stubble, garish makeup, dated garments or hair, and overtly sexy garments lower credibility and trust.

4. **Be consistent.** Product inconsistency has killed many brands. When you speak at a weekend retreat or attend a client's golf tournament, dress as if you just left the polo match, not a garage sale. Trust and credibility are destroyed when you let your brand down, because they'll wonder which one is the impostor. Imagine seeing your airline pilot dressed in jeans and a T-shirt; you might decide to take another flight. Don't let your brand down by looking anything less than the polished professional you are.

CREATE A SIGNATURE IMAGE

To ensure that you are etched in the mind of others, it is necessary to craft a unique "signature image" so you will be remembered long after you've left the platform. Here are tips for getting started:

1. Choose Winning Colors

- Take the time to discover the colors that make you look better. One shade of blue, for example, will make you look healthy and vibrant; another shade of blue will make you look sad, tired, and boring. Studies at the Impression Strategies Institute have shown that most people don't know what they look good in and that they usually choose colors that make them feel safe. Once you *know* you look good, your confidence will soar.

- **Men:** Wear dark suits in navy blue, grey, or black for the most authoritative look. Navy blue, in particular, looks businesslike and authoritative on nearly everyone. In addition, if your budget is modest, a navy blue suit will look more expensive than its brown, grey, or black counterparts. Use caution when choosing black, as some people can look threatening in this color. Dark suits are not only authoritative; they are also more slimming, and fit-looking people are judged to be more successful.

- **Women:** In addition to the classic suit colors, you can also wear bold colors such as royal blue, ruby red, racing green, magenta, white, and royal purple. Assert your expertise by dressing like an authority, not a passive bystander.

- Most people do not look good in grunge colors, so avoid drab colors like olive green, basic brown, and most "earthy" tones. Neon colors also should be avoided, because they are deemed flashy. The darker the color, the greater the inherent authority; thus, pastels can make you look passive or timid. Pure white and lemon yellow are not pastels.

2. Choose Garments and Accessories That Suggest Authority

- Choose garments made of high-quality fabrics. They fall better and are more flattering to the figure, and they don't look rumpled at the end of the day.

- **Men:** Wear styles that flatter your physique. If you're fairly short, dress in one solid color from head to toe so you are visually elongated. If you're heavier than you'd like to be, wearing one unbroken color will also make you look slimmer. This means wearing a suit instead of tan trousers with a navy blazer, for instance. The best way to conceal a paunch is by wearing a suit. The jacket is always worn buttoned except when you are seated. Most men look better in a two-button suit; a three-button suit often looks "too buttoned-up." Avoid pinstripe suits (banker's stripes) unless you're presenting to those in banking or finance—this look is perceived as less friendly outside the financial arena.

- **Women:** Choose distinctive-looking jackets that are well-tailored to suit a woman's hourglass figure. Avoid shapeless blazer-style "daddy jackets." You don't want to look like a miniature man. Solid colors look more professional than patterns, and large patterns make you look larger. You will look taller (and slimmer) in a pantsuit in one unbroken color. However, skirted suits convey more authority, because they are more formal. Knee length is best for skirts.

- **Men:** Select ties with small repeating patterns instead of those with abstract patterns, floral prints, or cartoon motifs. Avoid "boxed sets" with matching shirts and ties, as they never look businesslike. Your tie must always dominate your shirt and suit. Think contrast, which means you will never again wear a blue tie with a blue shirt. Best shirt colors are white (the most formal), Oxford blue, French blue, and stripes in blue and white.

- **Women:** Bold accessories such as brooches and chunky hoop earrings make you look more important and authoritative. Avoid large hoops and all dangly earrings, as they are distracting and shout "teenager."

- Keep shoes simple and unobtrusive. Avoid shoes with square toes or very rounded ones. Plain pumps are best for women; avoid ultra-high stilettos because they give the impression you can't move freely. Classic cap-toed lace-ups are a good choice for men.

3. Women: Wear Professional Makeup.

- Professional makeup enables you to look more worldly and sophisticated. You also will be deemed more professional.

- The most natural-looking foundations have subtle pink undertones. Look for soft pink or orchid-toned blushers to harmonize.

- Avoid brown-toned lipstick. It makes you look washed out and dreary. For a natural look, try soft orchids; for a power look, try fuchsia, cherry red, or true red. Of course, the best color to select will depend on your skin tone. Avoid turquoise eye shadow, heavy black eyeliner, and black nail polish.

NOW IS THE TIME TO TRANSFORM YOUR IMAGE

We *do* judge a book by its cover, because the way you look and dress announces the outcome other people can expect from you. It also announces how you feel about yourself, and you'll be treated accordingly. If you want to walk into a room and own it, then you must own your image.

You may disagree with some of the principles set forth in this chapter. You may even feel insulted by them. However, if you follow the suggestions given, you'll put money in your pockets! And you'll own your image.

Ultimately, the way you dress defines who you are not only to others, but to the person in the mirror when you leave the house each morning. Get up in the morning and dress as if you are the No.1 speaker in NSA. When you change on the outside, people treat you differently, and then you change on the inside—*profoundly*. Image doesn't cost; it pays.

Sandy Dumont, CEO at The Image Architect, is a speaker and internationally known expert in the arena of professional image. She works with speakers, VIPs, and corporate executives, and she has presented on three continents. Sandy Dumont has produced numerous books, DVDs, and boxed sets on the subject of image and Branding for People®. Contact Sandy at Sandy@TheImageArchitect.com.

28

INSIDER SECRETS FOR MARKETING YOURSELF AS A SPEAKER

Pam Lontos, CSP, MA

Whether you're a new speaker or an experienced one, you always have to make sure that you're perceived as the expert and that you're getting your marketing messages out in the right way. But with so much hype and conflicting advice these days about the best way to market yourself, how can any speaker know the best path to take?

The following marketing tips are gleaned from my thirty years as a professional speaker, PR professional, and consultant. These are the strategies the top-tier speakers use on a regular basis but rarely talk about. Implement these today and watch your speaking career soar.

KNOW WHAT MAKES YOU UNIQUE

Yes, you're a speaker; however, if you're going to market and brand yourself as an expert, you have to know what makes you unique. So sit down and write out all the things that make you special and one-of-a-kind as a speaker.

Chances are there are many experts, just like you, in your niche or industry. You're not the only expert. So why should someone hire you over another speaker? What do you offer that no one else does? Some ways you can stand out include:

- **Your life story.** Did you survive a traumatic experience and end up stronger and wiser? Were you born into a high-profile family? Are you a survivor of a natural or manmade disaster?

- **Your business experience.** Did you grow a large business from nothing? Did you turn around a well-known organization? Were you a leader or manager of a high-profile company?

- **Your method or system.** Did you develop a system that consistently gets great results? Have you personally used your system to lose weight, build a business, sell a million copies of your book, etc.?

- **Your presentation style.** Do you include a lot of audience interaction and/or role-playing? Are you funny to the point that participants laugh 'til they cry? Do you sing, do magic, or have some other unique props?

Whatever you identify as your unique element, you need to promote that fact in all you do, just as Marti MacGibbon, ACRPS, CADAC II, ICADC, does.

Marti started her professional life as a successful stand-up comedian, performing at all the big-name comedy clubs. But then she became involved in an abusive relationship and couldn't find a way out. No matter how many times she tried to leave him, he'd find her and convince her to come back. One day she heard of an opportunity to work as an escort in Japan for a few months. She figured it was her only way to really get away from her boyfriend, so she went—only to find out she had been tricked. The escort service was really a human trafficking operation. Now she was really stuck. But Marti was certain she'd find a way out. A month later one of her "clients," who had ties to the Mob, helped her buy her freedom. Once back home, depression and post-traumatic stress disorder (PTSD) struck, and Marti turned to drugs for solace.

While this extraordinary story sounds sad on the surface, Marti tells it with her signature humor and wit, all while showing audience members how she turned her life around against insurmountable odds and how they can too.

By combining her unique compelling story with great humor, Marti stands out. How can you stand out?

Even if you're an experienced speaker with thousands of presentations under your belt, you still need to do this exercise. There are always newcomers in the speaking profession, so you have to continually differentiate yourself to stay on top.

IDENTIFY YOUR MARKETS

No speaker can successfully market himself to every sector of the population. Look at what makes you unique and choose one key industry or demographic that makes sense for you to speak to. For example, before becoming a speaker, I had years of experience in the broadcasting industry. As such, I initially marketed myself to that sector. Look back over your business and life experiences and decide which demographic you should target. It might be insurance, pharmaceuticals, manufacturing, or troubled youth.

Next, see if you can expand that market so you can have two distinct demographics to target—the first is a niche industry or sector, and the second is broader. For example, from my broadcasting niche, I branched out to general sales. I had one client whose niche was incarcerated teens who then branched out to the business sectors talking about overcoming past challenges. Look at what's a natural extension of your main topic and target that additional segment. You'll find that focusing on two key demographics will make your marketing efforts easier and more effective.

PROMOTE THE BOTTOM-LINE RESULTS YOU DELIVER

When marketing themselves, many speakers fall into the trap of constantly touting why they're so great. They say and write things like, "I do 100 presentations each year. People always invite me back. I'm the best speaker around." In truth, no one cares about attributes like that.

One of my clients was trying to get a corporation to sponsor his public speaking events. His first thought was to establish his wins and credits, so the prospects would know how good he was. I led him in another direction.

I suggested that he start by asking prospects a few key questions:

1. Who is your demographic—whom do you want to reach?
2. Why do you want to reach this group?
3. How can I help you reach that goal?

Once he had the answers to these questions, he was able to tell his potential clients how he could help them achieve their goals. In other words, he spoke to the company's bottom line. At the end of his presentation, his client expressed amazement with my client's ability to get to the heart of what they wanted—and the company agreed to sponsor his presentations. My client says he never would have accomplished that without first asking those questions.

The only way to know what matters most to a meeting planner or company decision maker is to ask. So find out what their goals are, and then show them how you can contribute to their success.

PICK UP THE PHONE

Studies show that each day, more than 294 billion e-mail messages are sent. Additionally, more than 8 trillion text messages were sent in 2011, and Twitter reports that more than 50 million tweets go out each and every day. The sheer amount of information people are being bombarded with is overwhelming. And while I agree that e-mail, texting, and social media are great tools to reach people, if you want to get more speaking gigs, then you need to start using one of the oldest marketing tools available: the telephone.

People buy from people they like and trust. If all you do is e-mail people and never talk with them or meet them in person, you're not giving decision makers an opportunity to like and trust you. Additionally, because so many speakers use nothing but e-mail, by picking up the phone and calling people, you'll stand out.

For example, when I provide a meeting planner with a demo video, as requested, I follow up with a phone call rather than an e-mail. Many times the meeting planner says something like, "I have 40 demo videos to review, and I just don't have the time. I'm so glad you called. I feel really comfortable talking with you, so I'd love for you to speak at our event."

WATCH YOUR WORDS

The power of verbal communication is a strong marketing tool, so when you do speak to someone, watch your words carefully. Rather than talking about yourself and why you'd be the perfect speaker for their event, always begin the conversation by building rapport. For example, if the person says something like, "I have to go pick up my daughter," or "I'm leaving for a trip tomorrow," you can ask,

"How old is your daughter?" or "Where are you going?" The point is to get them talking and feeling comfortable with you.

Once you build that initial rapport, it's time to find out their needs. Just as you wouldn't expect a doctor to start treating you without first knowing what's wrong, you can't talk about how great your results are until you know what issues/challenges they need to have resolved. Therefore, ask questions like:

- Who will be attending? Managers, operations executives, owners, secretaries, nurses?
- What is the theme or slogan of the convention/meeting?
- What are you looking for in a speaker?
- What speakers have you had in the past?
- What did you like best about that person?
- What did you like least?
- Does your group like audience participation?
- What kind of seminar do you want?
- Do you want entertainment or meat?

Depending on the topic or industry you specialize in, there may be some key questions you know are important to ask. Make a list of those and keep them by the phone so you don't forget them.

Always let the other person talk first, so you can reply to their statements rather than having them reply (often in rebuttal) to yours. For example, if you immediately say, "I encourage a lot of audience participation," then they may say, "Our people are engineers, and they don't like participation." While the audience participation may not be a requirement of your presentations, when you start there, it's hard to backpedal. This doesn't mean you have to change your topic or your uniqueness factor; it simply means you have to let questions, not statements, guide your conversation.

PARTNER WITH LOCAL CONVENTION BUREAUS AND LOCAL BUSINESSES

Another great marketing option is to contact the convention centers located in the big cities and even smaller resort destinations that are within a two-hour drive of your location. Tell them you want to join the convention bureau and get a list of all the upcoming meetings and events coming to that facility. You'll likely find that many associations will be having events in these places.

Once you learn that a particular association is coming for their meeting or convention, contact them and offer your services (again, find out their needs first). Because you're local and wouldn't have to spend precious time travelling across the country, offer them a local rate that's slightly less than your regular rate. Be sure to stress that you're a *national* speaker, but because you're nearby, they can get you for a local rate. An added advantage for them is that there are no airfare or hotel expenses for them to pay. The advantage for you is there is no travel time involved (which can often amount to two or three days of your time for a one-hour speech). The beauty of speaking at these sorts of local association meetings is that you'll be in front of decision makers from many different companies, and you don't have to travel to do so.

But don't stop at convention centers. Also contact local businesses with the same offer. For example, Diane Ciotta is a sales motivator. But rather than always traveling to her clients' locations, she wanted to get some local business. So she picked up the phone and started calling local businesses that could benefit from her topic, and she offered them the local fee. By doing this, in one day she secured $22,000 of business. And best of all, it's all local so she gets to be home for dinner every night.

MARKET TO NATIONAL GROUPS

While staying local is great, the national scene offers many more marketing opportunities. Thanks to the Internet, finding association meetings outside of your local area is easier than ever. Simply make a list of the associations in your industry. Go to their websites and look for meeting or event notices. Most associations list their upcoming events well over a year in advance. Read the various descriptions and needs posted, and reply to any that match your expertise.

If you're not well-known yet and think these associations only bring in famous people, think again. Often, meeting planners are looking for strong content. If you can provide that, then you have a chance. Granted, it may not be the keynote presentation, but they likely have numerous workshops and breakout sessions they need to fill where your expertise would be beneficial.

Additionally, when you speak to an association and have various company decision makers in the audience, offer something for free. For example, ten minutes before the end of your presentation, you can say, "I have a free audio about . . . (hiring, or weight loss, or management, or whatever your topic is). Give me your card and I'll e-mail you (or send you) the audio."

If you speak to 100 people and 20 give you their business cards, of those 100 decision makers you need to market to only 20. After all, why market to the other 80 and waste your time if they don't even want your free offering?

When you return to your office, send people what you promised them along with a nice note or letter, and enter their information into your marketing database for regular communications. Then a few weeks later you can call them and ask, "Did you get the material I sent?" and "Do you have any questions?" Talk with them about their needs as much as possible. Finally, ask, "Do you have any meetings coming up where you could use a speaker?" Now instead of a cold call, you have a warm call . . . and an open door for future marketing materials.

DON'T FORGET DIRECT MAIL

Finally, let's not forget that direct mail pieces (sales letters and postcards) are still a great way to market your speaking business. Key elements of your direct mail piece are:

- A strong headline that stresses how you're going to help their audience. Depending on your topic, you might talk about increasing sales, losing weight, making smarter hiring decisions, or increasing productivity.
- Testimonials from others in their industry who have attended your presentations.
- A breakdown of the problems they are likely facing AND your solution for each one.
- A mention of any relevant association meetings or similar types of companies you've helped.
- A list of any articles you've had published in an industry or association magazine.
- A call to action. Clearly state the next step you want people to take: "Call me today," "Visit my website," "Request more information."

Show people that you're "in the know" when it comes to their issues and that you're the best person to help them solve those challenges.

MARKET SMART

Being a speaker is one of the most rewarding professions I know. In what other career can you share your knowledge, travel the world, meet lots of interesting people, and make a difference in the lives of others? But to do all this well, you have to continually market yourself. By using the strategies outlined here, you'll be better able to stand out from the competition and market your speaking business to new levels of success.

Pam Lontos is president of Pam Lontos Consulting. Pam consults with speakers, authors, and experts in the areas of marketing, publicity, and speaking. Pam is a past vice president of sales for Disney's Shamrock Broadcasting, where she increased sales 500 percent. She is the author of *I See Your Name Everywhere: Leverage the Power of the Media to Grow Your Fame, Wealth and Success*. She is also a former speaker and the founder of PR/PR Public Relations. For more information on her consulting services, call (407) 522-8630 or e-mail PamLontos@gmail.com, or visit her online at www.PamLontos.com.

29

THE MYSTERIES OF MARKETING: A COMBO PLATTER OF PRACTICAL PRACTICES

Susan RoAne

While we all wish we had the Magic Marketing Wand, the reality is, there is no such thing. Although marketing, like every other element of business, has changed in the 30 years I've been in the speaking business, one thing hasn't changed: We have to do it.

We must plan and implement myriad marketing strategies, because building the proverbial better mousetrap (or presentation) is not enough to have the market beat an online or off-line path to our doors.

SOCIAL MEDIA: A MUST

Marketing has changed a lot since the days of cold-calling and writing and mailing letters. Fortunately, I was always willing and eager to jump aboard the latest and greatest technology to advance my business. I was an early adopter of computers and social media. I've had a website for 16 years (redone and revised many times), have slavishly worked on keywords, hired search engine optimization (SEO) specialists for more than a decade (my current genius has remarkable impact), have been on LinkedIn for more than seven years, had a Facebook page for four years, have been blogging for more than seven years, and have been tweeting for three and a half years. I also have a QR code. (A QR code is a matrix barcode, or two-dimensional code, readable by QR scanners, mobile phones with a camera, and smartphones, that directs people back to my website.)

24/7 MARKETING INCLUDES RETRO ACTIVITIES

Part of my marketing continues to be that *combo platter*: saying yes to invitations, showing up, and interacting with the strangers in any and every room. I still snail-mail handwritten (by my hand) notes and cards, send individual e-mail messages, and (I hope you're sitting down as you read this) I pick up the phone and talk to people! I even meet people face-to-face over coffee or a nosh.

As Carl LaMell, CEO of Clearbrook, an organization that serves developmentally challenged communities in Greater Chicago, reminded me: "Every handshake is marketing."

Some thoughts on the mysteries of marketing a speaking business:

1. There's no *one* way to market.
2. We must utilize *every* medium and modality.
3. The term "showing up" refers to all of the following: online, in people's inboxes, in the cloud, and good old-fashioned face-to-face. Those are the most memorable "handshakes."
4. We must "behave our brand." We can't speak on balance or wellness and look like we're going to explode from stress. I have to socialize with clients and be open to attending their receptions—regardless of whether I've flown across the country and am tired. If I don't mingle, then I'm not supporting my brand.

TALK TO YOUR MARKET

One of the most important marketing concepts I learned through writing my books is really simple: Talk to your market.

Listen very hard when the members of your market speak.

No need for expensive, fancy, and phony focus groups. Ask people who hire speakers and those in your audiences what they want, like, and need. We additionally have the advantage of using online social media to posit that question and garner data/feedback that we can extrapolate to reach conclusions and then adapt.

NSA was instrumental in helping me think and learn about and plan my marketing. I learned a lot from senior colleagues who spoke at chapters and shared their information, experiences, and hard-won wisdom.

Another truism: No amount of brilliant, effective marketing that turns into dates on a speaking calendar is a substitute for a compelling presentation that is well conceived, well crafted, well written, well delivered, and well received.

MY HMP (HINDSIGHT MARKETING PLAN)

1. Rather than put all my eggs in one speaking biz association basket, I joined different organizations, including:

   Women Entrepreneurs. I learned how to run a business from those who were running women-owned businesses in various categories: printing, car dealerships, elevator installation and repair, bookkeeping/accounting, training, image consulting, and even cosmetic surgeons!

   San Francisco Chamber. I immediately joined the education committee—a logical choice for this former educator. I participated and volunteered to chair and cochair different events that gave me access, opportunity, and practice. I worked every event and room, meeting many people who helped me grow from a teacher to a business owner to a keynote speaker. Because I had a network, I was able to make "warm" calls, not cold ones.

   Because he saw a need, one of the members of the education committee at the San Francisco Chamber who was an accountant for a Big Eight firm offered to give a business plan workshop for small business owners. The hook: We would walk away with a draft of our business plan. I'm forever grateful to Steve Mayer, founder and CEO of Burr, Pilger and Mayer, a prominent Bay Area accounting and consulting firm. I then invited Steve to do the same for NSA/NC members so we would have business plans.

2. I joined NSA after attending several meetings, consistently showing up and talking to everyone regardless of business standing/fame/purported success. There is something to learn from each person we meet. If there's not a "lesson," maybe we just get to make a friend. Call me Pollyanna, but that, to me, is a gift.

3. I was visible and *active*. No one had to tell me that joining was simply not enough. I knew this from my time in the National Women's Political Caucus and volunteer work with KQED, our PBS station.

4. When our stellar NSA speaker stars spoke at our chapters, I attended, listened, and took notes—and read them. When Jim Cathcart, CSP, CPAE, said his goal was to be an author who speaks, I paid attention. When Tony Alessandra, PhD, CSP, CPAE, spoke about inbound marketing and what we can do to "make that phone ring," I paid attention. When Sheila Murray Bethel, CPAE, invited me to observe her training session with a client group, I jumped at the chance to observe a pro. When Patricia Fripp, CSP, CPAE, offered a full-day workshop for new speakers, I immediately registered. When Judith Briles hosted a publishing workshop in her Palo Alto office, I signed up.

When Judith, who had published one of the first books on finance for women, *Financial Savvy for Women*, held up one of my articles for the *San Francisco Examiner* Careers series and said, "Suz, you can really write. *How To Work a Room* should be a book," I listened. Then she said, "Here's the name of my agent." And I followed up; another key to marketing success.

5. *How to Work a Room* outperformed everyone's expectations, was No. 1 on Book-of-the-Month Club's best-seller list, on many major best-seller lists including *Publishers Weekly* Audio Bestsellers, and launched an industry. Most of all, it launched and catapulted my speaking business and launched the current "networking" industry. How did a lot of this happen? That brings me to an important point on solving the Mysteries of Marketing.

6. To paraphrase Gypsy Rose Lee, "You gotta have a network." Call it a gimmick if you want, but having social, business, and extended family networks is a key to those "you never know" mysteries of marketing because of serendipitous meetings and benefits of connections. Stay with me on this one: A friend's husband's brother-in-law was CEO of Book-of-the-Month Club. I learned this at dinner at my friend's house. Because I had quoted my friend in *How to Work a Room* (written before she met him), her husband sent my book to his brother-in-law. It was simply serendipity.

7. Original material abounds! A snarky review in *The Wall Street Journal* turned into a funny/memorable opening signature story. How could I resist? Getting panned by the venerable *Wall Street Journal* proved to be a good omen!

8. Don't be afraid to speak up on issues that matter to you. It's a possible path along the Mysteries of Marketing journey. With an early menopause, I took a class at our local hospital with fourteen other women. We wanted to continue meeting after the class ended to explore this important phase of life. We called ourselves The Red Hot Mamas. A friend suggested I call a beloved reporter for the *Marin Independent Journal* because, as he said, "We men know nothing about this."

The headline was a grabber: "The Hottest Group in Town." It featured our group and the work we were doing. The article caught the attention of a reporter from the *San Francisco Examiner*, and that article caught the attention of Jane Gross, a health issues journalist for *The New York Times* based in San Francisco. Menopause and Marin County's Red Hot Mamas were on the front page of the Sunday *New York Times,* with a photo taken in my living room.

9. "Stand up and be counted" was a lesson I learned in Hebrew school from a very wise rabbi. He also cautioned us to speak up for others, not just ourselves. I had several speaking colleagues, whom I respected, tell me they were concerned that I'd be known as "the speaker with menopause." I had to make a decision. Potentially jeopardize my speaking career or make sure the next generations of women are informed, empowered to ask their doctors questions, and take control of their own bodies. It was a no-brainer. I had to do the right thing.

The New York Times feature caught the attention of a meeting planner in New York City who was planning a conference (no speaking fee) in San Francisco . . . while having hot flashes.

That no-fee gig turned into three paid programs that I can track, including one for Lockheed's Leadership program.

10. And what about free talks? I see them as "Planet Points" . . . doing something good that earns our right to be on this planet. Patricia Fripp's words were emblazoned on my brain: "Speaking begets speaking." It creates momentum and inbound marketing calls and brand awareness. We must treat the free ones as marketing opportunities and give them the same 110 percent.

Case in point: I agreed to speak for free for a San Mateo, California, non-profit serving people in their forties and fifties who had been laid off. The reason I separated from my career as a teacher in San Francisco was that the school district had laid off 1,200 teachers, including me. I was fortunate to have turned this huge lemon into lemon soufflé. (I don't like lemonade.)

Unbeknownst to me, the fiancé of another speaker, who ran the Peak Performers seminars nationwide, sat in on my session. That free keynote turned into five fee-based engagements, including one in Chicago that my parents attended. It was the first time they had attended one of my presentations. My dad passed away shortly after, and I cherish that he was able to see and hear what I do for a living. Priceless.

RANDOM ROANE MARKETING THOUGHTS

Looking back on a 30-year career as a professional speaker, here is what I've found works:

Return calls. A client found me through a Google search and called. I called back, and she was shocked to hear from the actual speaker. The other two people she contacted never returned her call.

Talk to clients. Forget about creating some phony phone mystique. Be a person to the people who want to hire you.

Be nice to everyone. Forget about assessing people's titles and positions before you give them the time of day. That is the short-range thinking of the self-absorbed. Don't listen to those who give you "methods" to bypass the gatekeepers. Be nice to them, as they can open the gates for you.

Stay in touch with clients that you like (and some you don't). Do so digitally and "old school."

The "begetting" may take time. Every speaker has a story of a presentation that emerged after a decade. People call when they have a need for our subject, not because we want to fill a calendar.

Social media are a must. Be findable. Be proactive on LinkedIn and join its various industry groups. Be sure you have a Facebook business page; consider joining Twitter; assess Google+ and join if it fits your plan.

Trademark your original intellectual property. Enough said.

Don't pick people's brains. Honor their time and expertise.

Solicit advice from people you trust. Separate the wheat from the chaff. If something sounds logical but doesn't feel right, don't do it. Or say what Gary Vaynerchuk says in *Crush It*: "It's not in my DNA."

Don't sell dreck. Just because you have the ability to sell your audios as MP3s, CDs, etc., don't rush into it. Make sure you have a script for listening, not reading, and a producer who will catch your sibilant esses and mistakes. Don't put your byline on something just to have a product to sell. Make sure it's quality and something you'll be proud of in 10 years when someone buys it at a resale shop. The buyer could be your next best client. You never know!

Act as if your life is on YouTube. Better not to have to explain bad behavior.

Lend a helping hand. Share your sources, resources, recommendations, support, and knowledge willingly and freely.

Pay up if you've been the recipient of largesse. Return the boon. Not doing so is just plain foolish, shortsighted, and stupid.

ACKNOWLEDGE! Say thank you in a way that's commensurate with the gift you've been given. Don't know what to do? A donation to a favorite charity or local food bank in someone's honor is a nice touch.

Go "old school" with these ideas:

- Send handwritten notes (not always on business stationery). Write with your hand, not a font that resembles a mailing from Publishers Clearing House.
- Pick up your phone and chat the way Alexander Graham Bell intended.
- Invite people for coffee or lunch.
- Attend events for face-to-face time.

Marketing is a full-time job that includes many types of activities and must be done 24/7. It starts with a solid, meaningful message and a memorable presentation. I hope these words and thoughts I've shared become part of your Magic Wand to help you uncover some of the mysteries for marketing your speaking business!

Marketing is a MUST, not a choice!

- Decide:

  What business you're in (speaking, training, consulting, coaching, etc.)

  Who are the audiences for your business

  What fees will the market bear

  How you will reach your market

- Do your due diligence—read, research, assess your marketing options.

- Explore/list the many ways to market your speaking business.

- Choose which marketing methods will work best for you.

- Draft a written marketing plan as a part of your business plan.

- Investigate any marketing expert (even if the person is an NSA member) thoroughly before you pay a penny.

- Attend local and national NSA meetings and conventions where you will learn more than you can absorb. Then read your notes a week later!

- Be open to serendipity—those unexpected opportunities that appear that we didn't write in our marketing plan. (My manicurist introduced me to her Friday client who hired me to speak because she came in a day early for her manicure.) Ya never know!

Susan RoAne, aka The Mingling Maven®, is the author of the classic best seller, *How to Work A Room,* and *The Secrets of Savvy Networking*, among others, and is the leading expert on savvy business networking. She is an in-demand international keynote speaker and has been a member of NSA since 1983. She has been featured in media around the world, including *The Wall Street Journal*, *The New York Times*, *Sydney Telegraph,* Australia's *Today* show, and globally on the BBC throughout Europe, Asia, and Africa. Her clients are Fortune 500 companies as well as universities, associations, and nonprofits. Susan is known for her practical advice and for what the *San Francisco Chronicle* called "her dynamite sense of humor." Susan can be found at www.susanroane.com, Susan@SusanRoAne.com, and www.twitter.com/susanroane.

YOU'RE HIRED! USING SALES AND MARKETING TO BOOK MORE SPEAKING GIGS

Curt Tueffert

In the world of professional speaking, the tools of sales and marketing come in many shapes and sizes, packaged and customized, amateur and professional grade. The challenges are many when speakers desire to move from unknown to known; from "no time" to part-time; and from part-time to full-time.

This evolution often tests our comfort level with sales and marketing: Do we really need to master these twin tasks? Professional speaker Jim Jacobus, CSP, says, "Honor the Dream, Do the Work." Six simple words, yet encompassing a lifetime of experience as a professional speaker. We each have a story or life experience inside us, waiting to be shared with a group of people. Becoming a professional speaker—someone who can move people with emotion and logic, facts, and stories—requires both honoring the dream and doing the work that will get us known.

Since I focus on sales and sales management as a speaker, I'm expected to have the twin tasks of sales and marketing perfected. If I do not practice what I preach, or use what I recommend to my clients, then I am a charlatan—or worse, a hypocrite! Even as I coach/mentor speakers, I am constantly looking for ways to improve my sales and marketing skills to become that much better for my current and future clients.

SALES AND MARKETING DEFINED

Let's start by defining the terms *sales* and *marketing* as they relate to professional speakers. *Marketing* is the messaging we use to communicate our expertise for people who would be willing to pay our engagement fees. It's packaged in current and future delivery methods, including websites, videos, social media, direct mail, word-of-mouth networking, articles written, books published, etc. *Sales/selling* happens when we connect with another person for the express purpose of speaking for their company or association, or being considered as a speaker for their bureau. Selling is the action resulting from the efforts of marketing. The end goal: hearing the words "You're hired!"

YOUR MARKETING TOOL KIT

There are, of course, countless marketing methods you can use to grow your speaking business and improve your sales process. No need to use them all but rather experiment, take what you like, and leave the rest—based on how effective you find they are for your individual business, as well as the investment of time and money required.

Writing articles: Getting your name in print or digital media serves two purposes. First, it holds you accountable. Submissions to newspapers, magazines, trade journals, blog sites, corporate newsletters, and other venues require research and keep your expertise top-of-mind, allowing you to pull relevant information into the conversation based on fresh data. Second, article writing gets your name out into niche areas, laying the groundwork for your selling process and potential future speaking engagements. It's a step toward becoming an authority, that "known expert" your client absolutely must have for a future meeting.

The financial investment in writing articles is low, although the time and energy investment is high. (But if you work strategically, you can even get paid for it.) You have to have something of value to write about, and you have to package it in a style that draws in the readers of a specific audience.

Websites: Yes, we all have some type of website that people can check out— but here, we're considering how it markets you as a speaker beyond the look and feel. When I land on your site, will you draw me in with a newsletter sign-up, or a web store where I can purchase your products, downloadable content, and more? This is where your creative side comes out regarding marketing. When you draw people to your site, give them as many opportunities as you can to "take you home"—in exchange for their contact information. They get the value of the products you are offering, you get the opportunity to reach out for future marketing efforts (direct mail, direct e-mail, etc.).

Website creation and maintenance require both a financial investment and a time and energy investment. Keeping your content fresh and relevant are the two keys to a successful site.

Blogging (standard and video): There are many options today for hosting a blog site and embedding amateur or professional video. Like article writing, blogging gives you exposure—with the additional marketing dimension of auditory and kinesthetic connection. Video can be used to talk to, share with, or appreciate the people "on the other side" of the blog. People get the chance to hear and feel your style in your videos, as well as experience your expertise.

Blogging is a minimal financial investment, yet it can be a medium-to-high time investment, again with a goal of keeping the content current and relevant.

Direct mail: Yes, speakers can still use direct mail as a marketing tool—and it's as much about the message as ever. I've used direct mail to select groups as a connection tool to alert them to a book release, quotes from raving fans, or to debut a new offer at my website. I've used direct mail when seeking to connect with the attendees in a creative way prior to actual date of the event.

Far more than the other methods described here, direct mail ranges widely in the financial investment as well as the time investment—from simple postcards to fancy dimensional mailers.

E-mail newsletters: You might be thinking "been there, done that" regarding newsletters, and yet, they are a tremendously effective marketing tool when done with consistency and value. I've sent out a monthly e-mail newsletter for more than 11 years. My approach is to offer ideas, tips, techniques, and insights in my areas of expertise. It keeps my connection with the people I've met.

Newsletters are very low cost; the investment comes in the form of the time and energy to develop the content and to keep the consistency over time.

Social media: They're here to stay, so how can we best use them for marketing? My tactic is to dive in, create a profile, keep my mind open to creative ways to reach out to my groups, and be willing to change up the content. If that sounds a bit vague, it is by purpose and design. Social media marketing is still in its infancy. While the movement is worldwide, technology is ever changing, allowing more and more people to use social media on devices that are low cost, portable, and omnipresent. Yes, there is a place for your speaking expertise, inside the world of social media, today and in the future.

Social media require a minimal financial investment, but they come with the subtle demand of constant updating with content and value—and the not-so-subtle temptation of procrastination.

There's no magic marketing mix. As a new speaker, pick a few that you are comfortable with and begin using them. Anchor your expertise to the tools that you've found productive while keeping an open mind to new ones as they appear.

SELLING YOURSELF: ADOPTING A SALES PROCESS

Marketing creates and sustains awareness. Sales gets you more bookings. For some speakers, selling ranks right up there with root canals and TSA pat-downs, while others view it as just part of the deal—from getting nowhere to getting hired over and over again! During my 28-plus years in sales and sales management, I've tried many things to grow my speaking business. Creating an effective sales process is clearly the best way to accomplish that—and the following seven-step methodology can help you get there.

1. **Prospecting:** It all has to start somewhere. Who is your target audience, association, or niche? Why would they want to pay money to hear you speak? Do you have something of value that can only be delivered by you? These are all critical questions to be considered before you pick up the phone or type the e-mail. There are many resources available to assist you in the prospecting stage of the seven-step process. Once you've identified the groups that would benefit from your expertise, it is time to break the ice, pick up the phone, and start the process.

2. **Making a first impression:** It begins with your tone of voice and carries over to the ultimate phone conversation or face-to-face meeting with people who can assist you in reaching your goal . . . getting hired! During the prospecting stage, you learned the names of the people responsible for hiring speakers. Once you're this far into the sales process, you have to be 100 percent on your A-game when it comes to making and developing those connections.

3. **Gaining understanding (qualification):** Before you dive into the who/what/where/when/why of how good you are, seek first to understand who they are. This is a critical step in the process and should never be rushed. If you've made a good first impression, you stand a great chance to ask open-ended questions about them, their hiring process, who they like, what they like, why they like it, and how you can get on their short list of speakers to consider. You must gain as much of this intelligence as you can before you move to the next step.

4. **Demonstration/presenting:** Here, you tie your strengths and speaking expertise to the discoveries made in the understanding step. If you are not a born sales professional, this takes time—probably more than you think. You must gain confidence in your ability to understand what they are looking for and just how perfectly you fit into their needs.

5. **Conviction:** Here, on the fifth step, you know about them, they know about you, and perhaps, you have made it to the short list of possible speakers for their upcoming event. The sales process is designed to move you closer to your goal of getting hired simply by progression. The conviction step offers the decision makers compelling reasons to keep you on the short list—while eliminating others. Perhaps you are bundling additional services, you have added value, you come in early, or you stay later. Perhaps you have a list of influential testimonials and referrals that can be used to tip the scales in your favor. All these and more are the sales aids you need to create strong conviction in the hearts and minds of the decision makers.

6. **Closing:** This is simply the next logical step in the process, usually at their pace. Be careful not to rush them or come across as pushy, impatient, desperate, or rude. Remember, it is their wants and needs that determine the decision, with some influence by you as you add value in your areas of expertise.

7. **Follow-up:** Whether you secure the speaking gig or not, you've moved through the first six steps and have much more information about their decision process than when you began. Now you need keep TOMA: Top-of-Mind Awareness. The tools I use for following up include thank-you cards, greeting cards, newsletter subscriptions, and members-only specials of my products or services sprinkled throughout the year—anything and

everything to keep them thinking of me in a positive way. At any given point in time, they'll need speakers, trainers, coaches, and consultants, and your ability to follow up with professional, value-added material and genuine appreciation will create more reasons to serve them, year after year.

"You're Hired!" are the two sweetest words a speaker can hear. Using sales and marketing to connect and grow your business will give you a more consistent and profitable speaking career, more repeat engagements, and more steady income. The tools are right there: Take them, use them . . . honor the dream, and do the work.

Curt Tueffert is a professional speaker and the president of Brick Wall Motivation. He has more than 28 years in sales, marketing, and sales management and is the author of *201 Sales Motivators* and *5 Stones For Slaying Giants*. His areas of expertise include sales, management, customer service, motivation, and inspiration. Curt has a blog at www.BrickWallMotivation.com, his website is www.Tueffert.com, and his e-mail address is tueffert@aol.com.

STARTING FROM $0: 17 TIPS TO BUILD A CAREER

Joe Liss, CPA

"Sure, I'd be glad to help." With that somewhat terse e-mail response to a speaking opportunity, my life changed.

I'd been retired for about six months from a CPA practice of thirty years, and it began my trek from virtually no professional speaking income to a pretty active speaking schedule. Preparation, opportunity, and luck came together to produce tremendous results. When the opportunity arose, I relied on my NSA education and CPA experience to react and produce. The following tips illustrate specific ways I was able to capitalize when it counted.

TIP #1: BEWARE! THE ENEMY OF GREAT SUCCESS IS ACCEPTABLE SUCCESS.

The more settled and happy you are, the less you are inclined to risk what you have for something better. Prior to retiring, I was speaking professionally as part of my CPA practice—and really enjoyed it. The practice was successful, so it was difficult to risk that stability for even greater, albeit uncertain, success in some other venture. But after more than thirty years in public accounting, I decided I had had enough. I closed my practice in September 2010.

TIP #2: RECOGNIZE YOUR OPPORTUNITY COST.

Opportunity cost is an economic principle that measures the difference between investments. If your money is currently yielding 2 percent, but it could yield

5 percent elsewhere, the opportunity cost is 3 percent. By remaining in my CPA business, I believed I was missing a better opportunity.

During my "CPA life," I had assisted one of my oil and gas clients with a presentation to explain oil and gas taxation to investment advisers and other CPAs. In March 2010, the CFO, Alex (not his real name), was unable to make one of these presentations due to scheduling conflicts, so he e-mailed to ask if I could substitute for him. He was concerned that I had not presented for them in a while, wanted to discuss my fee, and mentioned that other presenters were being considered.

TIP #3: UNDERSTAND RISK REVERSAL.

Perhaps the single most effective marketing principle for expanding business is risk reversal, a technique I learned from Jay Abraham, a marketing guru based in California. Based on Alex's concerns, I wanted the company to assume no risk by hiring me—just like retailers who let customers return products if they are not satisfied. This dynamic shifts the customer's risk to the seller. I told Alex that if they were dissatisfied with the engagement, they wouldn't have to pay me. Combined with our prior history, that made it virtually impossible for him to say no, and they agreed to the deal.

TIP #4: ATTEND ALL EVENT FUNCTIONS TO WHICH YOU ARE INVITED.

I was asked to arrive the night before I spoke to attend a dinner with the host and attendees—which yielded an opportunity to incorporate input from that evening's discussions into my presentation. It enhanced the presentation's timeliness, and made it more tailored and personalized. The conference went better than I could have ever imagined—and reminded me how much I enjoyed speaking and how it invigorates me.

TIP #5: WORK WITH A NICHE SPONSOR.

Standard speaking engagements had always involved finding an audience and collecting fees from attendees. In this structure, speakers compete to present to companies or association audiences. The sophisticated marketers and more experienced speakers were always intimidating to me, and seemed to have a huge advantage. Having a niche sponsor (the oil and gas company) in my area of expertise afforded me the opportunity to bypass the traditional marketing techniques—since the sponsor made calls and booked me with their own audiences.

TIP #6: BE A SPONSOR PROFIT CENTER.

The goal of my sponsor is to raise investment money; my role is to encourage attendees to direct their clients to my sponsor's investment ventures. This is a fundamental difference from my other speaking engagements, which are viewed as costs to the provider. They're often educational, but not always directly related to producing more income. As a profit center for my sponsor, I'm providing direct access to investor dollars that were virtually impossible to tap otherwise.

TIP #7: NEGOTIATE WITH THE ECONOMIC BUYER.

Alan Weiss, CMC, CSP, CPAE, FCMC, NSA Hall of Fame speaker and management consultant, teaches that you must reach conceptual agreement about an engagement before memorializing that agreement in writing. Subsequent to speaking at the oil and gas event, I spent a lot of time talking with the company's marketing partner, Richard (not his real name). We discussed future engagements, company expectations, metrics to measure, and fees. Based on his prior experience working with presenters, Richard thought my fees were acceptable.

I put together a proposal and submitted it, as requested, to the owners of the company. Subsequently, Alex, the CFO, called me and said all the goals and processes were acceptable—but flipped his lid at my fee! Obviously, I had not been discussing price with the economic buyer, the person who would write my checks. I hadn't done a very good job at laying a foundation to get paid; I needed to ask more than one person who was responsible for approving my fee.

TIP #8: DON'T TAKE THE NEGOTIATION PERSONALLY.

In Roger Fisher's book *Getting to Yes*, he talks about separating the people from the issues. I repeated this advice to myself silently over and over, as Alex insisted on renegotiating the fee for every event. I found it offensive when he said that my pricing was ridiculous and that I wasn't being a good team member. I'd known

Alex for fifteen years, and it took everything within me to maintain my self-control. He'd call at inconvenient times, propose a take-it-or-leave-it offer, and demand an immediate answer. When I responded with a question, he would interrupt, saying he had to get into a meeting and that he needed my answer now. The stress and aggravation taxed my patience. I tried to reason with him in e-mail, used caller ID to avoid his calls, and returned calls when the time was to my advantage.

Funny enough, when not discussing money, Alex and I were friendly, just like old times. I learned that these methods were simply his tactics, and he didn't mean it personally. I needed to ignore his bluster and deal with the issues. If you get flustered or angry, terminate the session, refocus, and resume when you are calm, cool, and collected. Once you've said something, you can't take it back.

TIP #9: NEGOTIATE VALUE, NOT DELIVERABLES.

In my years as a CPA, it was drilled into me by associates, competitors, and clients that my products were things like financial statements and tax returns and that my inventory was my time. Accordingly, billing was based on products delivered and/or time at hourly rates. Once again, Alan Weiss taught me an important lesson: I don't deliver product or time, I deliver results. This altered the discussion from details of input and products to output and results. Alex preferred paying me based on an hourly rate. It took quite an effort to define value and shift Alex's thinking from hourly to value fees.

TIP #10: SPEAK ABOUT WHAT YOU KNOW, AND KNOW YOUR SUBJECT EXHAUSTIVELY.

By knowing my topic inside and out, I am able to concentrate on my audience and building relationships. Since I have a thorough knowledge of and familiarity with oil and gas taxation, I can pay attention to body language of my audience members, the questions behind their questions, and what they want to know, not just what I want to tell them. Best of all, I can have more fun! Knowledge and familiarity of my subject make everything flow, humor happens dynamically, and the atmosphere of professionalism is elevated.

TIP #11: KNOW YOUR AUDIENCE. TELL THEM WHAT THEY NEED TO HEAR.

Investment advisers aren't as concerned about the technical tax rules as CPAs are; they're more interested in selling aspects. CPAs are methodical and concerned about professional liability.

These differences have important implications in the content I present. An adviser conference is a 30,000-foot discussion, focused on sales techniques and how to present the product to client's advisers. The CPA meetings are far more technical, unmasking the mysteries of income tax code sections, liability issues, and tax reporting and preparation issues specific to oil and gas. The bottom line is that you need to find out what your audience needs to know. Are there new aspects to the industry of which they are unaware? Are there ways they might benefit from these changes? Let them know, and they'll see you as a resource rather than just a speaker—and they will hire you again and again.

TIP #12: WIIFM.

You've probably heard it a million times, so this isn't a radical or innovative tip. But the timeworn acronym about self interest is true: Audiences want to know WIIFM: *What's In It For Me?* At my initial conference, I garnered follow-up engagements by offering to speak in attendees' home cities if they gathered a group of CPAs (the audience they were having a challenge reaching) to learn about the tax issues involving oil and gas. Many of their CPA contacts already had clients with an oil and gas investment, which made a perfect opportunity for CPAs to learn more and better advise those clients. In addition, the seminar qualified for Continuing Professional Education (CPE) credits. Those credits can be costly, so free CPE is something that always catches the CPA's eye.

Two of the attendees took me up on my offer, delighting the oil company sponsor since it put their offering in front of more prospects, and more engagements came as word spread of the seminar's success. What can you provide to your attendees that they can't get elsewhere? What makes it impossible for them to say no to an opportunity to attend one of your sessions?

TIP #13: BECOME ALLIES WITH THE SALES FORCE; DON'T COMPETE WITH THEM.

There was a key difference between the initial conference and my follow-ups. The audience at the former was composed of investment advisers, while the audience at the latter included predominantly CPAs.

As a speaker, not eligible to be paid sales commissions, I don't compete with my sponsor's sales force. That gives them the comfort to sell me as added value to their prospects. The sales force tells investment advisers that if they get a group of CPAs together, the salesperson will get the company's hired gun to come show them the tax benefits of an oil and gas investment—with free CPE credits to boot. It's an attractive offer to prospects, and, best of all, requires no sales calls on my part.

TIP #14: LOOK FOR WAYS TO EXPAND YOUR EXISTING WORK INTO NEW OPPORTUNITIES.

I now tailor presentations for webinars, MP3s, books, etc., in order to diversify ways to get my sponsor's products in front of prospects. Because tax laws change constantly, my presentations must be constantly refined and updated. The sponsor is creating an education department to use my materials to expand the services they provide their prospects. They also have a need for financial statement and income tax consulting, so my background makes me a perfect candidate for that work, too. The relationship has gone far beyond speaker-for-hire.

TIP #15: PREPARE YOURSELF FOR OPPORTUNITY.

When I think back on the trajectory of my speaking career, I am reminded of President Kennedy's response to a child who asked him how he became a war hero. His response? "It was an accident; they sank my boat!" His training had, however, prepared him for being stranded in the Pacific Ocean. Similarly, my training prepared me for success when the opportunity was presented. I knew from experience that professional speaking was where my skills, abilities, and gifts merged.

TIP #16: FIND MENTORS.

Ten years in the NSA and thirty years as a CPA prepared me for this wild ride, but mentoring was vital as I learned so many lessons from professionals in the speaking industry. Watch the way Hall of Fame speaker Mark Sanborn, CSP, CPAE, commands respect. A weekend speaking trip with New Orleans speaker Bruce Wilkinson, CSP, taught me more about customer service than months of academic training could: Serve in any way possible, and you will be appreciated and remembered. Find mentors whom you admire and want to emulate, and you'll stay inspired and striving for excellence.

TIP #17: BE NICE, LAUGH, AND HAVE FUN!

When you are genuinely enjoying yourself, your audience senses it. You don't have to be a standup comedian or the life of the party . . . just be nice and have a good time. I love to laugh when presenting, and self-deprecation makes it easy for the audience to loosen up at my expense. When that wall between the audience and speaker drops, the learning begins. In that respect, NSA past president Naomi Rhode, CSP, CPAE, a member of the NSA CPAE Speaker Hall of Fame®, has been an inspiration—always smiling and enjoying herself, and viewing platform presence as a privilege, not a right. And she does more than talk about it . . . she lives it. What do you do to put the audience at ease? What do you do to make the wall between speaker and audience disappear?

What fun the speaking business is! Go to your professional functions, learn their lessons, get involved, and be prepared for your own thrilling journey when those special opportunities arise.

Joe Liss is a CPA, professional speaker, coach, business consultant, and oil and gas consultant. If something isn't enjoyable and worthwhile, he won't do it! You can e-mail Joe at JoeLissCPA@gmail.com

TURN SHINY PENNIES INTO MARKETING GOLD

Kristin Arnold, MBA, CPF, CMC, CSP

Congratulations! You have made it to the last chapter of this book. Perhaps you read it from cover to cover, or maybe you hopscotched between chapters. Regardless, your head is now likely swimming with all the possible ideas to build your speaking business. Consider this book to be full of "shiny pennies" of actions you can take to build your speaking business.

Therein lies the problem. All of these shiny pennies look great, don't they? As entrepreneurs, it's easy to commit to multiple strategies, only to get frustrated with the learning curve, misjudge the amount of time or resources needed, or become downright bored with the actual implementation. When we lose interest, we go in search of another shiny penny—without ever seeing the results of our efforts from the original.

This chapter will show you how to select the best pennies for your specific business model and how to stay on track—so you can turn your pennies into gold in your pocket.

So let's begin, shall we?

1. TAKE AN INVENTORY

Before you go after that new shiny penny that's caught your eye, take a look at what you are currently doing to market your business. Figure 32-1 lists the major business development activities described in this book. It is not a definitive list, but it represents the traditional strategies speakers use to promote their businesses. Feel free to add to this list if you are doing something else.

Figure 32-1 – Common Speaker Business Development Strategies

STRATEGIES	5 Absolutely Thrilled	4 Respectable	3 Adequate	2 Less Than Adequate	1 No Clue	Yes! Go Forward
Absolute Must Do Strategies						
Collateral Materials: Benefit Statement						
Collateral Materials: Bio						
Collateral Materials: Business Cards						
Collateral Materials: E-mail Signature						
Collateral Materials: Fee Schedule						
Collateral Materials: Introduction						
Collateral Materials: One Sheet						
Contact Management Database						
Website						
Active Strategies						
Attend: Events/Conferences of Target Market						
Attend: Networking Events						
Attend: Trade Shows						
Bureau Connection						
Client Referral Requests						
Client Testimonial Request						
Direct Mail: Gifts						
Direct Mail/E-mail						
Direct Mail/E-mail: Specialty Mailings						
Direct Mail/E-mail: "I'm in the neighborhood"						
Direct Mail/E-mail: Newsletter						
Direct Mail/E-mail: Sales Letter						
Exhibit: Trade Show						
Public Event: Association						

	5 Absolutely Thrilled	4 Respectable	3 Adequate	2 Less Than Adequate	1 No Clue	Yes! Go Forward
Public Event: Book Signing						
Public Event: Pro Bono Speaking						
Public Event: Showcase						
Public Event: Teleseminar						
Public Event: Webinar						
Solicit Sponsors						
Telemarketing: Cold Sales Calls						
Telemarketing: Referral Follow-up						
Visits: Client						
Visits: Prospect						
Visits: Bureaus						
Volunteer						
Passive Strategies						
Advertising						
Collaborate: Speakers in Same Space						
Collaborate: Speakers in Adjacent Space						
Collateral Materials: Action Shots						
Collateral Materials: Client List						
Collateral Materials: Headshot						
Collateral Materials: Press Clippings						
Collateral Materials: Media Press Kit						
Collateral Materials: QR Codes						
Demo Video						
Directory Listings						

	5 Absolutely Thrilled	4 Respectable	3 Adequate	2 Less Than Adequate	1 No Clue	Yes! Go Forward
Media: Press Release						
Promotional Materials: Handout						
Promotional Materials: Giveaway						
Publish: Articles						
Publish: Book/e-book						
Publish: Columnist						
Publish: Trade Journals						
Publish: Market/Customer Survey Results						
Publish: White Paper/ Special Report						
Radio						
Social Media						
Television						
Website: Search Engine Optimization (SEO)						
Website: Blog						
Website: Podcast						
Website: Video Blog						

2. ASSESS YOUR "GO FORWARD" STRATEGY

For each business development strategy you are currently using, rate your satisfaction with the returns you have received for your effort. We could make this into a big science project (note the cost/amount of resources dedicated versus the amount of business received as a result of that effort), but let's keep this simple: Give it a number that best describes the results you know or believe you are receiving for that specific strategy:

5–Absolutely Thrilled: No improvement needed
4–Respectable: May require some minor tweaking to get even better results
3–Adequate: It's a good strategy with some room for improvement

2–Less Than Adequate: May or may not be a great strategy

1–No Clue: Either it is too soon to tell or you don't know

Be honest with yourself. If you have a team of people (employees, contractors, or virtual assistants), bring them into the conversation.

Your "go forward" strategy should include only those activities that received a "3" or better. Note any improvements you want to make, and have a serious discussion about the viability of those activities receiving a "2" or a "1."

3. REFINE YOUR CURRENT MARKETING MIX

Take a good look at your remaining "go forward" strategies. They are grouped in three categories:

Absolute "Must Do": those strategies that every professional speaker must do to be credible in the speaking profession.

Active: those strategies that require your direct effort to connect with a prospect. For example, networking is a common active strategy. In order to implement a networking strategy, you need to go to networking events or attend them online. The strategy requires your active participation. Some active marketing strategies include:

- Attending events, conferences, networking events, trade shows
- Creating bureau connections
- Obtaining client referrals/testimonials
- Sending direct mail/e-mail (e.g., specialty mailings, gifts, I'm in the neighborhood, newsletters, sales letters)
- Exhibiting at trade shows
- Hosting public events: book signings, pro bono speaking, showcase, teleseminar, webinar
- Soliciting sponsors
- Telemarketing
- Visiting clients, prospects, bureaus, and meeting planners
- Volunteering

Passive: those strategies that work for you even when you are not present. For example, publishing an article requires an up-front investment of your time, but once it is published, it is up to the prospect to initiate the connection with you. Some passive marketing strategies include:

- Advertising
- Collaborating with speakers in the same or adjacent space
- Collateral materials: photos, client list, press kit, QR codes
- Demo video
- Directory listing
- Media/press release
- Promotional materials (e.g., handout, giveaway)
- Articles, books, e-books, columns, trade journals, market/customer survey results, white papers, special reports
- Radio interviews
- Social media
- Television
- Website content (e.g., blog, podcast, video blog)
- Website Search Engine Optimization (SEO)

As a general guideline, an emerging speaker (one with one to two years in the speaking business, with gross revenues less than $100k) should complete the "absolute must do" strategies and have no more than two active and two passive strategies working at a time. More than four total strategies for an emerging speaker indicates shiny penny syndrome: You'll do lots of different things without doing anything well. Focus on the top four strategies, aiming for a "4" or a "5" in each. If most of your strategies are hovering around a "3," you may want to reassess the number and mix of strategies in your "go forward" plan.

For the established speaker, you should have *at least* two active and two passive strategies working at a time (a score of "3" or above). Add additional strategies, one at a time, only after all strategies are operating at a minimum of a "3." Think of your strategies as a spinning plate: Once you get one strategy up and spinning well, you can add another plate to the mix!

How many active strategies do you intend to continue pursuing? _____

How many passive strategies do you intend to continue pursuing? _____

4. IDENTIFY YOUR NEW STRATEGIES

Once you have determined your current marketing mix, it's time to figure out which plate you want to add to the plan. Consider this book of best marketing practices as a springboard for fabulous business development ideas. Perhaps you have seen another speaker use a marketing technique that you felt was extremely effective. Or you have been inspired with a jolt of creativity and defined a new marketing strategy! Jot down the ones that grabbed your attention and that you feel would be a great fit for your clients and your brand.

A great marketing strategy fits these three criteria:

- *You are intrigued, interested, and passionate about implementing the strategy.* Don't just pick it because everyone else is doing it. You'll get bored easily and look for a new shiny penny.

- *There is market interest.* Don't just build it and expect that they will come. Test out your idea with some of your current clients. See if it will actually pique their interest enough to make them pick up the phone and call you to speak at their next event.

- *It is consistent with your brand.* Your marketing strategies should reflect the image you want to project into the marketplace.

Keep in mind, whatever strategy you choose, that you will need to adapt it to your own business model. The best practices in this book work for each specific speaker-author. It is a rare for a different speaker to be able to adopt the idea exactly as stated. Similar to buying a jacket off the rack at a department store, you will need to get it tailored (sometimes a little, sometimes a lot) for it to fit perfectly and to get that "5" you deserve.

Based on these criteria, identify the top three strategies you want to pursue. Now take a look at your "go forward" mix. Which of these three strategies would work best for you and your business right now? In three months? In six months? Is there a good balance of active and passive strategies for your business model?

Establish the order you will introduce your strategies—and don't add them until your other plates are spinning at least a level "3"!

1. _____

2. _____

3. _____

5. CREATE A SIMPLE PLAN

Take your first strategy and create a simple plan: Who is going to do what by when? Note what tools and resources you will need to successfully implement this marketing strategy.

Don't forget to look at ways to leverage your other marketing strategies. For example, if you are creating a new e-newsletter, you will want to update your website and use social media to get the word out.

If you haven't done so, now is the time to bring your team into the conversation. Ask your colleagues for their advice, consult with people who execute this strategy flawlessly, and tailor the strategy to be aligned with your marketing goals, brand, and market.

Most speakers think they have to do it all themselves . . . and this couldn't be further from the truth. You have other options to consider:

A–Automated solutions using off-the-shelf software or cloud solutions, such as eSpeakers or Infusionsoft.

C–Collaboration with other professionals who are looking for a similar outcome.

O–Outsourcing to someone with that specialized expertise. Typical examples include administrative, financial, web services, and graphic design.

D–Delegating it to an employee, family member, or even your friends!

E–Eliminating it. Do you really have to do that specific task? If you didn't do it all, what would have to happen to be successful? Challenge yourself to look at the problem differently.

Finally, ask yourself, "What is a successful outcome?" and "How will I know if I am successful?" These two questions point to how you will measure success. For an example of a simple plan, see Figure 32-2; Figure 32-3 shows a sample scorecard.

Figure 32-2 – Sample Action Plan

Strategy: E-Newsletter_____Active/Passive

Goal:

    Resources Required:

- Time: 20 hours to launch; 8 hours/month to maintain
- E-newsletter automation capability
- E-newsletter template. May need some graphic support.

Tools to Help:

    Automated e-mail system (e.g., 1shoppingcart, aweber, Mailchimp) ranging from $0/month to $99/month, depending on capabilities

    Metrics to show progress and/or results

        # sent

        # opened

        # of responses

ACTION	Responsibility	Deadline
Research different e-mail automation options	Kristin	March 1
Decide on automated e-mail system	Kristin/Jennifer	March 14
Import existing contacts into system	Jennifer	March 21
Develop newsletter template (header, layout, columns, etc.)	Kristin/Andy	March 21
Send out first e-newsletter	Jennifer	April 1
Update website	Jennifer	April 1
Post e-newsletter on social media outlets	Kristin	April 1

Figure 32-3 – Marketing Scorecard Example for the E-Newsletter

GOAL	METRIC	JAN	FEB	MARCH
	# sent			
50% of goal	# opened			
5% of opened	# of responses			

6. NOW DO IT!

Now that you have your simple action plan, theoretically, you and your team should be able to execute flawlessly. If only that were true! Stuff happens, shiny pennies distract, and before you know it, your plan has been delayed.

Try these techniques to keep you and your team focused and on track:

- *Monthly accountability meeting.* Have a formal meeting (even if it is just yourself) where you evaluate the status of your marketing strategies. Typically, your marketing meeting will review the pipeline, marketing strategies, and next steps. Don't forget to celebrate small successes that will eventually crescendo into a "5"!

- *Marketing scorecard.* Remember Step 2, where you rated your satisfaction with the returns you have received for your effort? A marketing scorecard will help you determine if you are receiving increasing value for your efforts.

- *Annual review.* Review your marketing mix each year, following the process outlined in this chapter.

TAKE YOUR PICK

There are myriad ways to market your speaking business. The challenge is to select the appropriate strategies to grow your business, given your time, talents, and resources. This chapter provides a process to help you evaluate your current strategies and to determine new strategies to grow your business. At this point, it is up to you to be deliberate—pick the strategies with the highest payoff—and intentional. Be mindful of the shiny pennies, follow through with your strategies, and watch the gold pour forth from your marketing efforts!

Kristin Arnold, MBA, CPF, CMC, CSP, is one of North America's most accomplished professional meeting facilitators. A consummate author, speaker, and trainer, she is on a crusade to make all events in the workplace more engaging, interactive, and collaborative. One of the first women to graduate from the U.S. Coast Guard Academy and the only woman stationed onboard a Coast Guard buoy tender, Kristin learned firsthand how to build high-performance teams, engage others in the workplace, and get the job done. She earned an MBA from St. Mary's College of California and teaches teambuilding at the Schulich School of Business at York University in Toronto. Kristin divides her time between Phoenix, Arizona, and Prince Edward Island, Canada. Visit www.extraordinaryteam.com.

ABOUT NSA

National Speakers Association (NSA) is a not-for-profit association with more than three thousand professional speakers as members. Founded in 1973, NSA is the leading organization for professional speakers. NSA offers the highly acclaimed Certified Speaking Professional (CSP) certification, online education programs, *Speaker* magazine, *Voices of Experience* audio publications, conferences, research, and networking opportunities. NSA is also a member of the Global Speakers Federation.

National Speakers Association
1500 South Priest Drive, Tempe, AZ 85281
480.968.2552 Fax: 480.968.0911
www.nsaspeaker.org

Made in the USA
Charleston, SC
06 July 2015